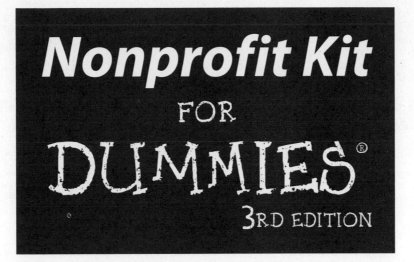

Nonprofit Kit
FOR
DUMMIES®
3RD EDITION

by Stan Hutton and Frances Phillips

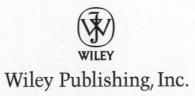

WILEY

Wiley Publishing, Inc.

Nonprofit Kit For Dummies®, 3rd Edition

Published by
Wiley Publishing, Inc.
111 River St.
Hoboken, NJ 07030-5774
www.wiley.com

Copyright © 2010 by Wiley Publishing, Inc., Indianapolis, Indiana

Published by Wiley Publishing, Inc., Indianapolis, Indiana

Published simultaneously in Canada

For general information on our other products and services, please contact our Customer Care Department within the U.S. at 877-762-2974, outside the U.S. at 317-572-3993, or fax 317-572-4002.

For technical support, please visit www.wiley.com/techsupport.

Wiley also publishes its books in a variety of electronic formats. Some content that appears in print may not be available in electronic books.

Library of Congress Control Number: 2009940868

ISBN: 978-0-470-52975-1

Manufactured in the United States of America

10 9 8 7 6 5 4 3

WILEY

About the Authors

Stan Hutton became involved in the nonprofit world after co-founding a nonprofit organization in San Francisco. Since that time, he has worked as nonprofit manager, fundraiser, consultant, and writer. He served as executive director of the Easter Seal Society of San Francisco and a fundraiser for Cogswell College. For five years, he wrote for and managed a Web site about nonprofits for About.com. He has worked at the San Francisco Study Center and the Executive Service Corps of San Francisco. He currently is a senior program officer at the Clarence E. Heller Charitable Foundation.

Frances Phillips is program director for the Arts and The Creative Work Fund at the Walter and Elise Haas Fund in San Francisco. She also teaches grant writing and creative writing at San Francisco State University. Previously, Frances worked as executive director of Intersection for the Arts and of the Poetry Center and American Poetry Archives at San Francisco State University; and as a partner in the public relations and fundraising firm Horne, McClatchy and Associates. Frances serves on the boards of the California Alliance for Art Education, Community Initiatives, Grantmakers in the Arts, and GreatNonprofits; and she is co-editor of the Grantmakers in the Arts *Reader*.

Dedication

We dedicate this book to the devoted nonprofit managers, staff members, volunteers, and board members who are working long hours to improve living conditions, advance the arts and learning, and protect the environment.

And to our daughter, Alice, who also is a writer.

Authors' Acknowledgments

This book started with our agent Maureen Watts, who had the idea and approached us to write it. Many thanks to her, and to project editor Tim Gallan, copy editor Jessica Smith, acquisitions editor Stacy Kennedy, and technical editor, attorney Gene Takagi, who guided us through shaping and revising our manuscript for this edition. We also thank our colleagues who gave us permission to include examples of their work on the CD that accompanies this book, and Laura Gigounas for her advice.

We owe much of our knowledge of the nonprofit sector to a remarkable array of professionals with whom we have worked. It is impossible to list everyone who has helped and inspired us but we would be remiss if we did not name a few. Lori Horne, Jean McClatchy, and Ginny Rubin showed Frances the satisfaction of raising money for good causes. She is grateful to the boards of the Poetry Center at San Francisco State and Intersection for the Arts for giving her a chance to be a nonprofit executive director; and to her current and past colleagues at the Walter and Elise Haas Fund — particularly Bruce Sievers and Pamela David. Stan wants to add his thanks to Arthur Compton, Louise Brown, Neil Housewright, John Darby, Jan Masaoka, and Bruce Hirsch, all of whom have given him opportunities to work in the nonprofit sector and provided guidance along the way.

Publisher's Acknowledgments

We're proud of this book; please send us your comments through our Dummies online registration form located at `http://dummies.custhelp.com`. For other comments, please contact our Customer Care Department within the U.S. at 877-762-2974, outside the U.S. at 317-572-3993, or fax 317-572-4002.

Some of the people who helped bring this book to market include the following:

Acquisitions, Editorial, and Media Development

Senior Project Editor: Tim Gallan

Acquisitions Editor: Stacy Kennedy

Copy Editor: Jessica Smith

Technical Reviewer: Gene Takagi

Editorial Program Coordinator: Joe Niesen

Editorial Manager: Michelle Hacker

Editorial Assistants: Jennette ElNaggar, David Lutton

Media Development Specialists: Jenny Swisher, Shawn Patrick

Media Development Manager: Richard Graves

Cover Photo: © iStock

Cartoons: Rich Tennant (`www.the5thwave.com`)

Composition Services

Project Coordinator: Sheree Montgomery

Layout and Graphics: Carl Byers, Samantha K. Cherolis, Joyce Haughey

Proofreader: Bonnie Mikkelson

Indexer: Potomac Indexing, LLC

Publishing and Editorial for Consumer Dummies

Diane Graves Steele, Vice President and Publisher, Consumer Dummies

Kristin Ferguson-Wagstaffe, Product Development Director, Consumer Dummies

Ensley Eikenburg, Associate Publisher, Travel

Kelly Regan, Editorial Director, Travel

Publishing for Technology Dummies

Andy Cummings, Vice President and Publisher, Dummies Technology/General User

Composition Services

Debbie Stailey, Director of Composition Services

Contents at a Glance

Table of Contents

Introduction

• •

*I*t may sound corny, but we feel a certain sense of mission when it comes to nonprofits. We've started them, directed them, raised funds for them, consulted for them, volunteered for them, given money to them, and written about them. We've been associated with nonprofits in one way or another for more years than we care to remember.

Why have we continued to work for nonprofit organizations? Yes, we care about others and want to see the world a better place — our values are important to us. But, to be honest, that's not the reason we've worked for nonprofit organizations for so many years. We believe the reason is that we can't think of anything more interesting or more challenging to do.

Starting a new program is exciting. Getting your first grant is thrilling. Working with the multifaceted personalities that come together on a board of directors is fascinating. Learning a new skill because no one else is there to do it is fun. Seeing the faces of satisfied clients, walking along a restored lake-shore, hearing the applause of audiences — all are gratifying.

That's why we do it.

About This Book

We try to cover the gamut in this book — everything you need to know to start and manage a charitable organization, from applying for your tax exemption to raising money to pay for your programs. On the CD, you find supplemental information, including forms to help you create a budget, examples of grant proposals, and links to Web sites where you can find more help.

We also attempt to give a bird's-eye view of the economy's nonprofit sector. When you look at financial resources, for example, nonprofits are much like the rest of the world: Most of the wealth is held by relatively few nonprofit organizations; a respectable number of them are in the middle, and many more struggle to make ends meet.

We try to be honest about the difficulties you'll sometimes face. You probably won't be able to achieve everything you set out to accomplish, and you'll always wish you had more resources to do more things. Still, we can't imagine doing anything else. Maybe you'll feel the same way after you jump into the nonprofit world.

Conventions Used in This Book

When writing this book, we used a few conventions that you should be aware of:

- ✔ Anytime we introduce a new nonprofit-related term, we *italicize* it and follow it with a brief, easy-to-follow definition.
- ✔ Web sites and e-mail addresses appear in `monofont` to help them stand out.
- ✔ When we refer to nonprofit organizations, unless we say otherwise, we're talking about organizations that have been recognized as 501(c)(3) nonprofits and that also are considered public charities by the Internal Revenue Service (IRS).
- ✔ All corresponding CD elements are labeled with the chapter number and the order in which the element appears in the chapter. For instance, the first CD element in Chapter 2 is labeled CD0201.

What You're Not to Read

We'd love for you to read this entire book, because we worked so hard on it, but if you're pressed for time or just want to cut to the chase, you can skip the following elements:

- ✔ **Sidebars:** These gray-shaded boxes contain interesting info that's related to the topic at hand but isn't essential.
- ✔ **Paragraphs marked with the "Technical Stuff" icon:** The info contained here is completely skippable, but you'll enhance your knowledge and understanding if you take the time to read these tidbits.

Foolish Assumptions

When writing this book, we made some assumptions about who may be interested in reading it. Here are some of them:

✔ You have an idea that will help solve a problem in your community, and you believe that starting a nonprofit organization is the best way to put your idea into action.

✔ You serve on a board of directors and wonder what you're supposed to be doing.

✔ You work for a nonprofit and need some ideas about fundraising, managing your organization, or working with your board of directors.

✔ You're simply curious about the nonprofit sector and want to find out more about it.

If you're one of these people, we're confident that this book will answer your questions and give you the info you're seeking.

How This Book Is Organized

This book is organized into six parts. You don't have to read it from cover to cover; you can dip in for reference at any point — jumping from Part IV to Part II to Part V if you like. We won't tell anyone.

Part 1: Getting Started with Nonprofits

Read Part I if you want an introduction to nonprofits and information about establishing a nonprofit organization. You also can find a chapter to help you answer the question "Do I want to start a nonprofit organization?" If you decide that the answer is yes, we provide guidance for setting up a legal structure and winding your way through the IRS requirements.

Part II: Managing a Nonprofit Organization

This part covers the nuts and bolts of managing an organization — finding and hiring employees, setting up procedures (and responsibilities) for your board of directors, getting publicity for your programs, and recruiting and retaining volunteers. Planning and budgeting are two important aspects of keeping a nonprofit on track and in the black. And if you're managing a building or thinking of buying one for your organization, you can find some tips here.

Part III: Successful Fundraising

Part III focuses on the fundamental reality of nonprofit organizations — fundraising is essential. Start by creating your fundraising plan and then implement it by raising funds from individuals, writing grant proposals, running annual campaigns, and, if you're really ambitious, launching a capital campaign.

Part IV: The Part of Tens

This is the famous Part of Tens, containing information to keep in mind when evaluating your programs, suggestions about adapting during challenging times, and quick, practical advice on a topic that's dear to everyone's heart: raising money.

Part V: Appendixes

In this part, you find a glossary of terms that are commonly used in the nonprofit sector, along with a bibliography of organizations, and a list of reference books and Web sites that can help you continue to gain knowledge about all aspects of working and volunteering in nonprofits. You also can find information about using the CD that comes with this book.

And don't forget the accompanying CD itself! We collected examples of just about everything we could think of — letters, grants, budgets, contracts, and more — and put them on the CD in the back of this book to help guide you in your work. Along with the examples on the CD, you also can find a list of offices to contact to find out about nonprofits in your state and links to dozens of other useful Web sites.

Icons Used in This Book

We use the following icons throughout the book to flag particularly important or helpful information.

ON THE CD

This icon means that you can find more helpful information and management tools on the CD that accompanies this book.

The remember icon stands watch at information that you should keep ready for application.

You may not need this technical stuff today, but — who knows? — it may be invaluable tomorrow.

This icon is posted next to little hints and suggestions gleaned from our experience over the years.

Warnings are just what you think they may be. We alert you to information that can help you avoid problematic situations.

Where to Go from Here

If you're new to the nonprofit world, we suggest beginning with Chapter 1, where you find fundamental information to get you moving in the right direction. If you're familiar with nonprofits already but want to better understand your responsibilities as a board member, you can find the answers you need in Chapter 6. If you're a new board member and want to understand the organization's finances when spreadsheets are passed out at board meetings, we provide guidance about both making a budget and understanding financial statements in Chapter 10.

If you're like every other nonprofit worker or volunteer, you want to know how to get money for your organization. Chapters 13 through 18 cover this topic, so they're good places to begin.

Part I

Getting Started with Nonprofits

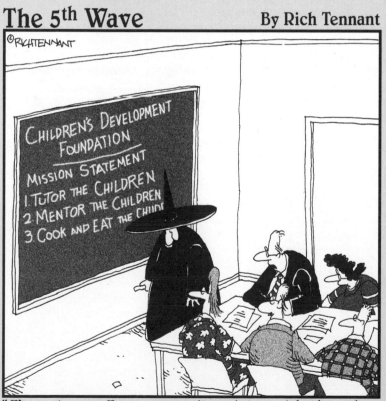

The 5th Wave — By Rich Tennant

CHILDREN'S DEVELOPMENT FOUNDATION

MISSION STATEMENT
1. TUTOR THE CHILDREN
2. MENTOR THE CHILDREN
3. COOK AND EAT THE CHILD

"I'm not sure I can reconcile point 3 with the other two points."

In this part . . .

In this part, we introduce the nonprofit sector and the key role that it plays in our society and economy. We define different types of nonprofit organizations, focusing on the kind that can receive tax-deductible contributions.

We walk you through the steps for starting a nonprofit organization: the questions you should ask, the planning you should do, the mission you should define, and the documents you need to master. We invite you to use all your skills, from dreaming to networking to filling in the blanks for the Internal Revenue Service (IRS).

After your organization receives nonprofit status from the IRS, you need to attend to various reports every year. Sound scary? Fear not — we show you the way.

Chapter 1

Tuning In to the World of Nonprofit Organizations

*I*t's a typical day in your hometown. Your alarm wakes you from a restful sleep and you switch on your radio to hear the latest news from your local public radio station. You hear that a think tank's study reports that economic indicators are on the rise and a new treatment regimen for arthritis is being tested at a health clinic across town. Plato, your Golden Retriever/ Labrador mix, adopted from the animal shelter when he was 5 months old, bounds onto your bed to let you know it's time for breakfast and a walk. Plato is followed by Cynthia, your 4-year-old daughter, who wants to go on a walk with you before she's dropped off at the preschool housed in the community center. You remember that you promised to bring canned goods to the food bank that's next door to Cynthia's school. You haven't even had your coffee yet, but already your morning is filled with news and services provided by nonprofit organizations.

You know that your public radio station is a nonprofit because you listen three or four times a year to its pledge drives, and you volunteer a few hours each month for the food bank, so clearly it's a nonprofit. But you may not know that the think tank is probably a nonprofit organization, just like the health clinic where the arthritis research is being tested and the animal shelter where you found Plato. It's likely that Cynthia's preschool and the community center where it rents its space are nonprofit organizations as well. Whether we realize it or not, all of us — rich or poor — benefit from the work of nonprofit organizations every day.

Sometimes nonprofit services are paid for mostly by tax-deductible donations and sometimes nonprofits charge a fee for what they do. Other nonprofits may enter into contracts with your city or county to provide services to residents. Usually, nonprofit organizations get their income from a combination of all these revenue sources.

The nonprofit sector isn't a distinct place — it isn't some plaza or district that you come upon suddenly as you weave your way through your day. It's more like a thread of a common color that's laced throughout the economy and our lives. No matter where we live or what we do, it's not easy to get through the day without being affected by the work of a nonprofit organization. So, in this chapter, we help you understand exactly what a nonprofit organization is and how to start and manage one.

So What's a Nonprofit Organization?

People hear the term *nonprofit organization* and picture Mother Hubbard's cupboard, as in awfully bare or zero bank balance. But in fact, some nonprofit organizations turn very tidy profits on their operations, and that's good, because cash flow keeps an enterprise humming, whether it's a for-profit business or not.

Comparing for-profits to nonprofits

The main difference between a for-profit and a nonprofit enterprise is what happens to the profit. In a for-profit company like Exxon, Microsoft, Disney, or your favorite fast-food establishment, profits are distributed to the owners, including shareholders. But a nonprofit can't do that. Any profit remaining after the bills are paid has to be plowed back into the organization's service program or kept in reserve. Profit can't be distributed to individuals, such as the organization's board of directors.

What about shareholders — do nonprofits have any shareholders to pay off? Not in terms of a monetary payoff, like a stock dividend. But in a broad, service sense, nonprofits do have "shareholders." They're the people who benefit from the nonprofit's activities, like the people who tune in to public radio or enroll their children in a nonprofit preschool.

Introducing the one and only 501(c)(3)

When we use the term *nonprofit organization* in this book, for the most part, we're talking about an organization that has been incorporated (or recognized in some way) under the laws of its state and that the Internal Revenue Service (IRS) has classified as a 501(c)(3) and determined to be a public charity. If the term 501(c)(3) is new to you, add it to your vocabulary with pride. In no time, "five-oh-one-see-three" will roll off your tongue as if you're a nonprofit expert.

Other kinds of nonprofit organizations *do* exist; they're formed to benefit their members, to influence legislation, or to fulfill other purposes. They receive exemption from federal income taxes and sometimes relief from property taxes at the local level. (Chapter 2 discusses these organizations in greater detail.)

Nonprofit organizations classified as 501(c)(3) receive extra privileges under the law. They are, with minor exceptions, the only group of tax-exempt organizations that can receive contributions from individuals and organizations that are tax deductible for the donor.

The IRS tax code describes allowable purposes of 501(c)(3) nonprofit organizations as serving religious, educational, charitable, scientific, and literary purposes.

Check out CD0101 for a more detailed list of the activities that 501(c)(3) nonprofits take on.

A sector by any other name

Not everyone thinks that *nonprofit sector* is the best term. That's because of the array of organizations with different kinds of nonprofit status. Some of these organizations are formed to benefit their members — like fraternities and labor unions — and don't share a broad public-serving intent. Another reason *nonprofit sector* may not be the best choice of terms is its negative connotation. After all, what's worse than not making a profit? But, as we point out earlier, and we remind you again in later chapters, not making a profit isn't the determining factor. Alternative terms that you may hear include the following:

✔ **Voluntary sector:** This term emphasizes the presence of volunteer board members and the significance of voluntary contributions and services to the work of 501(c)(3) organizations. In this definition, the organizations alone don't represent the meaning of *nonprofit;* the definition includes the vast web of their supporters who participate as volunteers and donors.

✔ **Independent sector:** This term emphasizes the public-serving mission of these organizations and their volunteers and their independence from government. (Independent Sector is also the name of a nonprofit organization that sponsors research, publications, and public programs about the sector.)

✔ **Charitable sector:** This term emphasizes the donations these organizations receive from individuals and institutions.

✔ **Third sector:** This term emphasizes the organization's important role alongside government and the for-profit business economy.

We use the term *nonprofit sector* throughout this book, but we want you to understand its limitations and be familiar with other commonly used terms.

Being a nonprofit organization doesn't mean that an entity is exempt from paying all taxes. Nonprofit organizations pay employment taxes just like for-profit businesses do. In some states, but not all, nonprofits are exempt from paying sales tax, so be sure that you're familiar with your local laws.

Finding Your Mission and Entering the Nonprofit World

People form nonprofit organizations in order to work toward changing conditions in the world, either for a specific group of people or society in general. The overall goal or purpose of a nonprofit is known as its *mission.* Taking the time needed to clearly outline a nonprofit's mission is time well spent because the mission guides the activities of the organization, helps the nonprofit's directors allocate resources wisely, and serves as a measure for evaluating the accomplishments of the group. We think developing a mission statement is so important that we devote an entire chapter (Chapter 3) to guiding you through this process.

Examining your personal mission before embarking on the path of launching a nonprofit is important. You're creating a legal entity that has responsibilities for reporting to both the state and federal governments. If the organization grows to the point where you must hire employees, you're responsible for paying regular salaries and providing adequate benefits. And although you can be compensated for your work as a nonprofit staff member, you can't develop equity in the organization or take away any profits at the end of the year. Chapter 2 has more information to help you make this important decision.

Setting up a nonprofit

Nearly all nonprofit organizations are established as corporations under the laws of a particular state. If you're located in Iowa and you plan to do most of your work in that state, you follow the laws in Iowa to set up the basic legal structure of a nonprofit corporation. Although you'll find some differences from state to state, in general, the process requires writing and submitting articles of incorporation to the state and developing *bylaws,* the rules under which the corporation will operate.

After your nonprofit is established under your state laws, the next step is applying for 501(c)(3) status from the IRS. This step entails completing and submitting IRS Form 1023. You need to specify in some detail the proposed activities of the new organization, and you're asked for projected revenue and expenses for the year in which you apply, and for start-up organizations, two years into the future. To be honest, you can't complete this form in one afternoon. It requires substantial time and thought to develop the necessary material. We discuss the incorporation and IRS application process in Chapter 4.

Making plans and being flexible

After you start managing a nonprofit organization, you'll discover that planning is your best friend. Every task from budgeting to grant writing requires that you make plans for the future. And you need to do a substantial amount of planning before you're ready to send in your IRS application for tax exemption.

Don't be frightened by this recommendation to plan. The act of planning comes down fundamentally to thinking through what you're going to do as well as how and when you're going to do it. Your plan becomes the road map that guides you toward achieving your goals and your nonprofit mission. Planning is something that you should pay attention to every day.

 You should always begin with a plan, but that doesn't mean that plans shouldn't be altered when the situation calls for it. Circumstances change; flexibility and adaptability are good traits to nurture if you're running a nonprofit organization. Chapters 7 and 10 cover planning and budgeting. Chapters 11 and 13 discuss planning for marketing and fundraising.

Bigger than a breadbox

The nonprofit sector is larger than many people realize. Here are some figures from the National Center for Charitable Statistics, based on IRS data, regarding the number of 501(c)(3) public charities in 2008 in the United States:

✔ More than 950,000 organizations were registered as public charities with the IRS.

✔ Assets held by these groups totaled more than $2.5 trillion.

✔ More than one-half of all the assets were owned by fewer than 2,200 charities.

✔ Nearly 80 percent of public charities had an annual gross revenue of less than $100,000.

Being Inspired and Inspiring Volunteers

The nonprofit sector is exciting. It encourages individuals with ideas about solving social problems or enhancing arts, culture, the environment, or education to act on those ideas. It creates a viable place within our society and economy for worthy activities that have little chance of commercial success. We think that it combines the best of the business world with the best of government, bringing together the creativity, zeal, and problem solving from the business side with the call to public service from the government side.

We also find volunteerism inspiring. Everyone has heard stories of tightly knit communities where neighbors gather to rebuild a barn. That spirit of pitching in to help is the best part of living in a community in which people share values and ideas.

Many people live in places that contain groups from a wide variety of backgrounds. The nonprofit sector provides an array of institutions in which all people can come together, with both those who resemble them and others who are unlike them, to work toward the common good. Volunteerism enables everyone to pitch in to rebuild "the barn" in a wide variety of contexts.

Applying the term *voluntary sector* to nonprofit organizations came about for a good reason. In the United States, according to the Bureau of Labor Statistics, 61.8 million people volunteered at least once between September 2007 and September 2008.

When you're working in a nonprofit, you'll likely be supervising volunteers — and they'll likely supervise you. What we mean is that (with very few exceptions) nonprofit boards of directors serve as unpaid volunteers. And if you're the executive director, your supervisors are the trustees or board members of the organization. At the same time, you likely depend on volunteers to carry out some or all the activities of the organization. You may even be a volunteer yourself.

The word "supervision" sounds harsh, and we don't mean to suggest that nonprofits are or should be run with an iron hand. The board of directors does have ultimate responsibility, however, for the finances and actions of a nonprofit organization, and, therefore, people serving in that capacity have a real duty to make sure that the organization has sufficient resources to carry out its activities and that it's doing what it's supposed to be.

We prefer to think of nonprofits as being an organized group activity. You need to depend on others to reach goals, and they need to depend on you. We talk about boards of directors in Chapter 6 and working with volunteers in Chapter 8. If your nonprofit employs paid staff or hopes to someday, Chapter 9 provides some guidance in hiring and managing employees.

Finding the Resources to Do Your Job

One distinctive feature of the nonprofit sector is its dependency on contributions. We devote many pages of this book — most of Part III — to advice about getting contributions through fundraising.

Gifts from individuals of money, goods, services, and property make up the largest portion of that voluntary support. This portion also is the oldest of the voluntary tradition in the United States and goes back to colonial times. Since the late 19th century, private philanthropic foundations have emerged as another major source of support, and more recently — particularly after World War II — the federal government and corporations became important income sources. Many nonprofits also sell some kind of service, and a trend in the sector shows earned income becoming a larger portion of total revenues.

Seeing where the money comes from

Among private, nongovernmental sources of support, gifts from living individuals — as opposed to bequests from people who have died — have always represented the largest portion of total giving, but philanthropic giving by foundations and corporations has been growing. Table 1-1 gives estimates of the sources of private contributions in 2008. The best fundraising approach for most organizations is to take a balanced approach that includes individual giving as well as grants and corporate contributions.

Table 1-1	Sources of Private Contributions: 2008	
Source of Income	*Amount of Total Giving in Billions*	*Percentage of Total Giving*
Individuals	$229.28	74.5%
Foundations	$41.21	13.4%
Bequests	$22.66	7.4%
Corporations	$14.50	4.7%
Total	**$307.65**	100%

Source: Giving USA Foundation — Giving USA 2009

Fundraising for fun and profit

Every nonprofit organization depends on generous donors for the cash it needs to pay its bills. Even if you have income from ticket sales, admission charges, or contracted services, you'll find that raising additional money is necessary to keep your organization alive and thriving.

You can see from Table 1-1 that individual giving is the largest single source of contributed income to nonprofit organizations. But you can't just sit waiting by the mailbox for the donations to begin arriving. Two basic rules of fundraising are that people need to be asked for donations and thanked after giving one. Chapter 14 focuses on raising money from individuals, Chapter 15 covers raising money with special events, and Chapter 18 discusses campaign fundraising, which is used when you need to raise extra money for your building or your endowment.

Grants from foundations and corporations make up a smaller percentage of giving to nonprofits, but their support can be invaluable for start-up project costs, equipment, technical support, and, sometimes, general operating costs. Keep in mind that the figures given in Table 1-1 don't apply equally to every nonprofit. Some organizations get most of their income from foundation grants; others get very little. Chapter 16 introduces you to resources to help you find potential grant sources. Chapter 17 takes you through the process of crafting a grant proposal.

Fundraising works better if people know you exist. That knowledge also helps get people to your theater or to sign up for your programs. Here's where marketing and public relations enter the picture. Chapter 11 helps you figure out what your media message should be and how to circulate it to the world.

Make no mistake about it, fundraising is hard work, but if you approach the task with a positive attitude and make your case well, you can find the resources you need.

Chapter 2

Deciding to Start a Nonprofit

● ●

In This Chapter

▶ Knowing the benefits and drawbacks of starting a nonprofit

▶ Starting off your nonprofit on the right foot

▶ Understanding who owns a nonprofit

▶ Looking at varieties of nonprofit organizations

▶ Examining the similarities and differences between nonprofits and for-profits

▶ Getting a fiscal sponsor to help you provide a service or complete a project

● ●

*M*aybe you've been thinking about starting a nonprofit organization for years, or maybe an idea to solve a social problem or provide a needed service recently popped into your head. It could be time to make your idea a reality. But before you file your incorporation papers, it's important to understand the positive and not-so-positive factors that can make or break your new organization. Like opening any business, starting and managing a nonprofit organization isn't a simple matter.

Take a look at the economy around you. Are existing nonprofit organizations in your community thriving, or are they struggling to find financial and volunteer support? In addition, are you equipped to manage money and raise funds — which isn't always an easy task even when business is booming — and can you inspire others to work with you whether they're board members, staff, or volunteers? After reviewing the pros and cons of starting your nonprofit organization, you may even decide that now isn't the right time to take this important step.

In this chapter, we pose some questions that you should think about (and answer) before you begin the process of incorporation and applying for tax exemption. If some of your answers point to the conclusion that your idea is worth pursuing but that now isn't the right time to start a brand-new nonprofit organization, we suggest you consider using a fiscal sponsor. As we point out later in this chapter, the benefits of fiscal sponsorship are many.

When we use the term *nonprofit* in this book, we're referring to organizations that have been recognized by the Internal Revenue Service (IRS) as public charities under section 501(c)(3) of the tax code. Later in this chapter, we describe some of the other kinds of nonprofits to point out the distinct attributes of these 501(c)(3) public charities.

Weighing the Pros and Cons of Starting a Nonprofit

Before you jump headfirst into making your nonprofit dream a reality, you should understand some basic facts about nonprofit organizations. We begin with some of the pros:

- You'll receive exemption from taxes on most income to the nonprofit.
- For some types of nonprofits, you'll have the ability to receive contributions that are deductible for the donor.
- You'll gain the possibility of receiving grant funds from foundations and corporations.
- You'll get the feeling that you're contributing to the solution of a problem or to the improvement of society.

Just about everyone would consider these facts to be positive, but they aren't the whole story. If you're thinking of starting a nonprofit to get rich or to avoid paying taxes, consider the following list of cons:

- Nonprofit employees' salaries are subject to income tax like all other compensation.
- You'll be required to file an annual report with the IRS. The complexity of the report increases as your nonprofit income increases. (See Chapter 5 for more information about reporting requirements.)
- You can't start a nonprofit organization to benefit a particular individual or family member.
- Competition for grants from foundations, corporations, and government agencies is tough, and so is getting donations from individuals. You'll be up against more-established nonprofits with successful track records.
- If you decide to move on to other pursuits, you can't take with you any assets accumulated by the organization you've built.

The bottom line is this: Think carefully about your motivation for launching a nonprofit organization. Remember that nonprofit organizations are permitted special privileges because they're formed to benefit the public, not individuals.

Doing Your Homework First

Beyond thinking about the challenges you'll face in starting and running a nonprofit organization, it's also a good idea to apply some common sense. Nonprofits don't operate in a vacuum and neither should you. Personal commitment and inspiration can take your organization far, but you also need to find out how your community will receive your particular idea. So before going full steam ahead with your nonprofit, investigate your competition, get community support, decide how to fund your organization, determine whether you're really ready to run a nonprofit, and develop a game plan. Read on to find out how to get your nonprofit off to the right start.

Checking out the competition

Just as if you were starting a business, you must examine your competition before starting your nonprofit organization. If you wanted to open a grocery store, you wouldn't choose a location next to a successful supermarket, because the market can bear only so much trade. This principle holds true for nonprofits, too. You may have the best idea in the world, but if someone else in your community is already doing it well, don't try to duplicate it.

If your area doesn't have a similar program, ask yourself why. Maybe your community doesn't have enough potential clients or audience members to support the project. Or maybe funders don't perceive the same needs in the community as you do.

Assessing the needs of your area is a good way to evaluate the potential market for your nonprofit's services. You may want to use some or all of the following methods to determine your community's needs:

- Telephone surveys or written questionnaires to a random sample of residents in your community
- Interviews with local foundation and civic officials
- Focus groups with people who are likely to benefit from the organization

For more details on assessing your community's needs, see Chapter 7.

Finding people to help you

Your chances of success increase if you begin with support from others, and the more help you have, the better. Sure, you can probably find an example of a single-minded visionary who alone battles through all sorts of adversity to establish a thriving nonprofit, but starting and running a nonprofit organization is essentially a group activity.

When starting a nonprofit, you need to find people to serve on the board of directors and to support your efforts with donations of money and volunteer time. The first people you usually identify as supporters are family and friends. How can they turn you down? In the long run, however, you need to expand those supporters to others who believe in the organization's mission (and not because you personally created it).

Some people hesitate to share their idea with others because they believe that someone may try to steal it. We think this fear is largely unfounded. No matter what it is, you'll be better off if you invite others to join you in the undertaking.

To find people to help you and support your organization, take every opportunity to speak about your idea before civic groups, religious groups, and service clubs. You can pass out fliers or set up a booth at a volunteer fair. Talk to your friends and co-workers. Put on your salesperson's cap and convince the community that it needs your program. If you're having a difficult time drumming up support, it may be a sign that you need to refine your idea or that others view it as impractical. You may need to think about going back to the drawing board.

Figuring out how you'll pay the bills

Funding your nonprofit organization is a big issue. Even if you begin as a volunteer-run organization and work from a home office, you still need funds for letterhead, supplies, equipment, postage, and insurance. You'll also have filing fees for your incorporation and tax-exemption applications. Many nonprofit start-ups are funded by the founder in the beginning. Are you able to pay all the start-up expenses before revenues start flowing to your new nonprofit?

Putting together a budget can help you decide whether the start-up expenses are manageable for you. You'll be creating lots of budgets sooner or later, so you may as well get an early start. Chapter 10 discusses more on budgeting and other financial issues.

If you aren't able to fund the operation by yourself in the early months, you need to make a compelling case that your new organization will provide an important service to the community and convince donors that you have the knowledge and experience to provide it. You may be able to solicit contributions from individuals before the IRS grants the organization tax-exempt status, as long as you reveal that your exemption is pending and complete any required registration. (These contributions become deductible to the donor if you receive the tax-exemption status and file for your exemption within 15 months of the date you incorporated.) Start-up grants from foundations or corporations are rare and next to impossible to obtain before the IRS recognizes your organization's tax-exempt status, so don't plan to receive any grants from outside organizations.

New organizations can avoid the awkward period between start-up and receiving tax-exempt status by beginning as a sponsored program of an existing nonprofit organization. This arrangement is known as *fiscal sponsorship.* We discuss fiscal sponsorship in more detail later in this chapter.

Taking a long, hard look in the mirror

Ask yourself whether you're the right person to start a nonprofit organization, and answer honestly. If your organization offers a service, especially in the health and social-services fields, do you have the qualifications or license necessary to provide those services? In addition to being professionally qualified, you also need to consider whether you feel confident about your management, fundraising, and communication skills.

When starting and working in a new nonprofit organization, you also need to be able to stretch yourself across many different skill areas. You may be dressed to the nines one day to pitch your project to the mayor or to a corporate executive, and the next day, you may be sweeping the floor of your office or unplugging a clogged toilet. In other words, you need to be versatile and willing to take on just about any task that needs to be done.

When potential donors are evaluating grant proposals, they certainly look to see whether the organization's leadership has the background, experience, and knowledge necessary to carry out the proposed program. This doesn't necessarily mean that you need to be an experienced nonprofit manager, but try to assess your background to see how you can apply your experience to the nonprofit that you hope to start.

Planning — and then planning some more

If there ever was a time to plan, this is it. Planning is what turns your initial idea into a doable project. Planning is also a good way to find potential holes in your thinking. For example, you may believe that your community doesn't have adequate animal rescue services. You may be right, but when you begin to break down the idea of starting an animal shelter, you may find that the project costs more money or requires more staff or facilities than you first thought it would. When armed with that knowledge, you can adjust your plan as necessary or scrap the idea altogether.

To begin planning, write a one- or two-page synopsis of your nonprofit idea. In your synopsis, include what you're trying to do and how you plan to do it. Then make a list of resources you need to accomplish your mission. Resources may include money, volunteers, and an appropriate space to carry out your activities. After you've prepared your synopsis and list of resources, talk to as many people as you can about your idea, asking for help and honest feedback about your project. The purpose of this planning process is to think your nonprofit idea through step by step. (If you need help in the planning process, take a look at Chapter 7.)

Understanding Nonprofit Ownership

We once received a telephone call from a man who was shopping for a nonprofit. "Do you know if there are any nonprofits for sale in New Hampshire?" he asked. Although this question doesn't come to us often, it illustrates a misconception about the status of nonprofit organizations. No one person or group of people can *own* a nonprofit organization. You don't see nonprofit shares traded on stock exchanges, and any equity in a nonprofit organization belongs to the organization itself, not to the board of directors or the staff. Nonprofit assets can be sold, but the proceeds of the sale must benefit the organization, not private parties.

If you start a nonprofit and decide at some point in the future that you can't or don't want to manage it anymore, you have to walk away and leave the running of the organization to someone else. Or, if the time has come to close the doors for good, any assets the organization owns must be distributed to other nonprofits fulfilling a similar mission.

When nonprofit managers and consultants talk about "ownership" of a nonprofit organization, they're using the word metaphorically to make the point that board members, staff, clients, and the community have a stake in the organization's future success and its ability to provide needed programs.

Benefiting the public

People form nonprofit organizations to create a public benefit. A nonprofit organization can't be created to help a particular individual or family, for example. If that were possible, we'd all have our separate nonprofit organizations. You can start a nonprofit to aid a specific group or class of individuals — everyone suffering from heart disease, for example, or people living below the poverty level — but you can't create a nonprofit for individual benefit or gain.

Just because you're working for the public's benefit doesn't mean that you can't receive a reasonable salary for your work. And, despite the name "non-profit," such an organization can have surplus funds — essentially, a profit — at the end of the year. In a for-profit business, the surplus money can be distributed to employees, shareholders, and the board of directors; however, in a nonprofit organization, the surplus funds are held in reserve by the organization and aren't distributed.

Accounting to the public

People are paying more attention to nonprofit organizations these days. A few examples of excessive salaries reported in the media and new concerns about how some nonprofits have spent donated funds have prompted donors, legislators, and the general public to ask more questions regarding nonprofit finances and management.

Although nonprofit organizations aren't public entities like governmental agencies and departments, their tax-exempt status and the fact that contributions are tax deductible require them to be held more accountable to the public than a privately owned business is.

We discuss nonprofit disclosure requirements in more detail in Chapter 5, but at a minimum, federal law requires that nonprofits file a report (for example, Form 990, Form 990-EZ, or Form 990-N) every year with the IRS. The amount of detail required in the report depends on the size of the nonprofit organization. States also have their own reporting requirements.

A word about excessive compensation

Although nonprofit employees have no absolute limit on the amount of compensation they can earn, the IRS does have the authority to penalize individuals (and organizations) who receive (or pay) excessive compensation. Whether the IRS considers benefits "excessive" depends on the situation. For instance, a staff member earning $100,000 annually from an organization with a budget of $125,000 probably needs to worry, but someone earning $100,000 from a nonprofit with a $5 million budget probably doesn't.

An employee who's found to be receiving excessive compensation may be required to pay an excise tax, and in dire cases, the nonprofit organization may lose its tax-exempt status. Chapter 5 offers more information on excessive compensation.

So, when setting your nonprofit's executive director's salary, take care that the amount of compensation is justified by salary surveys of similar organizations. Also factor in the local cost of living, the size of the nonprofit's budget, and the type of services being provided.

Federal law also requires nonprofits to make their three most recent 990 reports, as well as their application for tax exemption, available for public inspection. State and local laws in your area may require additional disclosures. Posting your 990 reports and other required documents on the Web is an acceptable way to meet disclosure requirements.

To get familiar with the 990 report, download a copy of it from the IRS Web site at www.irs.gov. You also can view completed 990 forms from other nonprofit organizations at GuideStar (www.guidestar.org).

Nonprofits Aren't One-Size-Fits-All

The words "nonprofit" and "charity" go together in most people's minds, but remember that not all nonprofits are charitable organizations. The most common examples are business and trade associations, political advocacy groups, fraternal societies, and clubs. Although these nonprofits enjoy exemption from corporate income taxes, people who donate to them can't claim a tax deduction for their contributions.

Most nonprofits, charitable or not, are incorporated organizations that are formed under the laws of the state in which they're created. Some nonprofits have other legal structures, such as unincorporated associations or trusts, but these are in the minority. The IRS may grant tax-exempt status to a nonprofit after reviewing its stated purpose. (See Chapter 4 for information about incorporation and applying for a tax exemption.) Nonprofit types are identified by the section of the IRS code under which they qualify for tax-exempt status.

In this section, we provide an overview of the types of nonprofit organizations and some of the rules and regulations that you'll be subject to if you decide to incorporate and seek tax-exempt status from the IRS. You may discover, for example, that your idea will have a better chance for success if you create a social welfare organization — a 501(c)(4) — or a for-profit business.

Knowing them by their numbers

Nonprofit organizations can be formed under the IRS code for many reasons other than charitable ones. To get a taste of the variety of these organizations, the following list summarizes various classes of tax-exempt organizations:

- **501(c)(3):** These organizations are formed for educational, scientific, literary, charitable, or religious pursuits; and also to test for public safety and to prevent cruelty to children and animals. Nonprofits in this category may be classified as public charities or private foundations;

the classification usually is determined by the source of support for the organization. Foundations are subject to additional reporting requirements. This book focuses on 501(c)(3) organizations that are classified as public charities. Contributions to these organizations are deductible for the donor.

- **501(c)(4):** These organizations are known as *social welfare organizations* because they're formed for the improvement of general welfare and the common good of the people. Advocacy groups tend to fall into this category because organizations with this classification are allowed more leeway to lobby legislatures as a part of their mission to improve the general welfare. Contributions to these organizations aren't deductible for the donor.

- **501(c)(5):** Labor unions and other groups formed to improve conditions for workers are in this category. These groups also may lobby for legislation.

- **501(c)(6):** Business and trade associations that provide services to their members and work toward the betterment of business conditions are placed in this classification. This category includes chambers of commerce and real estate boards, for example. Again, lobbying for legislation is allowed.

- **501(c)(7):** This section covers social clubs formed for recreation and pleasure. Country clubs and organizations formed around a hobby come under this classification. These organizations must be funded primarily by memberships and dues.

- **501(c)(9):** This type of nonprofit is an employees' beneficiary association that's created to pay insurance benefits to members and their dependents. It must be voluntary, members must have a common bond through employment or a labor union, and, in most cases, it must meet nondiscrimination requirements.

Several other 501(c)-type organizations are so specialized in nature that we won't go into them here. One of our favorites is the 501(c)(13), which covers cemetery companies.

Political committees and parties have their own special classification, too. They're recognized under IRS code section 527 and are organized for the purpose of electing persons to office. They have special reporting requirements and aren't required to be incorporated.

To get the full flavor of the various categories of nonprofit organizations, see the information at the IRS Web site (www.irs.gov) or review IRS publication 557.

Odd little rules and regulations to add to your file

Entire volumes have been written about IRS regulations and laws pertaining to nonprofits. But don't worry — we just want to give you an overview of some facts that may help you decide whether starting a 501(c)(3) nonprofit organization is your best choice.

IRS regulations can change from year to year. So it's always a good idea to look at the most recent version of IRS Publication 557 for the latest information.

Nonprofits and political activities

Nonprofits that are classified as 501(c)(3) public charities can't campaign to support or oppose the candidacy of anyone running for an elected office. If you want your organization to do so, you must instead form a political committee under IRS section 527. However, the stipulations on nonprofits lobbying for specific legislation are less clear. In the following list, we break down the stipulations for you a bit:

- ✔ **Social welfare organizations and labor unions** have more leeway when it comes to legislative lobbying than the 501(c)(3) organizations do. In fact, lobbying can be the primary activity of these organizations. Groups that lobby must inform their members what percentage of dues they use for lobbying activities, and they can't work toward a candidate's election.

- ✔ **Charitable organizations, or nonprofits that the IRS considers public charities under section 501(c)(3),** may participate in some legislative lobbying if it isn't a "substantial" part of their activities. The IRS doesn't define "substantial," so it determines this question on a case-by-case basis.

- ✔ **Public charities** can spend a higher portion of their budgets on lobbying activities if the organization chooses to elect the *h designation* (IRS Form 5768), which refers to section 501(h) of the IRS code. Electing the h designation requires more financial reporting to the IRS, but it allows the nonprofit to spend a greater percentage of its income on lobbying activities. The IRS allows more expenditures for *direct lobbying* (when members of the nonprofit talk with a legislator about an issue at hand) than for *grassroots lobbying* (encouraging members of the general public to contact legislators to promote an opinion about a piece of legislation).

- ✔ **Private foundations,** although they, too, are recognized under section 501(c)(3), may not participate in any legislative lobbying. The only exception to this rule is when pending legislation may have a regulatory impact on the foundation.

Penalties for engaging in too much political activity can include loss of your organization's tax exemption. However, going deeper into the details of these laws and reporting requirements is really beyond the scope of this book. So, if you're contemplating involving your nonprofit in serious legislative activity, consult an attorney or tax specialist for advice. Information also is available at the Charity Lobbying in the Public Interest Web site (www.clpi.org).

The situation with churches

Churches are in a category all by themselves. The IRS doesn't require them to file for a tax exemption, nor does it require them to file annual reports to the IRS. Some churches, however, do apply for an exemption because their social-service programs often include anything from preschools to soup kitchens. These programs can then apply for foundation funding and government grants or contracts to help pay the costs of providing the services.

It's highly unlikely that grants or contracts will be given to church programs that haven't been officially recognized as being tax-exempt.

Taxes, taxes, taxes

Nonprofit organizations may be subject to *unrelated business income tax,* which is also known as UBIT. When a nonprofit earns $1,000 a year or more from a trade or business that's unrelated to its exempt purpose, this income is taxable. Some corporate sponsorship funds also may be subject to UBIT if they're perceived by the IRS as advertising dollars. IRS Publication 598 (visit www.irs.gov to take a look at this publication) tells you all you need to know about this subject.

Some states exempt *some* nonprofits from paying state sales and use taxes. Check the laws in your state to see whether your organization is exempt from paying these taxes. The same is true of property taxes — it depends on your local jurisdiction. Your nearest tax assessor can tell you whether you have to pay property taxes.

Nonprofit employees must, of course, pay income tax on their salaries and other taxable compensation.

Nonprofits owning for-profits

Nonprofits can own for-profit businesses. We don't recommend it, because you're going to have enough on your plate, especially when you're starting out, but it is possible. The business is subject to all regular taxes, just like all other for-profit businesses. Profits from the business become assets of the nonprofit and must be used to further the organization's goals and programs.

Very small organizations

If your nonprofit has less than $5,000 in annual revenues, it doesn't need to apply for a tax exemption. You can even go a bit over $5,000 in a year if your average annual income over a three-year period is less than $5,000. When your income averages more than that amount, however, you have 90 days following the close of your most recent tax year to file for a tax exemption.

Even if your organization has revenues under $5,000, you may still need to file the IRS 990-N form. This form can only be filed online. Check the IRS Web site at www.irs.gov for the latest information about this requirement.

Nonprofit compensation

Nonprofit organizations have one common feature, regardless of their type: No board member, staff member, or other interested party can benefit from the earnings of a nonprofit. Instead, assets are forever dedicated to the purpose of the organization. If the organization dissolves, the nonprofit must transfer the assets to another organization that performs a similar function.

Just because assets are dedicated to fulfilling an organizational mission doesn't mean that people are required to work for nonprofit organizations for free. Nonprofits can and should pay reasonable salaries to their staff members, if they have any. But keep in mind the difference between paying a salary and splitting the profits at the end of year.

Comparing Nonprofits and For-Profits

Believing that nonprofit organizations have special advantages isn't uncommon. And to some extent, it's true. How many for-profit businesses, for example, get help from volunteers and generous donors? On the other hand, the advantages to owning your business exist, too. In this section, we discuss the similarities and differences between nonprofits and for-profits to help you decide the direction in which you should go.

How they're alike

We start with the similarities between the nonprofits and for-profits because, believe it or not, there are several. For instance, consider the following:

- Sound business practices are important to both organizations.
- Good planning based on good information is a critical factor in the success of both nonprofits and for-profits.

 ✔ Management skills, the ability to communicate clearly, and attention to detail make a difference whether you're working in a nonprofit or somewhere else.

 ✔ A little bit of luck doesn't hurt either type of organization.

A final similarity involves the term *entrepreneur,* which usually is used to describe someone who starts a new business. But any person or group that sets out to establish a nonprofit organization is entrepreneurial as well. After all, you're starting out on a path that may lead to great success, and you'll assume some risks along the way. We hope that you won't risk your house or your savings account to get a nonprofit going, but you may have uncertain income for a while.

How they differ

Although for-profits and nonprofits require similar professionalism and dedication from their leaders, they differ when it comes time to interpret their bottom lines and successes.

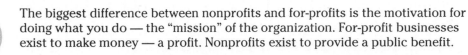

The biggest difference between nonprofits and for-profits is the motivation for doing what you do — the "mission" of the organization. For-profit businesses exist to make money — a profit. Nonprofits exist to provide a public benefit.

Evaluating the success of a for-profit endeavor is easy: Did you make money, and, if so, how much did you make? We're not saying this to cast stones at the capitalist system or to in any way disparage the millions of folks who work for profit-making endeavors. After all, the nonprofit sector depends on profits and wealth for its support. And, of course, nonprofits have to balance the books, too. Even nonprofits prefer to end the year with more money than they had when they started. They just don't call it profit; they call it a surplus.

For a nonprofit to be successful, it needs to change some aspect of the human condition; it needs to solve a problem, provide education, or build a monument. Because the goals of nonprofits are so lofty and progress toward achieving them is often slow, evaluating nonprofit success is sometimes difficult. That's why nonprofits often are said to have a *double bottom line* — that is, the financial results and the social change they create.

Using a Fiscal Sponsor: An Alternative Approach

If you're simply interested in providing a service, maybe you don't want to waste your time with the bureaucratic and legal matters that can complicate a new nonprofit start-up. Or maybe you have a project that will end after a year or two, or you simply want to test the viability of an idea. Why bother to establish a new organization if it's going to close when you finish your project?

You may not need to start a nonprofit to carry out the program you're thinking of starting. Instead, *fiscal sponsorship* may be the best route for you to take. In this approach, your new project becomes a sponsored program of an existing 501(c)(3) nonprofit organization. Contributions earmarked for your project are tax-deductible because they're made to the sponsoring agency.

A fiscal sponsor sometimes is called a *fiscal agent,* but this term doesn't accurately describe the relationship between a fiscal sponsor and the sponsored project. The term *agent* implies that the sponsoring organization is acting on behalf on the project, when really the project is acting on behalf of the organization. The project is simply a program of the sponsoring nonprofit.

This distinction may seem nitpicky, but it's an important one to keep in mind; after all, you must satisfy the IRS requirements for this type of relationship. The 501(c)(3) sponsoring organization is responsible to both the funders and the IRS to see that the money is spent as intended and that charitable goals are met.

Considering your options

Here are some important points to keep in mind if you decide to go the fiscal sponsor route:

- ✔ The mission of the fiscal sponsor must be in alignment with the project. In other words, if you have a project to provide free food to the homeless, don't approach your local philharmonic orchestra as a potential sponsor. Find a nonprofit that has similar goals in its mission statement.

- ✔ The board of directors of the sponsoring organization must approve the sponsorship arrangements. They are, after all, ultimately responsible.

- ✔ Both parties should outline a contract or memorandum of understanding detailing the responsibilities of each. See CD0201 for a sample fiscal sponsorship agreement.

- ✔ The fiscal sponsor customarily charges a fee for sponsoring a project, usually between 5 and 15 percent of the project's annual revenues, depending on the services it provides to the project.

- ✔ Some fiscal sponsors provide payroll services, office space, group insurance coverage, and even management support, if needed. Be sure to ask if these additional services are included in the fiscal sponsor's fee.

- ✔ Contributions to the sponsored project should be written to the sponsor, with a note that instructs that they be used for the project.

Some foundations are reluctant to award grants to fiscally sponsored projects, even announcing in their guidelines that they won't do it. One reason for this reluctance is their concern that boards of the sponsoring organizations exercise less oversight toward fiscal sponsorships than they do toward their agency's other programs. Those foundations also may be concerned that the sponsoring nonprofits only are providing convenient access to 501(c)(3) status to entities that don't qualify for that tax status from the IRS. Not all foundations share these prohibitions, however. Some, in fact, are proponents of fiscal sponsorship as a way of supporting new ideas and timely programs. You can read much more about foundations and grant proposals in Chapters 16 and 17.

Finding a fiscal sponsor

You may be able to find a fiscal sponsor near you by using the Fiscal Sponsor Directory (www.fiscalsponsordirectory.org). Some nonprofit organizations are formed with the sole purpose of providing fiscal sponsorship services. Another place to search is at your local community foundation. Community foundations have wide connections in the areas they serve and likely are aware of qualified fiscal sponsors.

If your area doesn't have a community foundation nearby, contact the nearest United Way office or another nonprofit that provides referrals and ask for help in finding the right agency to sponsor your project.

You don't want to go with just any fiscal sponsor. You have to do your homework to find one that fits your needs. First determine whether the sponsor's mission covers the type of program you'll be offering. Then do a little research to find out whether the sponsor is trustworthy. For example, you can perform an Internet search for the fiscal sponsor's name. Does its name appear in news stories detailing nonprofit malfeasance or other skulduggery? Ask others in your community, including individuals who are knowledgeable about nonprofit activities in your town.

The following is a helpful checklist for vetting a fiscal sponsor. Ask the sponsor these questions to determine whether it's a good fit for your project:

✔ Do you charge for specific services, such as access to insurance programs, over and above your basic sponsorship fees? What additional services do you offer?

✔ Do you allow sponsored projects to hire salaried employees, and do you provide payroll services and access to health insurance?

✔ Do you provide coaching and mentoring in nonprofit management and fundraising?

✔ How frequently do you write checks to pay bills? What's the frequency and format of financial reporting for the sponsored program?

✔ Do you require projects to have a minimum annual income?

✔ Do you formally acknowledge gifts and donations?

✔ Do your potential foundation funders make grants to fiscally sponsored programs?

Fiscal sponsorship as a first step

Using fiscal sponsorship as a temporary solution while establishing a new nonprofit corporation and acquiring a tax exemption can be an effective approach for the following reasons:

✔ You avoid the period when you have a nonprofit corporation but no tax-exempt status.

✔ You have an opportunity to test the viability of raising funds for your idea.

✔ You have time to establish an organizational infrastructure and to create a board of directors in a more leisurely manner.

✔ You can pay more attention to building your program services in the crucial beginning stages of your project.

Chapter 3

Writing Your Mission Statement

• •

In This Chapter

▶ Understanding the role of a mission statement

▶ Creating an effective mission statement with everyone's help

▶ Using your statement to make organizational decisions

• •

A good *mission statement* clearly states a nonprofit's purpose — including who benefits from its work — and how it works to fulfill that purpose. The process of developing your mission statement is important because it can help you refine your ideas, test them with others, and inspire those involved in the mission-writing process.

Mission statements can be one-liners or huge essays that go on for two or three pages. We suggest aiming for something brief, but in between these two extremes. A mission statement contained in one line resembles an advertising slogan, and a long, rambling statement is rarely read or remembered, even by the board of directors and staff members.

You need to spend some time thinking about what you want to include in your mission statement, because it defines what your organization hopes to accomplish. Your mission statement should be clear to people you work with daily as well as to the long-lost cousins you come across at your aunt's retirement party.

After you've decided on your organization's mission statement, you can use it as a touchstone to return to when making decisions about your nonprofit's activities. You'll include your mission statement in your 990 tax report to the Internal Revenue Service (IRS), in brochures, and in grant proposals. You may even print it on your business cards or coffee mugs.

In this chapter, we give you some guidance about how to create a simple yet compelling mission statement.

Mission Statement Basics

The mission statement is an organization's center. We were tempted to use the word *heart* rather than *center,* but we think that's stretching the metaphor a little. Or we could have said that mission statements are living, breathing organisms from which all organizational life flows, but that would truly be going too far. People are at the heart of and bring the life to an organization. Mission statements just help give this human energy direction.

Can organizations operate without good mission statements? Yes, and some do. We're sure that some organizations out there haven't looked at their mission statements since the Carter administration, and they're still doing good things. But social and environmental conditions have changed since the 1970s, and organizations have likely adapted to those changes. An organization's chances of success in making that adaptation are better if the organization and the people associated with it know exactly why it exists, what they're trying to do, and how they're going to do it.

A mission statement should state the organization's purpose, how the purpose will be achieved, and who will benefit from the organization's activities. Organizational values and vision also may be included. The mission also should be

- **Memorable:** You want to carry it around with you at all times.

- **Focused:** You want it to be narrow enough to focus the activities of your organization but broad enough to allow for growth and expansion.

- **Easy to read:** Your statement should be written in plain language so it doesn't need a set of footnotes for folks to decipher it. Be sure to limit your use of adjectives and try to avoid jargon.

Working with a purpose

When thinking of your organization's purpose, think of your desired end result. What would you like to see happen? What would the world (or your community) be like if your organization succeeded?

To say that you have to have a purpose seems almost too basic. Maybe you're thinking to yourself, "Of course I have a purpose. Why do you think I bought this book? I want to start a nonprofit to [fill in the blank]." But we bring up this point because clarifying the purpose is basic to a mission statement.

For example, you may know that you love cats and dogs and have always wanted to work with them, but that isn't the same thing as identifying a non-profit organization's purpose. Here's an example taken from a mission statement for a humane society in Texas: "Animal Friends' mission is to provide temporary shelter for homeless puppies, dogs, kittens, and cats until responsible, loving homes can be found."

This sentence doesn't describe Animal Friends' facilities or how it recruits and trains volunteers, but it does clearly state which animals it serves and that it doesn't intend to foster them as long as they live, but to place them in good homes. And if someone came to Animal Friends with a ferret, a pony, or a tarantula, its staff would know to refer that person to another shelter.

Knowing and understanding your organization's purpose is essential to making important organizational decisions. It also is a fundamental tool to use when asking for money, recruiting board members, hiring and motivating staff, and publicizing your activities.

Putting the beneficiaries on a pedestal

If you've determined your purpose, you probably know the primary beneficiaries of your activities. Their needs — be they kittens or egrets — make your mission compelling. Defining who will benefit from your nonprofit helps to focus your organizational activities and is an essential ingredient in your mission statement.

Some organizations have a more general audience than others. If your purpose is preserving historic buildings, the beneficiary of this activity may be current and future residents of a city, a county, or even a state. It also may be the workers you train in the crafts needed to complete the building restorations.

Describing how you accomplish your goals

After you know your organization's purpose and who benefits from its work, the next step is deciding how you're going to make it happen. Mission statements usually include a phrase describing the methods your organization will use to accomplish its purpose. Think about the activities and programs you'll provide to achieve your goal. Take a look at these examples:

✔ To indicate how it will accomplish its goals, the Animal Friends' mission simply says, "This is accomplished by a dedicated staff of employees, volunteers, and board members."

✔ The National Audubon Society's purpose "is to conserve and restore natural ecosystems, focusing on birds, other wildlife, and their habitats for the benefit of humanity and the earth's biological diversity." How does the society accomplish that goal? Its mission statement explains, "Our national network of community-based nature centers and chapters, scientific and educational programs, and advocacy on behalf of areas sustaining important bird populations, engage millions of people of all ages and backgrounds in positive conservation experiences."

When describing how your organization addresses its purpose, you don't want to be so specific that you have to rewrite your mission statement every time you add a new program. At the same time, you want your mission statement to be concrete enough that people reading it (or hearing you recite it) can envision what your organization does.

Envisioning your future with a vision statement

Simply put, a *vision statement* is your dream — your broadly described aspiration for what your organization can become. Although vision statements can describe a future desired condition as a result of the organization's activities, they're more typically applied to the organization itself. Usually, the statement includes phrases like "the best" or "recognized as a leader."

Here's an example of a vision statement from a fictitious agricultural policy think tank.

> *The Agricultural Economics Institute will encourage excellence in its staff by providing opportunities for collaboration and professional development. The Institute's research projects and position statements on agricultural matters will be widely reported in the media and referred to in the setting of state and national agriculture policy.*

Some nonprofits include their vision statements in their mission statements, and others don't. We believe that holding a dream is a good thing, and we see some truth to the statement, "If you can't conceive of doing something great, you can't do it." Still, we encourage you not to spend an excessive amount of time shaping your vision statement. Focusing on a clear purpose and concrete means for addressing it is more important.

Keeping your focus narrow at first and broadening over time

The narrower your mission statement, the easier it is to convey your organization's purpose and activities and focus your attention and resources on achieving success. If you start out with a mission to benefit all man and womankind, you're likely to frustrate yourself and your board. In this situation, you likely would be trying to work at a scale that far exceeds your organization's resources.

However, keep in mind that you can always change your mission statement. As your organization achieves initial success and you determine that it's time to expand, you may want to review — and possibly broaden — your mission as a part of your organizational planning process.

Check out two examples of a mission statement from the same organization — seven years apart. CD0301 was adopted in 1995; CD0302 is a revised mission statement adopted in 2002.

Keeping your statement short and sweet

In keeping with our notion that a good mission statement is easily expressed, we tend to favor short, pithy statements over long, rambling ones.

We understand, however, that some organizations want to describe their aims and activities more fully than what can be captured in one or two short sentences. For those organizations, we suggest that you begin your mission statement with a short summary that states simply what your nonprofit hopes to accomplish, how it plans to do it, and for whom. This succinct version can be printed on brochures or used as an introductory statement on your Web site. Then you can prepare your longer statement, which includes all your organization's programs.

Writing the Mission Statement

You probably already have a good idea of your purpose (but if you don't, check out the earlier section "Mission Statement Basics"); however, the task before you is to refine that idea so it's simply stated in a few words and to officially get it down on paper. Frankly, it is easier to have an individual draft and refine the statement's wording, but we highly recommend that you invite your board, staff, and volunteers to participate in identifying the statement's key content — your organization's goals, purpose, programs, and vision. The act of creating or refining a mission statement can motivate and even inspire them.

While inspiration may be your goal, as you gather your group's ideas and begin to write your statement, it's also important that your written statement be clear. In the following sections, we recommend a process for inviting participation and achieving clarity.

Getting input from your group

Whether you're working with a newly formed nonprofit or a long-running institution, everyone on your board or planning committee needs to agree on the mission statement. We recommend holding a meeting to solicit their input. The biggest advantage to this kind of group activity is achieving full buy in from everyone involved. After all, you want people to believe and accept the organization's mission statement. If they don't, they likely won't stay around to help (or won't do a good job of upholding that mission while they're there).

For groups that are working to establish a mission statement for a new non-profit organization, we recommend that you find an outside facilitator to guide the group through the inevitable discussions about priorities and the direction of the new organization. Finding a neutral person who can bring an outsider's perspective to the group's deliberations is extremely helpful. A facilitator also takes responsibility for managing the group so you and your colleagues can be full participants in the meeting. If you aren't near a *nonprofit support organization* (a nonprofit that helps other nonprofits with technical assistance), ask other organizations near you for suggestions.

Bring a few prewritten suggestions to the group meeting. Present them as drafts and ask for feedback. After an initial discussion among the group, give each member index cards or sticky pads and have them write down three ideas they feel strongly about keeping as a part of the mission.

After you collect everyone's written ideas, read them all aloud and — as a group — organize them so that similar ideas are grouped together. These notes should identify for you the key ideas that belong in your mission statement. Also be sure to ask whether anyone thinks an important idea is missing. If not, you're ready to assign someone to draft the mission statement.

Drafting the statement

A group process is essential to identifying the core ideas that belong in the mission statement, but when it comes to putting words on paper, we recommend that you choose your best writer and turn her loose.

We aren't fans of committee-written prose. We've sat in meetings where committees discussed adjective choices and the placement of commas without apparent end. The result of such efforts is usually murky writing that requires several readings to interpret the meaning. After a draft is on paper, feel free to bring it back to your group for their final thoughts and approval on content, grammar, and word choice. Until then, however, assign only one person to work on the draft.

When finalizing the wording of your statement, the best advice we can offer is to stay away from jargon and flowery rhetoric. Avoid the buzzwords that are currently popular in your field. In fact, this is good advice in any kind of writing — grant proposals, memos, letters, and so on. You don't want your audience scratching their heads and wondering, "What does that mean?"

Here's an example of a vague, unclear mission statement:

> *The Good Food Society works to maximize the utilization of nutritious food groups to beneficially help all persons in their existence and health by proclaiming the good benefits of balanced nutrition.*

You probably get the idea that this organization wants people to have better eating habits so they can enjoy better health. But try reciting this statement to someone whom you're trying to convince to contribute to your organization. Can you say tongue-tied?

Long, multisyllabic words don't make a mission statement more impressive. If anything, they have the opposite effect. Instead of using the preceding statement, try something like this:

> *Believing in the value of good nutrition, the Good Food Society aims to improve public health by providing information about the benefits of a balanced diet to parents of school-age children through public education programs.*

This mission statement may not be perfect, but it states the organization's values, its long-term goal, the targeted group, and a general method for accomplishing the goal — all the ingredients of an effective mission statement.

Imagine that you're riding in an elevator with someone who knows nothing about your nonprofit. You have 15 seconds to describe your organization's purpose and activities. Doing so is easy if you have a clear, short mission statement. Even if you have a longer mission statement, develop a 50- to 75-word spiel that you can recite from memory.

Living by Your Mission

You've brainstormed, drafted, and refined a short statement that clearly identifies your organization's mission. Congratulations! Now that you have put considerable thought and time into this exercise, what are you going to do with it? You'll use your mission statement in practical ways, of course. For instance, you'll likely

- ✔ Incorporate its description of the organization's purpose in your articles of incorporation (see Chapter 4 for additional details).

- ✔ Include it in brochures, on your Web site, and in other marketing materials.

- ✔ Use it to complete IRS Form 990 — the tax statement you'll file in one form or another each year.

Your mission statement also resembles the pin that holds the needle of a compass: You'll use it to chart your direction. Here are some examples:

- ✔ When you have to make a decision about creating new programs or setting priorities, your mission statement should guide you as to whether they're appropriate to your organization.

- ✔ When your board and staff sit down to create a new three-year plan, they'll first revisit and commit to the mission statement. All other discussion about setting goals and refining programs should be tested for appropriateness against the statement.

- ✔ When you need to cut your budget and eliminate programs or activities, your mission statement should guide you to protect those programs that are core to your organization's purpose and vision.

Chapter 4

Incorporating and Applying for Tax Exemption

In This Chapter

▶ Forming a nonprofit corporation

▶ Writing your organization's articles of incorporation

▶ Applying for an Employer Identification Number

▶ Creating bylaws — the rules of your nonprofit

▶ Scheduling board meetings

▶ Going for IRS tax exemption

*I*f you want to provide programs and services as a nonprofit organization, you need to set up the legal structure for your organization and apply for its tax exemption. Before you begin fulfilling your mission, you must take care of these tasks, which require attention to detail and ample planning.

This process usually consists of forming a nonprofit corporation under the laws of your state and then submitting an application to the Internal Revenue Service (IRS) requesting that your organization be recognized as tax exempt.

In this chapter, we provide you with a guide to the incorporation and exemption process for a 501(c)(3) public charity. We also give you suggestions about where you can go for help. Keep in mind that we aren't attorneys, and the information in this chapter isn't meant to be legal advice. Although many nonprofits are formed without the aid of legal counsel, we think that consulting an attorney is a good idea, even if it's only to review your work. After all, you're taking on legal responsibilities. Why not be certain that you've done everything correctly?

For quick reference, we've put together a checklist for forming a nonprofit organization (CD0401).

Creating a New Entity — the Corporation

The first legal step in creating a nonprofit organization almost always is forming a corporation. A *corporation* is an entity or an organization that has legal standing. It's established by a group of individuals — the incorporators — under the laws of the state in which it's formed.

We say the first step is "almost always" forming a corporation because exceptions do exist. In the United States, for example, associations, trusts, and sometimes limited liability companies can operate as tax-exempt nonprofit organizations. And charitable groups with less than $5,000 in annual revenues, as well as churches, aren't required to apply for tax exemption. Here we focus on the most common legal structure for nonprofit organizations: the corporation.

One advantage of creating a corporation is that the individuals who govern and work for it are separate from the abstract thing they create. Although board members can be liable for the corporation's actions if they don't exercise their duties and responsibilities carefully, in most cases corporations protect individuals from personal liability. So it's helpful to think of a corporation as separate from the people who start it, because, well, it is.

When you establish a corporation, you're creating an entity that's expected to continue in perpetuity. In other words, the corporation you create goes on living after you decide to do something else or after your death. Corporations can be closed or dissolved, but you must take legal steps to do so. You can't just take down your shingle and walk away.

Looking to your state law

In the United States, corporations are created and regulated under the laws of the state in which they're formed. Although the way a corporation is formed from state to state has more similarities than differences, you do need to create your nonprofit so that it conforms to the peculiarities of your state. Some states, for example, require a minimum of three members to belong to a board of directors; others require only one. (Flip to Chapter 6 for more information about boards of directors.)

Check out CD0402 for information about where to get specifics about incorporating in your state. Usually, the secretary of state's office handles incorporations. Some states have an incorporation package that includes the forms you need to file. You also can find state contact information on the IRS Web site at www.irs.gov.

Considering your corporation's governing documents

Think of a corporation as a tiny government with a constitution and laws. To set down the rules under which the organization will operate, you need to prepare the following important documents:

- **Articles of incorporation:** The *articles of incorporation* make up the document that creates the organization. It names the organization and describes its reason for existence. In the case of a nonprofit corporation, it specifies that the corporation won't be used to create profit for its directors. The articles are signed by the corporation's incorporators, usually three people, who may or may not end up being directors of the organization.

- **Bylaws:** A corporation's *bylaws* specify how directors are elected and the length of their terms, the officers and their duties, the number of meetings to be held, who is and isn't a member of the corporation, how many members or directors are required to be in attendance for a quorum to be present, the rules for director attendance at board meetings, and the process through which the bylaws may be amended. They also may list the standing committees of the board and grant or limit particular powers of the trustees.

As you draft these documents (see the "Writing the Articles of Incorporation" section later in this chapter for more specific information about writing them), remember that you're creating the legal rules under which your nonprofit will operate. Both articles of incorporation and bylaws may be changed by following the laws of your state (in the case of articles of incorporation) or the rules described in the bylaws.

Deciding whether to have members in your corporation

Corporations may have members. They may even have different classes of members — voting and nonvoting, for example. In general, having members in your corporation adds additional responsibilities to the governance of the organization. If you have members, for instance, you need to have membership meetings, probably at least one per year, and the members will be involved in choosing directors for the organization.

Depending on state law, you usually have the option to create membership conditions in either the articles or the bylaws. If you have a choice, we recommend adding these conditions in the bylaws, which are easier to amend than the articles of incorporation.

We don't advise having members unless you have a very good reason to do so. However, you may want to get as many people involved in your organization as possible, and having members is one way to achieve this goal. If your nonprofit is a neighborhood-improvement group, for example, including as many people as possible in the governance of the organization may be important.

Many nonprofit organizations have "members," with membership cards and special rates on admissions to performances or exhibits. Don't confuse this kind of membership, which is a marketing and fundraising strategy, with legal membership in a corporation. You're free to start a membership program of this type without amending your bylaws or your articles of incorporation.

Choosing your corporation's name

Choosing a name for your new corporation may be one of the most important things you do as you set it up. A nonprofit's name is a little like a mission statement (see Chapter 3 for more on mission statements). Like your mission statement, you want your organization's name to suggest the types of programs and services you offer and the people you serve.

If your programs provide home health services to people over 65, don't name your nonprofit something generic like "Services for the People." Also stay away from names that are so abstract that they have no meaning at all. A name like the Reenergizing Society prompts more questions than it answers. What or who is being reenergized? How are clients being reenergized? And why are they being reenergized? Instead, use concrete, descriptive terms.

To avoid possible embarrassment, check the acronym that results from your organizational name. The Associated Workers For Union Labor, for example, isn't a title you want to abbreviate on your letterhead.

Also be careful that you don't select a name that's easily confused with that of another organization. Before you decide on a name, do an Internet search to see whether any other companies or organizations already have that name. The state agency that accepts your application for incorporation has procedures for ensuring that two corporations in your state don't end up with exactly the same name. However, these procedures can't help you uncover organizations with the same name in other states or with names that are similar and could be confused with your name. To help ensure that you have a distinctive name, you may want to include the name of the city or region where your organization is located — Tap Dancers of Happy Valley, for example.

You also can search the Trademark Electronic Search System (TESS) found at www.uspto.gov to determine whether the name you have chosen is trademarked by another organization. If you want, you can register your own trademark with the federal government and with the state in which you incorporate.

If you incorporate your organization under one name and then decide that you aren't totally pleased with it, you can amend the incorporation papers you filed with the state. Often, however, organizations find it easier to register another name as a DBA, which stands for "doing business as." The original corporate name continues to be your organization's legal name, but you can use the DBA name on letterhead, annual reports, and press releases — everywhere except legal documents. A county office usually handles this type of transaction. Check your local laws for more information.

Writing the Articles of Incorporation

We assume that you have the articles of incorporation papers you need from the appropriate state office. (If not, use the state-by-state list on CD0402 for contact information.) That office may even have provided sample articles of incorporation and instructions about how to prepare your own. Pay close attention to the instructions and follow them step by step. It may be as simple as filling in the blanks. Although articles of incorporation can be amended, it requires filing additional forms and paying more fees, so it's better to spend time getting them right the first time. In this section, we give you some general guidance on drafting your articles. However, note that the sample articles may not coincide exactly with your statement requirements.

The articles need to be signed by the incorporators of the corporation. In some states, three incorporators are needed; in others, you need only one. If the articles need to be notarized, the signatures must be added in the presence of a notary public. Most states charge a fee for filing for incorporation. If your state requires a fee, include a check or money order with the articles and any other required forms.

Crafting a heading

You must put a heading on your articles so they can be identified. The heading should be something like this one:

Articles of Incorporation of the XYZ Theater Company, Inc.

Sometimes you're required to add a short paragraph after the heading, stating that the incorporators adopt the following articles under the [cite the state code number under which you're filing] of [give the state name].

Article 1

You insert the name you worked so hard to choose here in Article I. It's as simple as writing a sentence like this one:

The name of the corporation is the XYZ Theater Company, Inc.

Could it be any easier than that?

Article 11

Some states require that you affirm that your corporation is *perpetual,* (which means that it's intended to exist forever). If your state does require that affirmation, put it in Article II. You can include something like this:

This corporation shall exist in perpetuity unless dissolved.

However, chances are that the state will give you the language to use if it's needed.

Article 111

Article III is a good place to state the organization's purpose. This article is probably the most important, because state authorities and the IRS review it to determine whether your organization qualifies as a charitable entity.

IRS Publication 557 contains information about the language needed in the articles of incorporation as well as sample articles. You can download this publication from the IRS Web site (www.irs.gov).

Remember that 501(c)(3) organizations must be organized for a charitable, religious, educational, literary, or scientific purpose. (See Chapter 2 for more on various classes of nonprofits.) You've already created your mission statement, right? If so, stating your purpose shouldn't be too difficult. (If you haven't created your statement yet, check out Chapter 3.) Using the XYZ Theater Company as an example, your purpose may look like this:

This corporation is established to provide theatrical productions of new and classic plays. It also will work to strengthen the theater arts, support emerging playwrights, and encourage persons to enter the acting profession by providing scholarships and grants to theater arts students and by promoting the benefits of dramatic entertainment to the general public.

This article also must include a statement of exempt purpose under the IRS code:

> *This corporation is organized exclusively for charitable, literary, and educational purposes, including for such purposes the making of distributions to organizations that qualify under section 501(c)(3) of the Internal Revenue Code or any corresponding section of any future federal tax code.*

You must state that no proceeds of the corporation will enrich any individual, except that reasonable compensation may be paid in exchange for services to the corporation. Finally, in this article, you must note that if the corporation is dissolved, any assets remaining will be distributed to another corporation that serves a similar purpose and qualifies as a tax-exempt, charitable organization under the provisions of 501(c)(3) of the Internal Revenue Code. You don't need to identify a particular nonprofit corporation; you just need to affirm that assets will be distributed to one serving a purpose similar to yours.

Article III may be the most critical for getting your nonprofit corporation established and, ultimately, approved for tax exemption by the IRS. If your state doesn't provide good examples of the language required in this article, ask a lawyer about the requirements in your state.

Article IV

All articles of incorporation identify the name and address of an *agent of the corporation,* someone to whom mail can be addressed. This address is considered the address of the corporation until changed. Include the person's name and street address. Post office boxes usually aren't allowed to be used as addresses.

The agent of corporation doesn't need to be a director or incorporator of the corporation. This person can even be your attorney.

Article V

Put the initial directors' names and addresses in Article V. This is not required in many states. For example, an attorney can serve as incorporator. Immediately after incorporation, she can appoint initial directors.

Article VI

In Article VI, you list the incorporators' names and addresses. *Incorporator* simply refers to the person or people who are creating the corporation. Often, the incorporators and the initial directors are one and the same. And again, whether you need one or more depends on your state requirements.

Article VII

If you want your corporation to have members, you define the qualifications for membership in Article VII. You can define classes of membership — voting and nonvoting, for instance. If you don't want members, all you have to say is, "This corporation has no members." Better yet, refer the question to your bylaws, which are easier to amend if you change your mind. If that's what you decide to do, you can use this language:

> *Membership provisions of this corporation are defined in the bylaws.*

Corporate members aren't the same as the subscribers to a PBS station or the members of a museum or zoo, for example. Members of a corporation have the right to participate in governing the organization.

Article VIII

You may not need an Article VIII in your articles of incorporation. Some forms have a blank space here to add additional provisions. We don't recommend adding any unless you're sure you know what you're doing. Maybe your group is adamant that all future directors must be elected by 85 percent of the membership. Such a provision probably would ensure that you'd never elect new directors, but who knows? Use this blank space cautiously.

Signed, sealed, and delivered

After you finish writing your articles of incorporation, they must be signed by the incorporator(s) and mailed to the appropriate state office with the required fee, if any, enclosed. Usually you only mail the original articles to the state office, but sometimes a state office requires one or more additional copies.

Your next step is to wait. It's hard to say how long the response will take — it depends on the efficiency of the state office and the volume of incorporation papers it receives. For a surcharge, some states offer an opportunity to expedite processing.

Simply creating a nonprofit corporation doesn't make your organization tax exempt. You also need recognition from the IRS (see the section "Applying for Tax Exemption" later in this chapter) before your nonprofit is a "real" nonprofit.

If your articles are in order and your corporate name passes muster (meaning that no other organization in the state has the same name), you receive a certified copy of the articles, stamped with an official seal. Guard this piece of paper as if it were gold. Make copies and put the original away for safe-keeping in a fireproof box. You've taken the first step toward starting your nonprofit. Congratulations!

Obtaining Your Employer Identification Number, or EIN

The first thing to do after you complete your incorporation is to apply to the IRS for an *Employer Identification Number,* or EIN. Even if you don't plan to hire employees anytime soon, you need this number for your application for tax exemption and for all your state and federal reports. The EIN is a little like a Social Security number for organizations. It will be attached to your nonprofit forever.

Getting an EIN is easy and free. Submit IRS Form SS-4, which you can download and print from www.irs.gov. You also can complete the online application. It's even possible to apply by telephone. As IRS forms go, this one is simple and straightforward and only one page long. If you do apply by phone or complete the online application, it's a good idea to download Form SS-4 beforehand to get an idea of the questions you'll be expected to answer.

Choose only one method to apply for your EIN. Don't send in IRS Form SS-4 AND apply by telephone. You may end up with two EINs, a confusing situation for everyone.

The name of the applicant isn't your name; it's the name of your new organization. As with the incorporation papers, you need to identify an individual as the principal officer and include his Social Security number on the form. Here are some of the other items you need to fill out, line by line:

- ✔ **Line 9:** If your organization is a church or church-controlled organization, check that box in section 9a. If it's not, check the "Other Nonprofit Organization" box. Specify what sort of nonprofit organization you are. In most cases, "charitable" is sufficient. In 9b you're asked in which state your organization is incorporated.

- ✔ **Line 10:** Most likely, your reason for applying for an EIN in Line 10 is "started a new business."

- ✔ **Line 11:** In Line 11, the date on your incorporation papers is the date the business was started.

- ✔ **Line 12:** This line asks for the closing month of your organization's accounting (fiscal) year. (See the later section "Dealing with financial information" for an explanation of a fiscal year.)

- ✔ **Lines 13 and 14:** These lines relate to the number of employees you intend to hire and your expected payroll tax liabilities over the coming 12 months. You can enter "0" and "No" if your organization doesn't plan to hire staff in the year ahead. If you do intend to hire people for whom you'll have to pay payroll taxes, you'll need to check IRS withholding tables (www.irs.gov) and estimate the amount of payroll taxes that will be due to the IRS.

- ✔ **Line 16:** This line asks you to check the box that describes your organization's principal activity. You can check "Other" here. Be a little more specific when describing your activities in the blank space. You may say "Charitable — Arts," for example.

The IRS estimates that you'll receive your EIN in four to five weeks if you apply by mail. You'll receive your EIN immediately if you choose the online application option.

You can apply for an EIN by telephone by calling the IRS Business and Specialty Tax Line at 800-829-4933. The person named as the principal officer on the form must make the call. Be sure that you have completed the SS-4 Form before you call. An IRS worker takes your information over the phone and assigns an EIN to your organization. You must fax or mail the form to the appropriate IRS office within 24 hours of making the call.

Even if your organization is an unincorporated association or a trust, you still need an EIN number if you plan to apply for a charitable tax exemption.

Developing Your Organizational Bylaws

Bylaws are the rules by which your organization operates. As with articles of incorporation, different states have different requirements about what needs to be included in the bylaws, so it's important to contact the appropriate agency in your state to get the specific information you need. Use the state contact information on CD0402 to find the office in your state.

In general, bylaws guide the activities of your organization and the procedures of your board of directors — how many directors, the length of their terms, how they're elected, what constitutes a quorum, and so on. Bylaws are divided into articles just like the articles of incorporation are. Because more detail is included in the bylaws, however, the articles themselves are divided into sections (and subsections, if needed) to address various aspects of the articles.

Bylaws can always be changed. However, amending the bylaws almost always requires more than a simple majority; usually two-thirds of the directors must agree to a bylaw change.

If you review the bylaws of ten different organizations, you'll find variation in the order in which articles are presented. For example, you may find the board of directors specified in Article III or Article V. Bylaws also vary in how specifically they spell out what's required. Some bylaws specify the number and type of standing committees; others give the board president the responsibility of making those specifications. If you don't address a particular question in your bylaws — setting a quorum, for example — most states have a default position in their code that applies to the governing of nonprofit corporations.

Check out CD0403 for a general guide to creating bylaws for your new nonprofit.

Holding Your First Board Meeting

Your organization's first board meeting is more or less a formality, but documenting it is important because it officially kicks off your new nonprofit corporation. If you've named directors in your articles of incorporation, each one should be present at the meeting. The first order of business is to elect the officers of the organization. For your second order of business, pass a resolution authorizing the board or its designate to open the necessary bank accounts. You need a copy of this resolution to open an account.

Prepare minutes of the meeting, and keep them with your articles of incorporation. We say more about keeping records in Chapter 5, but now is a good time to start a *board book* — a loose-leaf notebook containing a copy of your articles of incorporation, bylaws, and the minutes of your first board meeting and every board meeting to follow.

Applying for Tax Exemption

The final step in becoming a tax-exempt charitable organization is to apply for tax exemption from the IRS. Keep in mind that "tax exempt" doesn't mean that you're exempt from *all* taxes. You don't have to pay taxes on the organization's income, and donors who contribute to your 501(c)(3) organization can claim a tax deduction. But if your nonprofit employs staff, it's required to pay payroll taxes like any employer. And your liability for sales and property taxes depends on your state and local laws. If your nonprofit has income that's unrelated to its charitable purpose, you're required to pay taxes on that revenue as well.

To apply for tax exemption, you request what's known as a *determination letter* or *ruling* — a letter from the IRS stating that it has determined that your organization qualifies as a tax-exempt organization under the applicable sections of the IRS code. You'll send copies of this letter to foundations, government agencies, and state tax authorities — in short, to anyone to whom you need to prove that yours is a tax-exempt nonprofit organization.

Be sure to check with your state about what you need to do to register your nonprofit as a tax-exempt organization. Registration and reporting requirements vary from state to state. Chances are you received this information when you contacted your state office to begin your incorporation process; if you didn't, contact the appropriate state government office for more details. You can find contact information for all states on CD0402.

You request tax-exempt status by submitting to the IRS the Application for Recognition of Exemption or IRS Form 1023. You can download the form from the IRS Web site at www.irs.gov. Be sure to download the form's instructions at the same time and read the next section, "Tackling Form 1023."

Who doesn't need to apply

If your organization is a church, a church aux-iliary, or an association of churches, you don't need to apply for tax-exempt status. Also, if your nonprofit had income of less than $5,000 in any previous year in which you operated, and if you don't expect your revenue to grow beyond this limit, you aren't required to submit an application.

Keep in mind that you still may apply for tax exemption even though you aren't required to

do so. Having a determination letter from the IRS acknowledging your tax-exempt status has some advantages. For example, you need to show proof of your exemption to get a bulk mail permit from the U.S. Postal Service. It's also a public acknowledgment stating that contribu-tions to your organization are deductible to the donor. If you hope to receive foundation grants, your organization should be recognized as tax exempt by the IRS as well.

Tackling Form 1023

Yes, Form 1023 is long, and yes, it's a little scary. If you can get help from your accountant or attorney, we recommend that you do so. Don't discount getting help from your friends and associates, either. Two heads are usually better than one.

Read the instructions carefully. The application package includes line-by-line explanations as well as the various schedules that you may need to submit if you're applying as a church or school, for example. If a schedule isn't required for your type of nonprofit, don't submit a blank one. Toss it into the round file (also known as the trash can).

Understanding the difference between public charities and private foundations

Public charities and private foundations are both 501(c)(3) organizations (see Chapter 2 for more on these types of organizations), but you should understand the important differences between them before you begin com-pleting the application for tax exemption.

Private foundations have different reporting requirements from public chari-ties and may be required to pay excise taxes on their income. Contributions to private foundations are deductible, but not to the same extent as contribu-tions to public charities.

One important determination that the IRS makes based on your application for tax-exempt status is whether your organization is classified as a public charity or a private foundation. Part X of Form 1023 addresses this question. We assume that you're striving for public charity status, so check the "No" box in line 1a and skip to line 5.

Establishing public charity status

The IRS applies several measures to determine whether an organization is a public charity. Generally, for a nonprofit to be considered a public charity, it must receive one-third of its revenues from public sources. It's complicated, and we can't cover all the nuances and technicalities here. But, fundamentally, it comes down to how much of your organizational income you get from the public.

A 501(c)(3) nonprofit organization wanting to be considered a public charity will undergo what's referred to as the *public support test.* To pass this test, the nonprofit needs to demonstrate, over a four-year average, that one-third of its revenue comes from contributions from the general public, support from government agencies, or grants from organizations that get their support from the public, such as United Way. So if your organization's average revenue is $60,000 per year and at least $20,000 a year comes from donations, state grants, and support from United Way, you're home free. Your nonprofit will be considered a public charity under code section 509(a)(1) and 170(b)(1)(A)(vi).

But what if your organization doesn't get a third of its revenue from the public? Fortunately, it may be able to qualify under another test that gives more leeway on the percentage of public support. Under this test, only 10 percent of total revenue needs to come from those public categories. But your organization also must demonstrate that it has an ongoing fundraising program that's reaching to the public for more donations. Other factors also are considered. If the nonprofit's contributions come in many small gifts rather than a few large ones, it's more likely to be given public charity status. It's even better if your organization's board of directors is broadly representative of the community. And if the organization makes its facility available to the general public, that's another feather in its cap.

A 501(c)(3) organization that expects to get a substantial portion of its revenues from fees related to its exempt purpose (but less than one-third of revenues from investment income) may qualify as a public charity under code section 501(a)(2).

When you get to Part X of Form 1023, you need to check a box indicating which public charity classification you seek. If you aren't sure — and, frankly, who would be? — you can let the IRS decide which category you fit by selecting the "i" box. Take schools as an example. To apply as a school, you have to submit Schedule B. Your school must provide regular instruction and have a student body and a faculty. In other words, you can't just start an organization and call it a school.

Every IRS rule has an exception or two, and qualifying as a public charity is, well, no exception. Churches, schools, hospitals, public safety testing organizations, and a few others are automatically considered public charities. If you have an intense interest in this rule, read Chapter 3 of IRS Publication 557, which is available from the IRS Web site at www.irs.gov. If you think your organization falls into one of these categories, check the appropriate box in Part X, line 5 (a through f) and answer the questions on the appropriate schedule included with Form 1023. But we don't recommend doing so unless you're absolutely certain that you know what you're doing. If you need further advice regarding these categories, we suggest you consult an attorney.

Until recently, a newly established nonprofit organization applying for a tax exemption usually requested an "advance ruling" on its public charity status. Typically, based on the sources of projected revenue given in the application, the IRS granted "temporary" public charity status for a period of five years. After this five-year period, the IRS reviewed the sources of the nonprofit's support over the previous years and, if the public support test was met, issued a "definitive" ruling of public charity status.

The advance ruling period has been eliminated. Organizations seeking to be classified as public charities will be considered as such if they can demonstrate in their Form 1023 application that the status is a reasonable expectation for the future. The public charity status is considered permanent unless and until substantial changes are seen in the organization's sources of support. This change in IRS procedure grants some leeway in an organization's sources of support for the first few years of its existence.

Describing your activities

In Part IV of IRS Form 1023, you need to attach a narrative description of your charitable activities and how you plan to carry them out. You must provide more detail here than you have in your articles of incorporation or in your mission statement. The IRS wants you to list what you're going to do in order of importance, approximately what percentage of time you'll devote to each activity, and how each activity fulfills your charitable purpose.

When you fill out this form, chances are you haven't started operating yet, so you're simply listing *proposed* activities. If you've created a business plan (which we recommend), refer to the plan to make sure you cover all your activities. (Refer to Chapter 7 for help with planning.) If you've been operating your organization, explain what you've been doing and how it relates to your charitable purpose.

A nonprofit that provides family counseling and public education about strengthening families may say something like this in Part IV:

> *The charitable purpose of the Claremont Family Counseling Center is to promote the benefits of positive family interaction in the following ways:*
>
> *The primary activity will be to provide professional family counseling services, on a sliding scale fee basis, to families in Claremont County and surrounding counties. No family will be refused service due to the inability to pay for services, and services will be available to all members of the general public. (75 percent)*
>
> *The center will maintain a Web site that provides referral information, suggestions for strengthening family interactions, reference materials concerning families, and e-mail and bulletin board posting capabilities. (10 percent)*
>
> *Staff members will present information about families to local schools, service clubs, and churches through multimedia presentations. (10 percent)*
>
> *Brochures will be prepared and distributed on request. (5 percent)*

You're asked more questions about your specific activities in Part VIII of Form 1023, including, for example, how and where you intend to raise funds, whether you operate a bingo game or other gaming activities, and the extent of your involvement with foreign countries and organizations. Answering yes to these and other questions in Part VIII means that you must attach explanations.

In Part VIII, you're also asked whether your organization will attempt to influence legislation. If you answer yes, you're given an opportunity to elect section 501(h) of the IRS code by filing IRS Form 5768. If you do so, your organization's expenses for allowable lobbying activities are measured by a percentage of your revenue. Chapter 5 has more information about this subject.

Reporting salaries and conflicts of interest

The IRS revises its forms from time to time. In the past few years, Form 1023 has been revised to include more questions about staff salary levels, board member compensation, and business and family relationships of board members and staff. If you pay or plan to pay any staff member or consultant more than $50,000 per year, you need to report this fact. If you compensate or plan to compensate members of your board, this information also must be shared on Form 1023.

You're also asked whether the organization has a conflict of interest policy and whether compensation has or will be set by comparing salaries of your staff to salaries of similar organizations. Although the IRS says these practices aren't required to get a tax exemption, they are recommended. The instructions for Form 1023 contain a sample conflict of interest policy statement. We suggest having your board adopt a conflict of interest policy based on the IRS model.

Part V of the application stretches over two pages and clearly is a reaction to increased public and legislative concern about financial abuse and self-dealing in both the nonprofit and business sectors. We say more about the increased scrutiny aimed at the nonprofit sector in Chapter 5. It's important to keep in mind that nonprofits are, in a sense, "quasi-public" organizations because the government is granting them special status as tax-exempt organizations.

Dealing with financial information

The IRS wants to see financial information. (Surprise, surprise.) New organizations have to estimate their income and expenses for three years — the current year and two years following. Making financial projections sends shivers down the backs of many folks, but it's really not that difficult. Ideally, you've made plans for your nonprofit already, and you can take the figures from your business plan. If you haven't written a business plan, now's a good time to do so. See Chapter 7 for planning information and Chapter 10 for help in creating a budget.

When you estimate your income, keep in mind the requirements for qualifying as a public charity (check out the earlier section "Establishing public charity status" for more details). Diverse sources of income are important, both for qualifying as a public charity and for the stability of your nonprofit.

You also need to choose your annual accounting period. This period is usually referred to as your *fiscal year*. It can be any 12-month period you desire. Most organizations choose as their fiscal year either the calendar year (January 1 through December 31) or the period from July 1 to June 30. Most government agencies operate on a July 1 through June 30 fiscal year, and nonprofits that get support from government grants and contracts often prefer to operate on the same basis. Some organizations offering services to schools set the fiscal year to correspond with the academic year. But the choice is yours. You can set your fiscal year from November 1 to October 31 if you want.

Your first accounting period doesn't need to be a full 12 months; in fact, it probably won't be. If you form your organization in September and select a calendar year as your fiscal year, your first accounting period covers only four months, September through December.

If you have an accountant, seek advice about the best accounting period for your organization. Remember that your fiscal year determines when future reports are due to the IRS and also when you prepare year-end financial reports for your board of directors. The annual 990 report is due, for example, four and a half months after the close of your fiscal year. So if your fiscal year is the same as the calendar year, the report is due on May 15. If you always spend early May traveling to the Caribbean, you may want to pick another accounting period.

Collecting the other materials

In addition to the completed tax-exemption application, you need to submit as attachments conformed (exact) copies of your articles of incorporation and the certificate of incorporation, if your state provides one. The bylaws of your organization should be submitted, too, but remember that bylaws alone don't qualify as an organizing document.

Put your organization's name, address, and EIN on each attachment and specify the section of the application that each attachment refers to. (The earlier section "Obtaining Your Employer Identification Number, or EIN" provides more details on obtaining your organization's number.) The application package you receive from the IRS has a checklist of the materials that must be included. This checklist must be included with your completed application package.

Every nonprofit applying for tax exemption must have an organizing document. Usually, this document is the articles of incorporation, because most nonprofit organizations are incorporated. However, in the United States, associations, trusts, and, in some states, limited liability companies also may apply for tax-exempt status. An organizing document for an association may be the articles of association or a constitution; a trust is usually organized by a trust indenture or deed.

Paying the fee

The fee for filing IRS Form 1023 is $850 for organizations that have had or anticipate having revenue of more than $10,000 per year. If your organization has been operating without a tax exemption and has income of less than $10,000 per year, or if you anticipate having revenues of less than $10,000 per year in the future, the fee is set at $400.

We don't recommend trying to save $450 on the application fee unless you're certain that revenues to your organization will remain under $10,000. We understand that the $450 difference in the fees can loom very large for a start-up nonprofit, but why play with fire? Although the penalties for misstating your income aren't clear, we wouldn't want you to find out the hard way.

Send the fee when you mail the form with all its appropriate attachments and schedules. Keep a copy of everything for your records. Then take a break! You deserve it.

Getting along until the exemption comes

After you file your tax-exemption application, your organization is in never-never land for a while. You don't have your exemption yet. Although making an accurate prediction is difficult, the IRS can take between three and six months to act on your application. The process may take longer if the application is returned for corrections.

During this period, your organization can operate and even solicit contributions. However, you must tell donors that you've applied for a tax exemption and are waiting to hear from the IRS. Assuming that your application is approved, if you submitted Form 1023 and the other required materials to the IRS within 27 months from the time you established the organization, your tax-exempt status is retroactive to the date of incorporation. Another option is to use a fiscal sponsor during this period. (See Chapter 2 for information about using and finding fiscal sponsors.)

If your organization had been operating for a longer period before you submitted Form 1023, the exemption may be retroactive only to the date on which you submitted the application. In this case, you also need to include Schedule E with your application.

Check with your state officials to find out what steps should be taken to have your tax exemption recognized by your state's government. If you didn't receive this information when you incorporated your organization, you can find contact information for the appropriate state office on CD0402.

Chapter 5

Safeguarding Your Nonprofit Status

In This Chapter

▶ Making public disclosures

▶ Avoiding trouble over pay and politics

▶ Sending Form 990 to the IRS

▶ Filing state and local reports

*N*onprofit organizations are private organizations, but because they're granted special tax status and presumably are acting on behalf of the public, they're required to disclose more information than privately held for-profit companies are. Nonprofit status is a privilege.

A good way to think about it is to compare nonprofits to companies that sell shares of stock to the public. These companies must follow the rules and regulations set forth by the Securities and Exchange Commission about disclosing financial information. Nonprofits in the United States must follow the rules of the Internal Revenue Service (IRS) to make financial information available for public scrutiny. In some cases, state and local governments also have disclosure rules.

Your nonprofit organization can get into trouble with authorities in a few ways. However, keeping your nonprofit status isn't difficult if you follow the rules. This chapter lays out the reporting requirements that you need to follow and some pitfalls to avoid in order to maintain your 501(c)(3) public charity status. See Chapter 2 for more on 501(c)(3) organizations.

We don't aim to scare you! Just keep good financial records and stick to your mission, and you'll be fine.

Disclosing What You Need to Disclose

Disclose is a funny word, isn't it? It seems to imply that you're hiding something that must be pried from your clutches. Don't think of it that way. The IRS regulations that lay out the rules for disclosure refer to "the public inspection of information." That's much more genteel. In this section, we briefly cover what you are and aren't expected to disclose to the public.

What you do need to show

What information must be disclosed to the public? (Sorry, we can't help ourselves. We like the word.) It's simple, really. Your three most recent filings of IRS Form 990 and your IRS Form 1023 application for tax exemption — if you filed for your exemption after July 15, 1987 — must all be available to the public. If you have unrelated business income and must file the 990-T Form, the three most recent filings of this form also must be disclosed.

If you have a question that this chapter doesn't cover, refer to IRS Publication 557, which you can find at www.irs.gov.

Form 990 is the annual report that you must file with the IRS. We talk more about filing the 990 later in this chapter, but in a nutshell, it's a report of your annual finances and activities as a nonprofit organization. The IRS has created three versions of the 990 Form, and the version you file depends on your nonprofit's gross receipts and total assets held. Don't panic! We get into that later.

Current IRS regulations state that the three most recent 990 reports and attachments to the report must be available for public inspection at the organization's primary place of business during regular business hours. A staff member may be present during the inspection, and copies may be made for the person requesting them. If you make copies on your own copier, you can charge the same as the IRS charges: $0.20 per page.

The information provided in this chapter is about 501(c)(3) organizations that are considered public charities. If your organization is a private foundation, special disclosure rules apply especially to you. Check with the Council on Foundations (www.cof.org) about disclosure requirements.

If you work out of your home or you really have no primary place of business, you can arrange to meet at a convenient place or mail copies to the person who requested them. You have two weeks to do so. The information also can be requested in writing, and if it is, you have 30 days to respond.

If you applied for your exemption after July 15, 1987, you must include your application for exemption and all the supporting materials submitted with it in the information you make available for inspection. Although the IRS doesn't say so, we assume that you include your articles of incorporation and your bylaws, if you attached them to your application.

You need to know the rules and regulations about public inspection of nonprofit materials, but frankly, in the many years we've been working for nonprofits, no one has ever asked to see our 990 forms. This doesn't mean that you won't be asked, however. Follow the Boy Scout motto and be prepared.

On your 990, you will need to disclose compensation paid to board members. This information will be available for public inspection, as will employee salaries and contractor payments over $100,000 per year.

What you don't need to show

You don't need to reveal your donor list. Donors who contribute more than $5,000 must be named on Schedule B of your 990-EZ or 990 report, but 501(c)(3) public charities aren't required to make the information public.

Other items that may remain private include the following:

- ✔ Trade secrets and patents
- ✔ National defense material
- ✔ Communications from the IRS about previous unfavorable rulings or technical advice related to rulings
- ✔ Board minutes and contracts

IRS regulations go into more detail, but we think the preceding four items sum up the major points. If you have questions about a particular item, consult your attorney or tax advisor.

The public disclosure rules offer a nice tool for anyone who gets a bee in his bonnet and wants to harass your organization. So if you start getting request after request after request, check with the nearest IRS office. IRS officials have the authority to relieve you of the disclosure responsibilities if they agree that harassment is occurring.

Check your state and local government requirements to see whether your nonprofit must make other information available under local laws.

Using the Web to satisfy disclosure requirements

You can avoid the hassle of photocopying your Form 990s by placing the required information on the Web. If you do so, be sure that you post an exact copy of the materials, not a summary or a retyped copy. You can scan material with a scanner and put it on your Web site as a graphic, but the best way to do it is to put the materials in PDF format by using Adobe Acrobat, available from Adobe (www.adobe. com).

GuideStar (www.guidestar.org) keeps a database of basic information about U.S. nonprofit organizations as well as PDF files of 990 returns. You can add information about your nonprofit to the GuideStar database. Some states also maintain Web databases of 990s of nonprofits incorporated in their jurisdictions. Remember that you need to make available your three most recent 990 returns and your application for exemption.

If someone arrives at your office and asks to inspect your 990s, you still need to allow them the privilege. Web access to the materials only relieves the responsibility of mailing out copies.

Avoiding Excessive Payments and Politicking

Paying excessive compensation and engaging in campaign politics can get a charitable nonprofit organization in trouble. It doesn't happen often, but you need to be aware of the rules.

Determining a reasonable amount of pay and benefits

In past years, if the IRS discovered wrongdoing in a nonprofit, it had little recourse but to take away the organization's exempt status. However, when revised tax laws were passed in 1996, the IRS gained the authority to apply "intermediate sanctions" in cases of excess benefits for nonprofit staff or disqualified persons associated with the nonprofit. Board members and their family members — really anyone who can influence the organization's activities — are disqualified persons.

Excess benefits can include excessive salaries for staff members or a business deal arranged to benefit a disqualified person in which the nonprofit overpaid for a service. So if you sit on a board of directors that decides to rent office space from your uncle at two or three times the going rate, you and your uncle may be in trouble. If you do decide to rent from your uncle, be sure that you can document that you're paying a market rate rent. Also, you shouldn't participate in the board vote about renting the space.

An excessive benefit for a nonprofit staff member is any sum that's above a "reasonable amount." You're probably thinking, "What's a *reasonable* amount?" and you're right to ask the question. In the case of executive compensation, it's up to the board of directors to find out what a fair salary is for nonprofit managers in your area and for an organization of your size and scope.

If the IRS finds that someone in your nonprofit has received an excessive benefit, the financial penalties are severe. A 25 percent excise tax is levied on the excess amount, and the full excess amount (including the tax) must be paid back to the organization in less than a year. If payment isn't received in that time, the tax can go up to a healthy 200 percent.

Here are three tips to avoid excess benefits problems:

✔ No board member should participate in a board decision that benefits herself or her family. Certainly, no executive director should participate in setting her own compensation.

✔ Rely on credible independent information about reasonable costs in business deals and compensation matters.

✔ Document the reasons that you make the decisions you make.

We don't want to frighten you with visions of huge tax bills. We're not saying that you can't pay nonprofit staff well or that you have to undertake a scientific study to determine fair compensation. Use your head, be reasonable, and exercise caution.

Document board decisions by keeping minutes of board meetings. You don't need to keep a verbatim record of board deliberations, but you want your minutes to reflect the discussions that take place and the decisions that are made. Maintain what's known as a *board book* — a loose-leaf notebook that contains copies of your articles of incorporation, bylaws, amendments to bylaws, notices sent to announce board and membership meetings, and a chronological record of your board meeting minutes.

Using caution when getting involved in politics

We aren't saying that you shouldn't get involved in politics, because it's your right to do so if you want. If you want to give your personal support and endorsement to a candidate, by all means do it. But be sure to separate yourself from your nonprofit organization when you do. Nonprofits in the 501(c)(3) category can't support or endorse candidates for political office.

If you want to talk to your legislator about the passage of a bill that benefits your clients, go ahead and make an appointment. But if you find yourself traveling to your state capital or to Washington, D.C., on a regular basis, step back and consider how much organizational time and money you're spending on the activity. Charitable nonprofits can spend an "insubstantial" amount on direct lobbying activities. If it's 5 percent or less of your organizational budget, you're probably within the limits allowed, according to the people who pay attention to these things.

Be more cautious with what's known as *grass-roots lobbying,* or attempting to influence the general public to vote in a particular way. If lobbying is important to your overall mission as a 501(c)(3) public benefit nonprofit, you can elect the "h" designation, which requires more financial reporting to the IRS but allows you to spend more money on these activities. To do so, file IRS Form 5768 after you have a look at the regulations in IRS Publication 577.

Why all the fuss? Understanding the increased scrutiny

Nonprofit organizations face increasing regulation and public scrutiny in the years to come. Why? Three reasons come to mind:

- ✔ Concern about how nonprofit organizations use contributions that are made for disaster relief efforts

- ✔ A series of widely reported cases in which some nonprofits, both public charities and private foundations, have paid very high salaries to executives and trustees and otherwise pushed the limits of ethical behavior

- ✔ The number and degree of corporate accounting and insider trading scandals that have been revealed over the past few years in the for-profit sector

These factors have focused more public and legislative attention on how nonprofit organizations (and for-profit corporations) operate and how their affairs are regulated.

Greater accountability is being asked of nonprofit leaders, both managers and board members, in how money is raised, how conflicts of interest are avoided, and how funds are spent, especially for salaries and expenses. The Minnesota Council of Nonprofits has developed a set of principles, referred to as the *Principles and Practices for Nonprofit Excellence,* that provide good overall guidance in this area. You can read about these principles at www. mncn.org/info_principles.htm.

If you're involved with a start-up nonprofit that's operating on a shoestring, you may be asking yourself why you need to worry about getting paid too much. And you're right; you probably don't need to worry. But you should stay informed of changes in reporting requirements and the need to have good, ethical operating policies in place, keeping good financial records, and documenting your organizational decisions with board and committee meeting minutes.

If you're already involved with a medium or large nonprofit, you should be aware of the need for independent financial audits and board policies that address excessive compensation, self-dealing, whistle-blowers, and conflicts of interest.

Because the regulatory situation is always changing, and because it varies from state to state, we suggest visiting the Web sites of Independent Sector (www.independentsector.org) and BoardSource (www.boardsource. org) to keep abreast of the latest developments.

Reporting to the IRS

The formal name for the report that nonprofit organizations must file annually is *Return of Organization Exempt From Income Tax,* and the IRS calls it the "annual information return." Everyone else refers to it as "the 990." It *is* IRS Form 990, after all. Depending on a nonprofit's gross receipts and total assets held, a version of this report must go to the IRS each year. The IRS made substantial revisions in its reporting requirements beginning with the 2008 tax year, and this section helps you sort through those changes.

The IRS uses gross receipts to determine which 990 Form your organization is required to file. *Gross receipts* refers to all funds that come into the nonprofit during the tax year before any expenses are subtracted. For example, if you held a special event that brought in $20,000, but you had expenses of $8,000 for a net income of $12,000, your gross receipts for that event are $20,000. This figure is added to grants, fees for service, contributions, and any other income to determine your gross receipts for the year.

No matter what report you file, it must be postmarked no later than the 15th day of the 5th month after the end of your annual accounting period; in other words, after the close of your fiscal year. When you filed your application for exemption, you selected your accounting period. If you use the calendar year as your fiscal year, your 990 has to be out the door on May 15. You can apply for an automatic three-month extension. If you need even more time, you can apply for an additional three-month extension — if you have a good reason.

The IRS has three versions of the 990: The 990-N, 990-EZ, and the long Form 990. The report you file depends on the total gross receipts (and total assets) of your nonprofit organization. We focus on the 990-N and 990-EZ in the next couple sections, but we do provide some advice for the long Form 990 as well. Most important, if your nonprofit organization is big enough to require filing the long Form 990, we advise that you seek professional help.

Using the 990-N

The 990-N is required for all 501(c)(3) nonprofit organizations (with the exception of churches and church-related organizations) that have annual gross receipts of $25,000 or less. This simple form must be filed electronically; in fact, the IRS refers to this form as an e-Postcard, so you need a computer, Internet access, and an e-mail address.

The due date for filing this form is the same as for the 990-EZ or the long Form 990: the 15th day of the 5th month after the close of the tax year. However, at present there's no penalty for late filing. You can't file before the end of the tax year.

If your organization fails to file a 990-N for three consecutive years, its tax-exempt status will be rescinded.

The Urban Institute handles 990-N filings for the IRS. Go to `epostcard. form990.org` and follow the instructions. If your organization is new or if you haven't filed a 990-N before, you need to register to obtain a login ID.

The 990-N asks for the following information:

- ✔ Legal name of the organization and any other names under which it's doing business
- ✔ A mailing address and a Web site address, if you have one

> ✔ The Employer Identification Number, or EIN, of the organization (See Chapter 4 for more on EINs.)
>
> ✔ The name and address of the principal officer, which is likely either the executive director or board president (use the organization's address as the address for this individual)

You'll also be asked for the organization's tax year (the same as the fiscal year), whether the nonprofit normally has $25,000 or less in gross receipts, and whether the organization is still in business.

Taking it easy with the 990-EZ return

We're the first to admit that filing IRS forms is intimidating. You have a lot of fine print to read and the instructions are a good test of the importance of close reading. That said, the instructions are complete and most terms are well defined. You can make your task easier by getting help from your accountant or attorney.

Keep in mind when reading the instructions that the 990-EZ report is used for categories of tax-exempt organizations other than 501(c)(3) public charities. This can be confusing unless you attend closely to the instructions. Because the 990-EZ is used for other types of nonprofits, be sure to check the 501(c) box and write in "3" in the empty parentheses in the "J" section.

Fill in the identifying information at the top of the form. If you've filed in past years, you'll receive a package of forms in the mail with a peel-off label that you can use for your name and address. Be sure to add your EIN. Also check the correct box to indicate whether you're using a cash or accrual accounting method. If you need help with that question, see Chapter 10.

Be sure to include a phone number where the IRS and members of the public can contact your organization. Don't forget that the 990 is a public document. So, if you've had an address or name change since you filed your last report, check that box in the "B" section. If these changes have required amendments to your articles of incorporation or if this is the first time your organization has filed the 990-EZ, check the corresponding boxes. If your tax-exempt application is still pending, indicate that as well.

If your 501(c)(3) public charity received in the past year a contribution of cash, a grant, or property from a single individual that was valued at more than $5,000, *or* if a gift totaled more than 2 percent of your total grants and contributions, you must file Schedule B with your 990-EZ. If a person gives you two gifts of $2,500 within the year, you must file the schedule. If you don't have grants or gifts in this range, be sure to check the box in the "H" section to let the IRS know that you aren't required to file Schedule B.

The IRS doesn't require Schedule B to be disclosed to the public. If your organization must file its 990 report with its state to satisfy state reporting requirements, check about its disclosure requirements.

Parts 1 and 11

In Part I of 990-EZ, you report your financial activities over the past year. Chances are that the two lines that have the highest amount of revenue are line 1 (contributions, gifts, and grants) and line 2 (program service revenue, including government fees and contracts). You may have some income from membership fees for line 3 and income from investments or interest on a savings account for line 4.

Lines 5 through 8 deal with income from sales of materials or assets and income from special events. You're asked to report the costs and expenses associated with the materials sold and any direct expenses associated with special events. In other words, the IRS wants to see a net amount for sales and special events. The total you end up with on line 9 is your total revenue for the year.

If you had more than $15,000 in gross receipts from special events (reported in line 6A), you need to complete Part II of Schedule G. If any part of these gross receipts came from gaming, such as bingo, you also need to complete Part III of this schedule.

Don't confuse your total revenue with your gross receipts. Gross receipts include all the income you received from sales and special events before you subtract expenses.

Report your expenses on lines 10 through 16 in their appropriate categories and total the amount on line 17. Subtract line 9 from line 17, and you have your surplus (or deficit) for the year. This amount goes on line 18. We come back to line 19 in just a minute.

Part II includes lines 22 through 24, which is where you report your assets — cash, savings, or investments as well as property and equipment. (Equipment goes on line 24, other assets, with a description. Attach a page with an equipment list if you need to.) Total these figures for line 25.

Enter your total liabilities on line 26. They may include accounts payable, outstanding loans, and vacation time owed to employees, for example. Describe these liabilities in the space provided. If you need more space, list them on an attachment. Subtract line 26 from line 25, and you have your net assets or fund balance. Put this amount on line 27. If you pay off all your bills and sell all your assets, this amount is what's left over — in theory.

Notice that you need to report assets and liabilities for the beginning of the year and the end of the year. (If this 990 report is your first, you provide only end-of-year totals.) Refer to the form you submitted last year for these figures.

Now go back to line 19 in Part I. Enter your net assets from last year's form on this line. If an adjustment to your net assets was made during the year (usually done by an accountant), enter the figure for this adjustment on line 20 and attach an explanation. On line 21, enter the amount of your net assets at the end of the current year.

That's it for reporting your financial activities on the 990-EZ form. It *was* easy, wasn't it?

Parts III and IV

Part III of 990-EZ asks you to state your primary exempt purpose. This statement doesn't need to be long like the one you wrote for your Form 1023 application; a few words will do. You also need to describe your programs, their objectives, how many people you served, and a total cost for each program. You find spaces for three separate programs, but if you have only one program, that's fine. If you have more than three, attach an additional sheet describing them.

Part III includes a space to report grants in each program area. This space is for grants made *by* your organization, not grants *to* your organization. You probably didn't make any grants, but if you did, report them here.

Part IV requires a list of your directors, with the board officers identified, and key employees and their addresses. The only key employee you need to report here is the executive director, if you have one. You also need to state how much time is devoted to each position each week and record any compensation received, including salary, retirement benefits, and expense allowances. If you need more space than what's provided on the form, attach an additional sheet. Because this information is public, most nonprofits use the organization's address for board members and staff, not home addresses.

Parts V and VI

You're likely able to check no to the questions in Part V of 990-EZ or leave the items blank. But several things may need your attention.

- ✔ If you've amended your bylaws or articles of incorporation since you filed your last report, check that item and include a copy of the amended document when you send in the form.

- ✔ Line 35 refers to income that may have come to your organization through activities not related to your charitable purpose. This is called *unrelated business income,* and if it totals more than $1,000, you must report it on Form 990-T. You may be liable for taxes on this income. If you think your nonprofit has income in this category, you would be wise to consult an accountant. (For more on unrelated income, check out the nearby sidebar "How the IRS decides whether income is unrelated.")

- If your organization loaned or borrowed money during the year from a director, trustee, or key employee — or if it has outstanding loans from the previous year — you should check yes on Line 38a, fill in the amount on Line 38b, and file Schedule L, Part II.

- In Part VI, Lines 46 and 47 ask whether your organization engaged in political campaigns on behalf of a candidate or engaged in lobbying activities. If you can legitimately answer no to these questions, do so and move on. If you have questions about your nonprofit's engagement in these areas, seek advice from an attorney.

Campaigning for a candidate under the banner of your nonprofit organization is a serious matter that ultimately could cause loss of your tax exemption. An "insubstantial" amount of lobbying is allowed for 501(c)(3) public charities, but this is an area filled with shades of gray and shouldn't be taken lightly. Nonprofit organizations can engage in nonpartisan voter registration and public education activities, but to be on the safe side, you should seek professional counsel.

- List all employees and contractors who were paid more than $100,000 during the last year. Chances are, especially if yours is a start-up organization, you can put "NA" in these sections.

Be sure to have an officer of the organization sign and date the form. If you used a paid tax preparer, she must sign as well.

How the IRS decides whether income is unrelated

The IRS definition of *unrelated business income* is based on three questions: Does the income come from a trade or business? Is it regularly carried on? Is it not substantially related to the organization's exempt purpose?

To better understand what these questions mean, consider an extreme example. The Juniper Avenue Young People's Club, a 501(c)(3) nonprofit with the mission of providing recreational opportunities, mentoring, and job-skills training to adolescents, decides to open a shoe repair business. They rent a storefront space, purchase equipment, hire employees, and begin soliciting business. The shoe repair shop does very well. In fact, in the first year of operation, income exceeds expenses by $10,000. The club uses the money to pay some costs incurred in working with young people in the neighborhood. The problem is that the shoe repair shop has no relationship to the club's charitable purpose. In this case, the club is required to file Form 990-T and pay appropriate taxes on the $10,000. That's okay, however, because the club realized a profit that can be applied to some of its program costs.

However, what if the club opens the shoe repair shop with the purpose of providing training in the shoe repair trade to adolescents in the neighborhood? In that case, chances are good that any income from the business would be considered "substantially related to the organization's exempt purpose," and the unrelated business income tax (known as UBIT) wouldn't be due on any proceeds.

Schedule A

All 501(c)(3) public charities that submit the 990-EZ must complete and submit Schedule A so the IRS can apply the public support test to determine whether your organization qualifies as a public charity. (Refer to Chapter 4 for a discussion of the public support test.) Although it's a little more complicated and there are other ways to pass the test, in a nutshell, public charities must receive one-third of their support from the public.

During the first five years of a nonprofit's existence, data is collected but the test isn't applied. So even if you're sending in your first 990-EZ, you need to provide the information requested on Schedule A.

In Part I of Schedule A, you're asked to check one box from Lines 1–11. Most 501(c)(3) organizations that are the subject of this book check either line 7 or line 9. Line 7 applies to organizations that qualify as public charities under section 170(b)(1)(A)(vi); in this case, you also need to complete Part II of Schedule A. Line 9 applies to organizations that qualify as public charities under section 509(a)(2). Organizations checking this box must complete Part III of Schedule A.

The IRS refers to the appropriate code section for your nonprofit in the letter of determination (tax-exemption letter) it sends you after you file your IRS Form 1023 application for exemption.

Parts II and III both ask for information about sources of financial support for the organization for the current tax year and the four previous years. If your organization has been in existence for less than this five-year period, you only have to provide information for the year or years in which your nonprofit has been active. Also, you don't need to compute the percentage of public support in Section C in either part until you have completed your sixth year of operations.

Using the 990 report

The IRS made substantial changes in the 990 Form that must be used by 501(c)(3) public charities with gross receipts of $1 million or more or assets of $2.5 million or greater when reporting activities for the 2008 fiscal year. For the 2009 fiscal year, all organizations with $500,000 or more in gross receipts or assets of $1.25 million or higher must file the long Form 990. By the 2010 fiscal year, organizations with gross receipts of $200,000 or more or assets of $500,000 or greater will be required to tackle the full 990 experience.

The revised 990 Form puts an increased emphasis on accountability and transparency in nonprofit organizations, which reflects growing public scrutiny of nonprofits. The first page of the form is a summary of the more-detailed information that follows. You have to describe your mission or "most significant activities" in the first question of Part I. In addition to questions about the number of board members, employees, and volunteers, you must present a summary of the detailed financial information requested in the final pages of the report.

Make no mistake, completing this report requires more time and effort than the 990-EZ. The newly revised long Form 990 spans 11 pages and is accompanied by 16 separate schedules. Although you won't be required to complete all the schedules, you may need to submit some of them, depending on the circumstances of your organization. One section of the 990 is a checklist with questions that that must be answered yes or no. Usually a "yes" answer triggers a requirement to complete one of the 16 schedules.

The IRS estimates that more than 16 hours is needed to learn about the 990 Form and nearly 24 hours is required to complete the form. We think this may be an underestimate. The instruction booklet contains 71 pages of dense reading. Answering the questions and providing the information required on this form should be a team effort. And, if at all possible, we recommend that a member of that team be a qualified accountant. It wouldn't hurt to have an attorney on board either. If you decide to undertake the task of completing the long form without the assistance of professional help, start early and plan to spend lots of time with the instruction manual.

Providing financial information

When you use the long Form 990, you'll be asked for more-detailed financial information than is needed for the 990-EZ Form. The IRS wants to know more about where you get your money and where you spend it. Also, all your expenses must be allocated to one of three categories: program, management and general, and fundraising costs, and you'll need to provide a detailed balance sheet. (Chapter 10 includes more information about financial recordkeeping.)

The IRS wants to know what method of accounting you're using and whether you're following certain accounting standards. You'll also be asked whether your financial statements were audited or reviewed by an independent accountant. If so, the IRS will ask whether your organization has a committee that provides oversight to the preparation of financial statements and audits.

If it looks like your organization will be required to file the full 990 report in the next year or two, start now to set up the accounting system you need to collect the appropriate information.

Describing your programs

In the long Form 990, you're asked to describe the program achievements of your three most expensive programs and whether any programs were added or eliminated in the year for which you're making the report. If you did make significant changes in your program offerings, you need to describe them on Schedule O.

The 990 report is a public document and is available for public review, so you need to be sure to take the time to describe your activities and program achievements completely and clearly and without the use of excessive jargon.

Looking at management and governance

The sections relating to members of the board (the IRS refers to the board as the "governing body"), board policies, and highly compensated and key employees are perhaps the most changed from the previous version of the long Form 990.

For example, in the newest version, you're asked how many board members are independent. An *independent* board member can't be compensated as an officer or employee of the organization or receive more than $10,000 as an independent contractor of the organization. He or a member of his family also may not engage in a business transaction with the organization or a key employee that would trigger the requirement to submit Schedule L.

Also, although not required by the IRS code, the 990 asks whether the organization has established written policies for when it's appropriate to get rid of old documents. (Destroying old documents relates to protecting whistleblowers and guarding against conflicts of interest.) Finally, in the board sections, the organization also must note whether a process exists for setting the compensation of the executive director and other key employees.

Getting your 990 to the IRS

Your 990 report (whether it's the 990-EZ, 990-N, or long Form 990) needs to be postmarked on the 15th day of the 5th month after the close of your financial year — unless, of course, you request an extension. Check the most recent version of the instructions to find the address to which the report should be sent. You can file the 990 reports electronically if you want. Go to www.irs.gov/efile for instructions on electronic filing. The 990-N can only be filed electronically.

Large organizations that have assets worth more than $10 million and that submit more than 250 IRS reports in a year must file their 990 returns electronically.

Reporting to Your State and Local Governments

You'll almost certainly have reporting requirements for your state and possibly your local government, especially if you provide services under contract. Sometimes reporting to the state is as simple as completing a one-page form, attaching a copy of your 990, and paying a small fee.

More and more states (and some local governments) require registration for fundraising activities. Be sure to check local laws.

Some states require a separate financial form, although we think that most follow the federal form closely. You'll probably get all the needed reporting information when you ask for the incorporation packet, but if you didn't or you aren't sure, check with your state office that regulates nonprofit corporations. The contact list provided for Chapter 4 (CD0402) is a good resource.

Part II
Managing a Nonprofit Organization

The 5th Wave   By Rich Tennant

"Does anyone know anything about Federal Grants and bookkeeping? Bob, you spent some time in a federal prison, what are they looking for?"

In this part . . .

In this part, we introduce the major aspects of managing a nonprofit. The subjects — planning programs, devising sound budgets and financial oversight, choosing and maintaining facilities, attending to insurance, marketing your programs, and hiring and supervising employees — may sound familiar to anyone who has run a for-profit business. But some important skills are found only in the nonprofit sector: For instance, how many profit-making businesses depend heavily on volunteers to meet their goals? Part II answers that question, too.

Chapter 6

Building Your Board of Directors

Some boards of directors do miraculous things. Others just muddle through. But no nonprofit organization has an ideal board of directors all the time. You may get the impression that your board is so disorganized that you may as well close up shop and go fishing. Don't despair. Boards can always get better, and many nonprofits do excellent work with boards of directors that would send shivers down the backs of most nonprofit consultants. The purpose of this chapter is to help you understand how nonprofit boards work in a perfect world. (We don't live in a perfect world, though. So please keep that in mind while reading.)

We're the first to agree that working with a board can drive you a little batty sometimes. Doing all the work yourself may seem easier, but the strength and success of a nonprofit organization grows from its board of directors. It's surprising what a group of people working together can accomplish. You'll find building a good board and working with its members to achieve your mission to be worthwhile.

Understanding the Functions of a Nonprofit Board of Directors

A *board of directors* (which we refer to simply as "a board" from here on) is a group of people who agree to accept responsibility for a nonprofit organization. A board is responsible for ensuring that the nonprofit organization is fulfilling its mission. It makes decisions about the organization, sets policy for the staff or volunteers to implement, and oversees the nonprofit's activities. Raising money for the nonprofit is another important responsibility that many, but not all, boards assume. Board members almost always serve without compensation; they're volunteers who have no financial interest in the nonprofit's business.

A nonprofit organization doesn't have owners like a for-profit business does, but a board of directors guides and oversees the organization like an owner might. No one owns city, state, and federal governments either, so citizens hand over the responsibility of running the government to elected officials. We expect those officials to govern the affairs of our city, state, and nation. The job of a nonprofit board is similar; in fact, it's referred to as *nonprofit governance*. Everything you need to know about this type of governance that you can't find here can be found in *Nonprofit Law and Governance For Dummies* by Jill Gilbert Welytok and Daniel S. Welytok (Wiley).

Key board role: Preserving public trust

A board's primary governance responsibility is *fiduciary,* or to uphold the public trust. Laws in the United States give special rights and privileges to nonprofits recognized by the Internal Revenue Service (IRS) as public charities. Primarily, these nonprofits earn the right to exemption from corporate income tax and the right to receive contributions that are tax-deductible for the donor. The government gives nonprofits this special status because they provide a public benefit. A board's leadership and oversight keep the organization's focus on that public benefit and make sure that these rights and privileges aren't abused.

Suppose that a nonprofit begins with a mission to rescue stray cats. People who support this idea make contributions to the nonprofit with the belief that their money is being spent on programs to help the plight of stray cats. But, unknown to the donors, the nonprofit begins to spend its money on programs to support preschool education. Supporting preschool education is a worthy goal, but it's a long way from the original purpose of helping stray cats. So, in this example, even though the nonprofit is using those contributions for a good cause, they're not being used as the donors intended or to fulfill the organization's original purpose.

A nonprofit that collected funds for helping stray cats but instead used the funds for the personal benefit of the board members and staff would be even worse. This dishonest act is serious and possibly a crime. Aside from potential felony fraud charges, such an activity violates IRS rules and can result in the revocation of the nonprofit's tax-exempt status.

In a for-profit business, net earnings (meaning profit) at the end of the year can be shared among the company's owners or stockholders. If nonprofit board members decide to divide surplus funds among themselves, it's called *inurement,* a big word that can be more or less defined as personal enrichment, which is not allowed in the nonprofit world. Board members and staff — or anyone, for that matter — can't personally benefit from nonprofit funds except for compensation for services provided or for reimbursement of expenses. A board must not only ensure that the nonprofit is doing what it set out to do, but it also must make sure that funds are spent properly. If a board does nothing else, it must be sure that these standards are adhered to.

Keep in mind that a board's responsibilities are legal responsibilities. BoardSource, a nonprofit organization providing information and services for nonprofit boards, outlines three duties that must be upheld: care, loyalty, and obedience. Although they sound like vows one may take when entering a monastery, they actually describe established legal principles. Here's what we mean:

✔ The duty of care refers to the responsibility to be a prudent board member. In other words, board members must pay attention to what's going on and make decisions based on good information.

✔ The duty of loyalty means that a board member must put the organization's welfare above other interests when making decisions.

✔ The duty of obedience requires that board members act in accordance with the nonprofit's mission, goals, and bylaws.

Other board tasks

In addition to the legal and fiduciary responsibilities, a nonprofit board performs other roles, too, including those described in the following sections.

Providing a guiding strategy

A board guides the overall planning and strategy of a nonprofit organization. At the most basic level, this job means reviewing the organization's mission statement and goals on a regular basis. Every nonprofit should have an organizational plan. Turn to Chapter 7 for more information on planning.

Hiring and working with the executive director

A nonprofit board is expected to hire the organization's executive director. Of course, many nonprofit organizations operate without paid staff, but if your nonprofit does have employees, finding the right executive director is one of the board's most important tasks. See Chapter 9 for information about hiring paid employees.

A board works with its executive director to set goals and objectives for the year. Board members shouldn't look over the director's shoulder every day, but they should have a good idea of the director's work plan and guarantee that her efforts are in line with the agency's purpose.

Overseeing the organization's finances

A board must see to it that the organization has the resources to carry out its goals. As part of this duty, many boards are active in fundraising. But a board also is responsible for reviewing the organization's budget and staying informed of the organization's financial situation. Nothing is more dismal than finding out, for example, that an organization hasn't been sending in its payroll taxes. Insist on good financial reporting. At a minimum, the board treasurer (or perhaps the executive director or bookkeeper, if you have one) should prepare quarterly financial reports and distribute them to your board.

Many people join boards because they care about and understand the nature of the service that the organization provides, but they may not be trained in bookkeeping and accounting. These board members should try not to let their eyes glaze over when the financial report is passed around at the board meeting, because part of a board member's job is to understand finances. If members don't understand the financial fine points, they should ask questions of staff and other board members and study Chapter 10 on nonprofit budgets and financial statements.

However, sometimes the problem is more than lack of comprehension. It may be that the financial information needs to be presented more clearly. If one board member doesn't understand the financial reports, you can be sure that other board members don't understand them, either. If your organization uses an outside accountant or bookkeeper to keep track of finances, ask for a brief meeting with him to explain how he has presented the information. Many nonprofit service organizations (see Appendix A) offer affordable workshops on nonprofit finances and recordkeeping to assist board and staff members; others have programs that place volunteers from businesses into nonprofits.

Working with an advisory board

Some organizations form *advisory boards,* which don't have governance responsibilities. Instead, their responsibilities depend on the type of advisory board it is. The following two types exist:

✔ Advisory boards that have members who actually provide advice and guidance because of their professional expertise

✔ Advisory boards formed so that prominent names can be listed on the organization's letterhead

We favor advisory boards that are asked for and give advice — even if it's only once per year. Some organizations also use advisory board appointments as a way of getting to know potential board members.

Sharing responsibilities

Defining roles causes problems for a number of nonprofit organizations. Should the board of directors be involved in day-to-day management decisions? No, probably not. An executive director and her staff don't need board members to approve every management decision that comes along. The board must trust the staff to run the organization. To put it simply, the board sets the overall goals and policies, and the staff implements them. But (and this is a big but) many nonprofits have limited staff or even no staff at all. What happens when the organization's work is done by the board and other volunteers?

In the case of volunteer-run organizations, board members must wear two hats. When they meet as a board of directors, they must see the larger picture and make group decisions that benefit the organization and its programs and clients. And, most important, they must exercise their fiduciary responsibilities. But when they have to do the hands-on work needed to provide the services and perform the day-to-day tasks of running a nonprofit, board members must act as if they're employees. They may even hold regular, unpaid volunteer jobs with job descriptions and scheduled hours. Confusing, isn't it? Still, this distinction should always be in the minds of those who serve as both board members and staff.

In any organization, building practices that create checks and balances is a good idea. These practices are particularly important when board members also act as staff. For example, an organization has better financial oversight and control when one person approves bills for payment, a different person signs the checks, and yet another person reviews the canceled checks and monthly bank statements. You don't *have* to use this system — it's just one way to make sure that everything is used and accounted for properly.

Finding the Right People for Your Board

You don't want just anybody to serve on your board. You want to choose the wealthiest, most generous members of your community who believe in what you're doing, will come to all your meetings, be advocates for your programs, provide honest and ethical oversight to the organization, and sweep the floor on weekends.

You won't find many board members who fit this description. Even so, the following three traits are critical to the success of the organization:

✔ Believing in your mission

✔ Being a good advocate on behalf of your programs

✔ Serving the organization as a careful and honest board member

Sure, having rich members who do the dirty work when needed is nice, but, most importantly, you must find board members who understand and believe deeply in what you're doing. Showing up for board meetings is a nice habit, too.

You also should think seriously about the skills that board members bring to your organization. Do you need an accountant to set up financial systems? A public relations specialist to help with media campaigns? An attorney to help with legal matters? Yes, you probably do. But don't expect the accountant to do your audit or the attorney to represent you in court. You need a disinterested professional to do that work.

Your board should reflect your organization's character and mission. A community-organizing group dedicated to collective decision making may want board members who work well together. A neighborhood development organization clearly wants board members from its neighborhood. A youth leadership organization may want to invest in future leadership by creating positions for youth members on its board. (*Note:* Before adding young people to your board, check with an attorney about whether your state laws allow minors to serve on nonprofit boards. If your state prohibits minors from serving, you can consider inviting them to serve on advisory committees.)

Although having a friend or two on the board is fine, be careful about overloading the board with golfing buddies and carpool partners. Boards need diverse opinions and honest feedback from members.

Keeping the board fresh

Building a board should be a continuing process. Therefore, we highly recommend that your organizational bylaws specify terms of service. Two three-year terms or three two-year terms are the most common terms for board service. Almost always, bylaws allow reelection to the board after one year's absence. Limiting terms of service helps you maintain a fresh supply of new ideas, which are more likely to come from people who are new to your organization. Plus, terms of service help you recruit new board members, because they know that their time commitment is temporary.

Persuading someone to take the plunge and join your board

Many people think that a board member's primary role is to raise money. In fact, a popular slogan addressed to board members who aren't raising funds is "Give, get, or get off." Harsh, isn't it? But nonprofits can't fulfill their purposes effectively without money, and board members who are taking an active interest in the organization's financial vitality are important. But a board member's role is broader than fundraising. Other roles include staying well informed about the organization's work, selecting leadership, setting policies, planning, overseeing, and serving as an ambassador for the organization. Many highly skilled volunteers think that they shouldn't serve on boards because they aren't wealthy, and this misconception represents a real loss to nonprofit organizations.

Some people also are reluctant to serve on boards for other reasons, including personal and financial liability. However, unpaid volunteers who aren't grossly negligent have some protection under the Volunteer Protection Act of 1997. If more information is needed about the possible liabilities of board members and other volunteers, we suggest that you get in touch with BoardSource (www.boardsource.org) or your state's association of nonprofit organizations through the National Council of Nonprofit Associations (www.ncna.org).

Organizations can protect their boards by purchasing directors' and officers' insurance (see Chapter 12). Generally, the organization's creditors can't come after its board members' personal wealth for payment. An exception is that the IRS can hold board members financially accountable when organizations fail to pay payroll taxes. But even the IRS will work with an organization to develop a payment plan and schedule to catch up on taxes. People are right to take the responsibility of board service seriously, but nonprofit board work also can be fun and satisfying.

To avoid having all your board members leave in the same year, stagger the years when terms expire. You can allow someone to serve an extra year or ask others to serve shorter terms.

If you're thinking about recruiting new members, drawing a grid is sometimes helpful. Along the top, list the skills you think you need on your board. Along the side, list your current board members and place check marks under the skills they bring to the board. This exercise helps you visualize the skills you need to watch for when you're looking for new members. Check out CD0601 for a sample grid for planning board recruitment.

So, where do you find board members? Start with your organization's address book. Who do you know who might make a good member and be willing to serve? Who benefits from your agency's work? Who are your agency's neighbors? Some cities have nonprofit support organizations that can help in this regard. Look at Appendix A for a list of these agencies. Also consider asking your funders for suggestions.

Even if you don't specify board terms, continuously recruiting new board members is important. As time passes, board members' lives may change in ways that draw them away from your organization. Many nonprofit organizations lose vitality when their boards don't refresh themselves with new members.

Big boards versus little boards

Opinions differ about the ideal number of board members. One school of thought holds that big boards are better because the members can divide work among more people, consider more diverse viewpoints, and reach into the community more extensively. Other people say that smaller boards are better because maintaining a working relationship with a smaller group is easier and decision making is better because the board has to consider fewer opinions. Those who support small boards also say that board members can easily become invisible in a large group, meaning that no one will notice if they don't do their share of the work.

We feel that there really isn't one right answer to the board-size question. Nonprofits vary widely in size, function, and type, so what works for one nonprofit may not work for another. Nonprofit board size is truly a case where the phrase "one size fits all" doesn't apply.

Following are some points to consider when setting board size:

- ✔ Start-up nonprofits tend to have smaller boards than more mature organizations. Start-up budgets tend to be smaller, and building a board of directors takes time.

- ✔ Boards that are actively engaged in fundraising for major gifts and special events tend to be larger because both fundraising techniques are fueled by personal contacts and friendships. The more board members you have, the more personalized invitations you can send to your next event. Some large cultural and arts institutions have 50 board members or more.

- ✔ Boards that govern nonprofits funded mostly by grants and contracts tend to have fewer members, perhaps an average of 10 to 12 members. Board members in these nonprofits usually have fewer fundraising responsibilities for the organization and frequently are representatives of the communities or clients served. They also may have professional experience in the types of service provided by the nonprofit.

It isn't unusual for the founder or founders of start-up nonprofit organizations to seed the board with personal friends. Within reason, this isn't a problem initially. However, as the nonprofit grows and matures, you should move beyond your own address book to find board members who have wider contacts in your community and who can bring an objective eye to the activities and plans of the organization.

Selecting board officers and committees

Typical officer positions of most nonprofit boards include president, vice-president, secretary, and treasurer. Sometimes the positions of secretary and treasurer are combined into one office. Your state laws may specify which officers are required. Seniority on the board, professional expertise, and skills at negotiating with and listening to others are common traits sought in a board's leaders. Ultimately, however, the board of directors chooses the officers. They're usually elected to two-year terms. Table 6-1 outlines the responsibilities of board officers.

Table 6-1	Duties and Responsibilities of Board Officers
Office	*Duties and Responsibilities*
President	Presides at board meetings, appoints committee chairpersons, works closely with the executive director to guide the organization, and acts as public spokesperson for the organization (but also may assign this responsibility to the executive director)
Vice-president	Presides at board meetings in the president's absence and serves as a committee chairperson as appointed by the president
Secretary	Maintains the organization's records, takes minutes at board meetings, and distributes minutes and announcements of upcoming meetings to board members
Treasurer	Oversees the organization's financial aspects, makes regular financial reports to the board, and serves as chairperson of the board finance committee

Check out CD0602 for more detailed job descriptions you can use.

If the board has *standing,* or permanent, committees, the board president appoints committee chairpersons. Typical standing committees include finance, development or fundraising, program, and nominating committees. Other possible committees that may be either standing or *ad hoc* — a temporary committee organized to deal with time-limited projects — include planning, executive search, investment, and facilities. Table 6-2 outlines the responsibilities of common standing committees.

Table 6-2	Responsibilities of Standing Committees
Committee	*Responsibilities*
Development	Sets fundraising goals and plans fundraising activities for the organization
Finance	Assists the treasurer in overseeing financial reports and making budgets
Nominating	Recruits new board members and nominates board officers for election to their positions
Program	Oversees the program activities of the organization

Board committees make regular reports to the full board about the organization's activities in their particular areas. Board officer terms and the number and type of standing committees are written into the organization's bylaws.

 If your organization is large enough to conduct an annual financial audit, your board may be legally required to appoint an audit committee. Be sure to check the laws in your state.

Executive committees are standard groups on some larger boards of directors. Usually the members of the executive committee are the officers of the board, but the committee also sometimes includes the chairs of the standing committees. The executive committee may hold regular meetings to set the agenda for the meetings of the full board and to advise the board president, or it may come together on an as-needed basis. Sometimes an organization's bylaws empower the executive committee to make decisions on behalf of the full board in an emergency or in other special circumstances.

Introducing new and prospective board members to the organization

Boards of directors exhibit all the characteristics of small groups, maybe even families: Friendships develop, alliances form, and disagreements occur. Over time, the group develops routines and habits that help make members feel comfortable with one another and help guide the board's work. When a new member joins the group or when a prospective new member visits, the existing members need to make that person feel comfortable and share with her the collective wisdom they have accumulated.

Invite a prospective board member to observe at least one board meeting before electing her to membership. That way, the new member gets a chance to see how the board operates, and the current members have an opportunity to size up the new person. Encourage the prospective member to ask questions. Also, if your nonprofit provides programs, such as childcare, a health clinic, or a music school, prospective board members should take a tour of the facilities before they join.

When asking someone to serve on your board, don't shy away from sharing a clear picture of the work to be done. You may be afraid that your prospect will say "no" if it seems like too much work. However, keep in mind that being asked is an honor, and contributing good work to a good cause is satisfying. Besides, if the person does decide you're asking too much of her, isn't it better to know now rather than later?

A packet of background materials about the organization and board procedures can help new members get up to speed quickly. The following information is useful for orienting new members:

- ✔ Board job descriptions
- ✔ Board minutes for the last two or three meetings
- ✔ Bylaws
- ✔ Calendar of organization's events and scheduled board meetings
- ✔ Description of board member responsibilities and expectations
- ✔ Description of programs
- ✔ Financial audit or financial statement
- ✔ Mission statement
- ✔ Names, addresses, and phone numbers of other board members
- ✔ News clippings about the organization
- ✔ Organizational plan (if one is available)

This information may seem like a lot of reading — and it is. But even if a new board member doesn't read everything from cover to cover, she at least has the reference material when she needs it.

We also suggest that the board president or the executive director meet with a new board member soon after she begins serving on the board, both to welcome her and to answer any questions.

Putting Staff Members on the Board

As a general rule, paid staff shouldn't be board members. The situation can get too complicated. For example, *conflict of interest* is always a potential problem. Awkward moments are likely when board and staff have different priorities, such as when employees want raises, but the board says no.

Some exceptions to the rule do exist, though. In fact, many nonprofits have at least one staff member on their boards. In start-up nonprofits, for example, founders frequently serve as both board members and staff members. This situation isn't surprising. Who's better suited to bring the vision and passion needed to create a new organization than the person who formed it in the first place? In many new nonprofits, of course, paying the staff isn't even possible; resources are so limited that all work is done on a volunteer basis.

If a founder or other staff member serves on the board, we recommend that he not be elected board president because doing so tends to keep all responsibility for vision and leadership in a single person's hands. Sharing that leadership can be an important first step toward broadening an organization's base of support.

Laws vary by state, but, in many cases, having a paid staff member on your board is permitted. For example, under California nonprofit corporation law, up to 49 percent of the members of a nonprofit board of directors is allowed to receive compensation from the nonprofit. But the standards of philanthropy set forth by the Better Business Bureau Wise Giving Alliance say that a board should include no more than one paid staff member. Check out the state contacts list from Chapter 4 (CD0402) for a list of state offices where you can get information about nonprofit corporation law in your state.

Using the Board to Full Capacity

If you spend any time around nonprofit staff, you'll probably hear a few complaints about the board of directors. They may say, "I can't get my board to do anything" or "I can't get them to face hard decisions or raise money." Worst of all, you may hear, "I can't get them to show up to meetings."

Motivating the board is an important part of any nonprofit leader's job. Keeping members well informed so they can make thoughtful, appropriate recommendations is essential. Sometimes, your most important task is gently steering the board's attention back to the organization's mission and immediate needs. Whether or not your nonprofit has paid staff, you can take steps to help the board do its work well.

The working relationship between the executive director (if you have one) and the board president is key to having an effective board and organization. Ideally, the relationship between these two leaders is one of respect and trust.

Encouraging commitment from board members

Getting members of a board to pull their weight sometimes seems like a problem that you can't solve. Not every board member will contribute equally to the work involved in governing a nonprofit organization. If everyone on your board shows up at every meeting, reads all the materials, studies the financial statements, and contributes to fundraising activities, consider yourself fortunate.

Here are some techniques that encourage full board member participation:

- ✔ **Board contracts:** Some nonprofits ask new board members to sign an agreement that outlines expectations for board service. The contract may include a commitment to contribute financially to the organization, attend all board meetings, and serve on one or more committees. Although board contracts aren't legally binding, they provide a clear understanding of responsibilities for each board member. With a board contract, no one can say he didn't understand what he was getting into when he joined the board. Check out CD0603 for a sample board contract.

- ✔ **Bylaws:** Organizational bylaws can state the requirements for board participation. For example, a board member may face dismissal from the board if he misses three consecutive board meetings.

- ✔ **Job descriptions:** Just like employees, board members often do better if they know exactly what they're supposed to do. Creating job descriptions for officers, committee chairpersons, and individual board members may clarify responsibilities and make them easier to fulfill. If a member isn't pulling his weight, a committee chair should speak with him and remind him of his responsibilities.

- ✔ **Reliance on board members:** Solicit opinions from members between board meetings. Use their expertise and recognize their contributions.

- ✔ **Self-evaluation:** Sometimes encouraging a board to look at itself motivates board members or encourages those who aren't pulling their weight to resign.

Board members fail to contribute equally to the work of the board due to time constraints, business travel, and just plain laziness. Give each member some slack. But if a board member's lack of participation impacts the full board, the decision is up to the board president (often in partnership with the executive director) to ask the member to reconsider his commitment to the organization.

To a great degree, each board member's work reflects his commitment to the organization's mission. Board members who truly believe in what you're doing do everything they can to help you succeed.

Making board meetings effective

Most board work is done in meetings, either with the full board or in committees. The board president is responsible for ensuring that meetings are well organized and begin and end at a scheduled hour. We can't think of anything that damages board effectiveness more than poorly organized meetings that don't stay on topic and continue late into the night. Nonprofit board members are volunteers; they aren't being paid by the hour.

If the organization has an executive director, the president may delegate some responsibilities for setting up meetings. Ultimately, however, part of the president's job is to see that board members have the information they need to make good decisions and that they do so in a reasonable amount of time.

Getting the members to show up

Saying how often a board of directors should meet is impossible. The glib answer: as often as it needs to. A meeting schedule really depends on the organization's needs and the amount of business conducted at board meetings. Some nonprofit boards meet only once a year, the bare legal minimum. These tend to be small but stable organizations with one or two employees. Most nonprofit boards meet more frequently than once a year; some meet quarterly, some meet every other month, and others schedule monthly meetings.

The advantage of having more frequent board meetings is that board members are more engaged in the governance of the organization. The disadvantage — especially if the agenda doesn't include much business — is that board members may be more tempted to skip meetings. Of course, the board president may call a board meeting at any time if the board needs to handle special business.

Some boards schedule meetings at the beginning of the year for the entire year. By entering these dates in their appointment calendars months in advance, board members are less likely to schedule other events on the same days and are more likely to attend the meetings. For example, if you meet monthly, you may schedule your meetings for the second Tuesday of each month. If you aren't this organized, always schedule the next meeting before the end of the present meeting. Doing so is much easier than trying to schedule a meeting by telephone or e-mail.

Some boards use a listserv or Yahoo! or MSN group to communicate between board meetings and to compile documents in an easily accessible place.

Having the best, most efficient meetings you can

If you're looking for some tips to ensure effective board meetings, check out the following ideas:

- ✔ **Ten days to two weeks before a board meeting, send an announcement of the meeting to all board members.** Include the minutes from the last meeting and an agenda for the upcoming meeting. Also include any committee reports, financial statements, or background research that the board will discuss at the meeting.

  If the meeting minutes include a list of tasks for board members to complete before the next meeting, it's a good idea to send members a rough draft of the minutes as soon after the meeting as possible.

- ✔ **Limit the length of meetings to two hours or less, if possible.** After two hours, especially if you're holding the meeting in the evening, attention begins to wane. If you must go longer than two hours, take a break. Offering refreshments is always a good idea.

- ✔ **Try to find a conference room for the meeting.** Holding a discussion around a conference table is much easier than holding one in someone's living room. The table offers a place to set papers, and people won't argue over who gets the recliner. It also sets the stage and implies that work is to be done.

  Avoid holding meetings in restaurants and cafes, if possible. The noise levels are too high to make good discussion possible, and all the activity is a constant distraction. You also have no privacy. Believe us — we've tried it!

✔ **Stick to the agenda.** Don't allow people to wander off topic. Some agendas set the time allowed for discussion after each item. You don't have to do this, but if your meetings have been veering off course, setting time limits may help control them. CD0604 and CD0605 are samples of common agenda types you can use as models.

✔ **Follow Robert's Rules of Order.** You don't need to be overly formal in your meetings (many board meetings are very casual), but having a basic knowledge of when to make a motion and when to call the question is helpful.

✔ **Thank your board.** Board members are volunteers who give time and money to your organization. Take every opportunity during meetings to make sure they're appreciated. Mention their names when appropriate in newsletters and media releases. Small gifts are sometimes useful but don't be extravagant. You don't want to be accused of wasting the organization's money.

Chapter 7

Planning: Why and How Nonprofits Make Plans

*T*he word *planning* can be intimidating. It brings up images of daylong meetings in stuffy conference rooms with consultants wielding marker pens. Of course, not all planning takes that sort of effort — perfectly good plans can be made with a pencil on the back of an envelope, or even just imagined in your head. People make plans all the time, from organizing a vacation to deciding how to get all the errands done on a Saturday afternoon.

Organization planning, however, requires more effort. It's a group project that calls for research, brainstorming, discussion, and, in the end, agreement on a goal and the strategies and tactics needed to reach that goal. Simply put, organizational planning is deciding where to go and how to get there. The planning process helps to ensure that everyone is headed in the same direction.

In this chapter, we cover planning for nonprofits in all its forms, from organizational planning to program planning to work planning. Plan to join us!

Why Spend Valuable Time Planning?

No organization has unlimited funds. Even the largest, wealthiest nonprofit needs to decide how to allocate its resources effectively. Planning helps you make decisions about how to spend your organization's money by answering questions such as "Is now the best time to invest in a new program?" and "Is it better to hire another staff person for the fundraising department, or should we hire a consultant?"

A nonprofit organization undertakes planning for the following reasons:

- ✔ To build a structure that guides its activities in pursuit of its mission
- ✔ To allocate organizational resources in the most effective ways
- ✔ To create a framework against which the organization's performance can be evaluated
- ✔ To adapt to changes in the external environment
- ✔ To reach agreement among board, staff, and supporters on desirable goals for the organization

Think of a plan as a blueprint or scheme describing what needs to be done to accomplish an end. In an ideal world, if your organization completes every step of its plan, you achieve your goals.

The *act* of planning is as important as the final plan itself. That's because, in theory, the planning group's decision-making process ensures that everyone understands what needs to be done and agrees that it's worth doing.

Making Your Organizational Plan

Organizational planning is what people usually think about when they consider planning. An *organizational plan,* usually covering a three- to five-year period, sets goals for the organization and describes the objectives that must be accomplished to achieve those goals.

The steps for successful organizational planning are as follows:

1. **Decide whether it's the right time to plan.**
2. **Look at your mission.**
3. **Assess the external and internal situation.**
4. **Hear from stakeholders.**
5. **Make decisions.**
6. **Write the plan.**

Planning is an ongoing activity. A formal effort to develop an organizational plan may occur only once every three to five years, but planning for the purposes of accomplishing objectives, creating a budget, and developing fundraising programs goes on all the time.

Getting ready

Make no mistake: An all-out organizational planning effort requires considerable time, energy, and commitment from everyone involved. Some nonprofits spend a year or more developing an organizational plan.

Don't jump into the planning process without understanding that it will add to your workload and complicate your life for a period of time. Also, keep in mind that you can't plan by yourself. If you're the executive director of a nonprofit organization who thinks that a full-bore planning effort is needed, but the board of directors doesn't agree with your assessment, don't try to start the process on your own. Take a couple steps backward and begin the work of persuading board members that planning is worth the effort.

Don't start the planning process if your nonprofit is in a crisis mode. It's tempting, for example, to launch an organizational planning effort if you just lost a major source of funding. But you have more immediate concerns to deal with in that situation. Delay organizational planning until you see a period of smooth sailing.

If you have the support, and foreclosure isn't hanging over your agency's head, the best way to get started is to form a *planning committee.* This small group of board members, staff, and one or two outside people can take on the role of guiding the planning process and, in the beginning, pull together the facts and observations that you need to make your planning decisions.

Working from your organization's mission

Reviewing the organization's mission statement is one of the first tasks facing an organization that's beginning the planning process. (Chapter 3 covers mission statements.) Ask yourself these questions:

- ✔ Is the problem we set out to solve still a problem?
- ✔ Should we fine-tune the mission statement to make it more specific, or should it be broadened?
- ✔ Does the mission statement contain enough flexibility to allow the organization to grow?

Is it long-range planning or strategic planning?

People often use the terms *long-range planning* and *strategic planning* as if they describe the same thing, but many planning experts make a distinction between the two. *Long-range planning* is setting a path to accomplish goals several years in the future. *Strategic planning* on the other hand, is making decisions based on the current state of affairs in your nonprofit and the outside environment.

We think both planning approaches are necessary. A nonprofit should have long-term goals that lead to accomplishing its mission, but nonprofit staff and board members also should always be thinking of the current situation and should be making choices that serve the organization and its clients today.

Keep your mission statement in mind throughout the planning process. At every turn, ask yourself: "If we do this, will we be true to our mission?" "Will this new program we're considering help us accomplish what we want to do?"

Surveying the external situation

Early in the planning process, you need to collect information about external factors that influence your nonprofit's operation. Someone, or a subcommittee of the planning committee, should find the answers to the following questions and distribute them to everyone on the committee before the formal planning meetings begin:

- ✔ Are other nonprofits providing similar services in the community? If so, how are our services different?

- ✔ What are the demographic trends in our area? Will these trends have an impact on the number of people who may need or use our services?

- ✔ What are the trends in the professional area in which our nonprofit operates? Are new methods being developed? Does the future show a shortage of professionally trained staff?

- ✔ How stable are the funding sources on which we depend? What about changes in government funding? Can we find new potential sources of funding?

The decisions you make are only as good as the information on which you base them. Therefore, it's important to find the best and most up-to-date data available that may have an impact on your organization and its programs.

Planning for uncertainty

No matter how well you plan, circumstances can, and probably will, change. So, of course, creating an organizational plan requires that you make assumptions about the future; sometimes these assumptions turn out to be wrong. Maybe, for example, another organization offers a better job to a key employee; maybe a dependable funding source drops out of the picture; maybe a major industry in your city closes its doors; or maybe new government regulations affect your programs. Unexpected events within your nonprofit or in your community can dump cold water on your carefully designed plans.

But this doesn't mean that your nonprofit should abandon planning. Fundamentally, planning is about making decisions. Decisions must be made, and they should be based on the best available information and the most careful thought you can muster. Ask yourself: Shall we invest in new fundraising software or shall we put the funds into our cash reserve account? Is this the best time to open a branch office in the suburbs or shall we acquire more office space at our current location?

You may want to collect information from the general public or a particular constituency of your nonprofit. Questionnaires and focus groups are two ways to get input from the public. Before you undertake either of these techniques, however, spend some time thinking about what you want to find out. Write a list of questions for which you want answers.

If possible, consult with someone experienced in preparing surveys, because the phrasing of questions affects the answers you get. Look for expertise in this area at local colleges and universities. If you can't get expert help in this area, consider doing a series of one-on-one interviews with fewer people, because a poorly conceived survey may give you bad information.

Bad information leads to bad decisions. Or, put another way, garbage in, garbage out. So, when gathering background information to guide planning decisions, take the time to get the most accurate, up-to-date facts available.

Looking at the internal situation

In addition to surveying the environment in which the organization operates, you need to expend some effort assessing the organization itself. Consider the following factors when doing an internal analysis:

- ✔ What are the organization's major accomplishments? What are its milestones?

- ✔ Is the board of directors fully engaged with the organization? Should any weaknesses on the board be filled? Is the board engaged in fundraising?

- ✔ What are the capabilities of the staff? Does the organization have enough staff to implement changes in how it operates? Is staff training needed?

- ✔ Has the organization operated within its budget? Is financial reporting adequate? Are appropriate financial controls in place?

- ✔ Does the organization have adequate technology? Do employees need additional training in using technological tools? What are its future equipment needs?

- ✔ Does the organization have a variety of funding sources? Are funding sources stable?

Scenarios for the future

Scenario planning, or scenario thinking, is an approach that involves imagining a particular future or futures in which your organization may find itself and then using those imagined futures to determine the strategies that your nonprofit needs to thrive in the years to come. But no one can predict the future, of course, and the practitioners of scenario planning don't pretend that they're prophets or seers. More than anything, this planning method provides a framework for deep strategic conversations among the leaders of the nonprofits, corporations, and government agencies that engage in it.

Scenario planning pushes you to define the most pressing issue facing your organization. In the beginning, you need to talk with as many stakeholders as possible to find the right question to ask. For example, if your organization works to overcome the digital divide — and provide equal access to information technology for everyone — you may want to think about whether you should focus your attention on access to technical education or the provision of affordable online tools.

After you've figured out the question you want to address — often the most difficult thing to do — you need to collect as much information as possible about trends that would impact access to technology. You may want to find out about future cost projections for computers, projected family income figures, trends in poverty rates, business trends in the technology industry, and efforts by local governments to provide wireless access to their communities, to name only a few.

Then you can begin thinking about how the future may play out by creating a description — some would say a story or stories — of possible future conditions. After you arrive at this point, you begin to talk about how your organization can make strategic decisions that will help it fulfill its mission in the future.

As with all planning exercises, scenario planning makes you think. We can't predict what the future will actually hold, but it's wise to consider whether we're on the right track or whether we could be doing something better.

Hearing from all your stakeholders

Unless you have a very small organization, you probably can't include every single person in the planning process. You do need to include all stakeholder groups, however. A *stakeholder* is someone who has a reason for wanting the organization to succeed. Paid employees and, presumably, members of the board certainly qualify. But although these two groups may be the most closely connected to the nonprofit, they're by no means the only people who have a stake in the organization's success.

In our view, you should include all the following groups in planning:

- ✔ Board of directors
- ✔ Community leaders
- ✔ Donors
- ✔ Staff
- ✔ Users of services
- ✔ Volunteers

Some organizations make the mistake of leaving planning only to the board of directors. Although the board does hold the final responsibility for guiding a nonprofit, the staff, clients, and donors have different perspectives on the nonprofit's operation that should be included when considering the organization's future.

If you don't have a client representative on the board (you probably should), organize a client advisory committee and empower the members to appoint one or two people to the planning committee. The same holds true for staff. Although we don't recommend that paid staff members serve on the board of the nonprofit that employs them, they should be involved in the planning process. Staff members often have information about the organization and the environment in which it operates that's crucial to the making of a good plan.

Check out the sample planning retreat agenda on the accompanying CD (CD0701) for some guidance in organizing your own planning retreat.

One purpose of organizational planning is to bring stakeholders together in pursuit of a common goal. People work harder to achieve the goals when they're asked to help set the goals.

Studying your organization's pros and cons

Be objective when looking at the pros and cons of your organization. It's tempting, for example, to put the best face on the activities of the board of directors. They're volunteers, after all. How much time do they really have to give to the organization? But if you avoid identifying important deficiencies because you don't want to hurt someone's feelings, your planning efforts will be handicapped by bad information.

The same advice holds true when evaluating staff strengths and weaknesses, and when assessing your external situation. For example, pointing out that the executive director needs more training in staff supervision may not be easy, but if you aren't honest, you can't identify problems, and positive change can't occur.

Guard against bias. Sometimes people get so close to the situation they're evaluating that they can't see the true picture with an objective eye. Include outside people who have no history with the organization and have no personal stake in the outcome.

Also, don't assume that all the people you interview know what they're talking about. Accepting statements without verification can lead to bad decisions. For instance, if someone says that getting a grant to pay the costs of a program start-up is a piece of cake, check with potential funders before you agree that it's an easy task.

Yes, honesty can create conflict. Be prepared for it. Set some rules when going into planning meetings. Make sure that all the participants have a chance to state their case. Demand that all the participants show respect for one another. Arguments can be productive if they don't disintegrate into shouting matches. Always place the emphasis on the organization, not on personalities.

Calling in the SWOT team

One common way to analyze the information you've collected is to perform a SWOT analysis. *SWOT* is an acronym for Strengths-Weaknesses-Opportunities-Threats. SWOT analysis is usually done in a facilitated meeting in which the participants have agreed-upon ground rules. If you prefer, however, stakeholders can complete their version of the analysis individually and then come together to discuss the results as a group.

For example, the results of a SWOT analysis for an organization providing counseling services to families may look something like the following:

Strengths

- ✔ The program staff is highly qualified and committed.

- ✔ Clients give program services a high-quality rating.

- ✔ The organization has a surplus equal to approximately five months of operating expenses.

- ✔ Program costs are funded largely by government grants.

Weaknesses

- ✔ The cost per client is higher than in similar programs.

- ✔ Most revenues are from government sources; contributed income from individuals is low.

- ✔ The programs aren't well known in the general public.

Opportunities

- ✔ Population trend predictions indicate that the client base will increase over the next ten years.

- ✔ Review of news coverage suggests that the media are showing increasing interest in covering issues that are important to nonprofit organizations.

- ✔ The organization has cash reserves to invest in growth.

Threats

- ✔ Local government (the primary funding source) will face a budget deficit during the next fiscal year.

- ✔ Over the past five years, program costs have increased at a rate of 3 percent a year.

A review of this SWOT analysis reveals an organization that has been successful in providing quality services and getting those services funded by government contracts. However, the responses also make it clear that the program's future may be in jeopardy if organizational change doesn't take place. Depending on a single source of income for most costs is a problem, especially because the funding entity apparently needs to make budget cuts in the next few years. Even if the program continues to be funded by the government, cost-of-living increases may cease because of tight financial needs. Over time, as program costs increase and funding remains stagnant, the organization runs a risk of not being reimbursed for the full costs of its programs.

On the positive side, this organization has time and resources to begin to diversify revenues. Little effort has been made to interest donors in supporting the organization's work; in fact, the programs are more or less invisible in the community. One strategy to increase revenue is to develop an annual campaign led by the board of directors and, at the same time, to work toward getting coverage of the nonprofit's programs in the local media.

As this example shows, one or more items often can be listed as both strengths and weaknesses. Here, for instance, you see the fact that programs are largely funded by the government as a strength, but it's also a weakness because it has created a situation in which the organization relies on a single source of funding.

Pulling it all together

After the research, analysis, and discussion, it's time to determine future directions and put the results into a final plan. Ideally, the plans of the organization will become apparent after sifting through and discussing the material assembled. If the planning group can't reach a consensus, more discussion (and perhaps more data) is needed.

We recommend using a professional meeting facilitator. A facilitator brings a neutral viewpoint to the proceedings and can be effective in helping a group arrive at a consensus about organizational goals — even goals that may be unpopular with some staff or board members.

Ensuring your goals make sense

Organizational goals need to be specific, measurable, and attainable within a set period of time. Don't set a goal like "In five years, the XYZ Tutoring Project will be the best tutoring program west of the Mississippi." You have no way to evaluate whether the organization is the best tutoring program west of the Mississippi, and even if you could determine the "best" program, the goal is so general and vague that you can't set objectives to achieve it.

Instead, an organizational goal for this program may be something like, "In five years, the XYZ Tutoring Project will provide tutoring services that are recognized by classroom teachers as effective in improving student performance." This goal can be measured. It's also attainable through implementing a series of strategies that may include better training for tutors, improved communication with classroom teachers to determine student needs, acquisition of computers to aid in tutoring sessions, and so on.

Clear and simple language is your friend

A common failing of planning documents (and grant proposals, for that matter) is the use of jargon and vague language. An organizational plan that uses such wording and lacks clarity does nothing to increase your credibility with your constituents or your funders. You don't want readers to ask, "What is it that they're going to do?"

If you have a choice between a five-syllable word and a one-syllable word, choose the one-syllable word. Don't try to impress people with your vocabulary. Clear, simple language is better than complex language.

Monitor your use of jargon as well. People working in a particular field or area develop special meanings for words that their colleagues understand. In a way, these words are a sort of shorthand that makes communication easier and faster. But avoid using these "professional" terms when writing a document for the general public. If you have no other alternative, be sure to define all terms.

Itemizing the parts that form your plan

When you reach a consensus about your organization's goals, assemble a written plan. The components of the plan should include the following items, in the order shown:

- ✔ An executive summary
- ✔ A statement of the organizational mission
- ✔ A description of the planning process
- ✔ Organizational goals
- ✔ Strategies to achieve those goals
- ✔ Appendixes that contain summaries of the background material used to determine the plan, including a list of the people who participated in creating the plan

Have a look at the sample outline for writing an organization plan (CD0702) for some help in getting started.

Assign the task of drafting the document to your best writer. When he finishes the draft, the planning committee should review it to ensure that the plan is stated clearly. Submit the final draft to the full board for approval.

Don't chisel your plan in stone

Although having a plan is important, flexibility in its implementation is just as important. Things change. Reviewing your plan is an ongoing activity; probably once a year, you should submit your organizational plan to a formal review by the stakeholders who developed it.

Suppose that your organization has decided through the planning process to begin offering after-school tutoring services but later discovers that another agency plans to do the same thing. In that case, don't move ahead until you consider the consequences of entering into competition with another nonprofit. If you face this situation, we recommend talking with the other nonprofit to find a common solution. Maybe a joint program is called for, or maybe you find that the other group is in a better position to offer the program. Don't force your decisions. If circumstances change, alter your plans.

Putting Plans into Action

Unfortunately, too many well-crafted plans end up in a drawer or on a bookshelf. Participants may have expended great effort to create the document, and board and staff may have formed close bonds during the planning process. But if the decisions made during that wonderful board/staff retreat at the charming lakeside inn aren't translated into goals, objectives, and outcomes, what's the point besides camaraderie?

No matter what sort of plan you create — organizational, fundraising, marketing, program, or a plan to help an employee structure his work — you need to break the larger, all-encompassing goals into smaller pieces so you can achieve your goals one step at a time.

Defining and setting goals, strategies, objectives, and outcomes

Getting lost in all the terminology of planning is easy. Goals, strategies, and objectives have been a part of planning for many years. Only in the past ten years or so have planning specialists put more emphasis on outcomes.

Here are brief definitions of the four terms, using a simple example of traveling from Chicago to New York to attend a professional conference:

✔ *Goals* are things your organization hopes to achieve. Goals can be set at the organizational level, the program or department level, or the individual employee level. Using a road trip as an analogy, a goal is traveling from Chicago to New York.

✔ *Strategies* are approaches or ways to achieve goals. Usually, more than one option exists. You can travel to New York by several methods: plane, train, automobile, or on foot. After considering the costs, your schedule, and your hiking ability, you decide to travel by car.

✔ *Objectives* are smaller steps that one must accomplish to reach a goal, and they're always stated in a way that can be measured. So on a trip from Chicago to New York, an objective may be to drive 325 miles on the first day. When you pull into the motel parking lot, you can check your odometer to see whether you've achieved your objective for the day.

✔ *Outcomes* describe the result of reaching a goal. In this example you've reached the goal — New York — and have signed in for your conference.

To see how all four terms come into play, look at the example of a plan in Table 7-1. Reading from top to bottom, you have the whole plan, from organizational goal to outcome.

Table 7-1	Organizational Goal to Outcome
What We Call It	*Example*
Organizational goal	Diversify income
Strategy	Increase individual contributed income
Strategic goal	Develop annual campaign
Objective 1	Compile prospect list
Objective 2	Create appeal letter
Objective 3	Mail appeal letter
Outcome	Organization is less dependent on a single funder

Don't get bogged down in terms. How you label the different steps in the planning process doesn't really matter all that much. The important thing is to understand that goals, strategies, objectives, and outcomes are a good way of talking about what you're trying to accomplish and how you're going to do it.

Creating a work plan

You can see in Table 7-1 that the objectives are general. You can add a way of measuring them by stating how many prospects you want to acquire, how much the appeal costs to produce, and how many appeal letters you plan to mail. But each objective in the table requires several steps. Here's where *work plans* come into play. Work plans break tasks into small steps so they can be easily managed.

Work plans grow out of organizational and program goals and are the nuts and bolts of planning. They're also called *action plans*. They contain specific objectives associated with a deadline for completion and a notation as to who's responsible for completing the task.

Sometimes grant proposals, especially proposals for government funds, require specific objectives described in a work plan. Individual employees also can develop work plans, either at their supervisor's request or simply as an exercise to help the employees organize their work. People also can use work plans to deal with an organizational crisis or a rapid organizational change or as management tools.

Think of a work plan as a blueprint. It provides a way to keep on top of what has to be done and when it needs to be completed. An action plan contains the answers to the following questions for each objective:

✔ What is the end result? (If possible, quantify the results. For example, three grant proposals will be submitted.)

✔ How long will it take to do the job?

✔ Who will be responsible for doing the job?

✔ What resources are needed?

A typical work plan may look like Table 7-2.

Table 7-2				Sample Work Plan
Objective	*By When*	*By Whom*	*Resources Needed*	*Date Completed*
Research three potential foundation funders	April 30, 2011	Allen	Foundation directory; Web search	April 28, 2011
Prepare three grant proposals	July 30, 2011	Allen	Program objectives; budgets	July 21, 2011
Follow up on proposals	September 15, 2011	Allen	None	September 10, 2011

Work plans require that a job be broken down into smaller tasks. In Table 7-2, for example, the three objectives can be split into even smaller tasks. The objective to complete three grant proposals can be divided into the individual steps for writing a grant (covered in Chapter 17):

1. Assemble the background information and support materials.
2. Develop the budget.
3. Write the first draft.
4. Revise and rewrite the draft.
5. Proof and assemble the proposal.
6. Submit the proposal by the deadline.

Be aware that you can take the creation of a work plan to the point of absurdity. For example, you can split the job of submitting a proposal into even smaller steps, such as finding the envelope, affixing proper postage, walking to the post office, and dropping the envelope in the mail slot. You see what we mean. Don't make work plans so detailed and specific that writing the plan takes more time than doing the work that the plan specifies.

Planning for Programs

Program planning is such an important part of nonprofit work that we think it needs its own section. Nearly all nonprofit organizations provide a service of one sort or another. The organization provides services through programs. A small nonprofit may have only one. Larger nonprofits may have dozens. No matter how many programs you have, you may be thinking of adding a new one or changing the ones you have.

Assessing needs

A *needs assessment* is an important part of program planning. If you're thinking of starting a new program, for example, a needs assessment to determine whether the program is necessary should be the first step you take.

A needs assessment is more or less a research project. You don't necessarily need to hold to the strict requirements of scientific inquiry, but just as you do when collecting information to help guide organizational planning, you should do everything possible to ensure that the information is accurate and free of bias.

Determining the questions to be answered

You probably already have a general idea of what you need to find out in your needs assessment. The most basic question is whether the program is needed. But in order to answer that question, a needs assessment should evaluate the answers to the following questions:

- **Are other programs providing the same service?** Obviously, you don't want to duplicate services if another organization is already doing the job. If you believe that your competition isn't doing a good job, that's another question. Jump to the second point.

- **How many people might use the service?** Getting a good estimate of the number of people the new program will serve is important. Doing so helps you justify establishing the program and helps you plan for staff needs.

- **Can and will people pay for the service?** If so, how much? This question brings us to how you'll fund the program. Can you expect 25 percent of your clients to pay the full fees for the service; 25 percent to pay 75 percent; 25 percent to pay 50 percent; and 25 percent to need full subsidies?

- **Do any special requirements for providing the program exist?** Does the program need to be near good public transportation? Is parking important? Will people come to the neighborhood where you're providing the services?

- **What are the trends?** Will the number of people using the service increase or decrease in the future? Is the population in your community increasing, decreasing, or staying the same? If you begin with 25 clients, how many clients do you expect to have in three years?

Finding the best data

Just as when you collect information for organizational planning, your goal in program planning is to get the most accurate, unbiased data available. Don't depend on only one source of information. Here are some ways to get the information you need:

- **Talk to colleagues in your community.** Ideally, you have relationships with the people and organizations that provide similar services. Ask their opinions about your ideas for new programming.

- **Look at census data.** The best sources for population information are the numbers collected through a census (www.census.gov). Some municipal and regional planning groups also publish population growth projections. These projections are estimates, but census data doesn't represent an absolutely accurate count of the people in your community, either. Get all the numbers you can get.

- ✔ **Visit a Foundation Center library.** By looking at funding trends, you can piece together a picture of what services are available and who is supporting them. You can find a Foundation Center library location near you at `foundationcenter.org`.

- ✔ **Get information from potential users of the service by distributing questionnaires and holding focus groups.** The questions you ask in large part determine the answers you get. If possible, find someone who has experience in preparing survey questions to give you a hand.

- ✔ **Look at similar programs in other communities.** Although you can't always depend on the experience of others fitting exactly with your particular situation, examining what others have done is always wise.

We've put together a needs assessment questionnaire (CD0703) as an example of a simple survey.

Some people say that they don't want to share an idea with others because they're afraid someone may steal it. Although you can't rule out the chances of this happening, we believe that it's a rare occurrence. In almost all cases, being open about your plans is a good idea.

Going beyond the needs assessment

Just because a new program is needed doesn't necessarily mean that your organization should be the one to start it. You need to take other factors into account before taking the leap into starting a new program. Consider the factors in the following sections when assessing your ability to start a new program.

Paying attention to the budget

A new program is almost always going to add expenses to your organizational budget. If we thought about it long enough, we could think of an example in which increased program costs aren't a factor, but we don't have all year.

To be sure that you don't get yourself into a financial hole, carefully project the extra costs you'll have from additional staff, increased space, equipment, and insurance. After you have solid expense projections, you have to project where you're going to find the added revenue needed to pay these costs.

If you're sitting on a surplus, be careful about tapping into this money for new program expenses. Program expenses recur every year; your surplus funds may not be there next year.

Evaluating organizational and staff capability

Does your organization have the knowledge and expertise to provide the program services? This question may not be a concern if the proposed program is merely an extension of what you've been doing. If your organization is branching out into new areas, however, be sure that you or someone in the organization has the credentials to provide a quality program.

Also pay attention to hidden staff costs. For example, consider whether your current program director will have sufficient time to provide adequate supervision for the new program.

Remembering special requirements

Check whether you need additional licensing or accreditation to provide the program. This issue is especially important for human services programs. For example, if you've been working with teenagers and want to expand to elementary and preschool children, find out whether your program space must meet additional code requirements in order to serve a younger client group.

Arts organizations also should be aware that adding new programs can create problems with building codes. For example, suppose you have a visual arts gallery that typically serves no more than ten people at a time. If you decide to hold poetry readings every Tuesday night and expect audiences of 50 or more, your building may not have enough exits.

Fitting it into the mission

From time to time, we're all tempted by the idea of doing something new. Gee, wouldn't it be nice if we could sell goldfish in the front lobby? But you have to ask yourself what selling goldfish has to do with your organization's mission. If you go too far afield, you'll be exploring unknown territory.

You can change your mission, of course, but you shouldn't do so without considerable thought. Altering a mission statement just to justify a new program probably isn't reason enough to do so.

Thinking long term

An idea that looks good today may not look good next year or the year after. Don't forget that costs rise year after year. Your staff appreciates raises occasionally. Try to imagine where the program will be five and ten years into the future.

To explain your program, take a tip from the business sector

If you were starting a new business and looking for investors, one of the first things you'd do is create a business plan. Nonprofits are wise to follow this model when developing a new program. A business model is useful in explaining the program and can form the basics of grant proposals when you seek funding.

Business plans should include the following information:

- An executive summary that covers the main points of the plan.

- An explanation of the need for the program and who will use it. (This information is comparable to the market analysis in a for-profit business plan.)

- A description of the program and your strategies for implementing it.

- Résumés and background information about the people who will provide and manage the program services.

- Three-year projections of income and expenses for the project, including an organizational budget for the current year.

Doing program planning as a team

As with organizational planning, program planning should be done as a group exercise. It doesn't have to be as extensive as the organizational planning process, but you get more acceptance of the new program and guard against omitting important details when you work with others to develop new programs.

Hindsight: Evaluating How You Did

Planning helps you move toward the future in an orderly fashion, but the goals and objectives that result from the planning process also encourage a nonprofit organization to look backward and evaluate its performance and (we hope!) its successes.

Evaluation is particularly important to nonprofit organizations because, unlike for-profit businesses, nonprofits can't evaluate their performance by showing a profit at the end of the year or increasing the value of their stock. Foundations almost always require that grant-funded projects be evaluated, and of course, you yourself will want to know how you're doing.

Selecting the right kind of evaluation

Evaluations come in many varieties. Sometimes they're as simple as documenting that the program did what it was supposed to do; more in-depth evaluations may test whether some anticipated change occurred as a result of the project. Elaborate and complex evaluations often require an outside professional evaluator.

Nonprofit organizations are concerned with three basic types of evaluation:

- ✓ **Process evaluation:** Did the project do what it was supposed to do? Often, this answer requires no more than simple counting. "This series of school concerts will have a combined audience of 1,500 children." To complete the evaluation of this statement, all you need to do is to keep audience attendance figures.

- ✓ **Goal-based evaluation:** Did the project reach its goals? Depending on the goal you're evaluating, this type of evaluation can be either simple or complex: "Establish an AIDS awareness program in the southeastern quadrant of the city that reaches 500 individuals during its first year." Determining whether a program was established is simple; figuring out how many people the program actually reached is a little more difficult. This answer depends, of course, on what method the project is using to reach people. In other words, you must define what you mean by "reach" before you start the program.

- ✓ **Outcome evaluation:** Did the project have the desired outcome? For example, if you oversee an AIDS awareness program, a desired outcome may be a reduced risk of contracting HIV. Evaluating such an outcome requires an in-depth study of the population in that section of the city to determine whether behavior changed in a way that reduces the chances of HIV exposure. The evaluator needs to collect or have access to baseline data about HIV exposure before the program begins in order to evaluate this outcome adequately.

Sometimes we use more than one type of evaluation on a project. Combining process- and goal-based evaluation is very common, for example. The type of evaluation you use depends on the requirements of your audience for the evaluation. For whom are you evaluating the program? Yourself? Donors? Funders, for example, may request that one or all the above types of evaluation be carried out on a project they're supporting. A board of directors may want to know whether your program is accomplishing its intended outcome. Ideally, every project is evaluated in all the ways mentioned above. In reality, evaluations take time and cost money that you may not have. Outcome evaluations in particular can be very difficult to accomplish.

Planning for evaluation

Setting up an evaluation framework after a project has started isn't impossible, but it's certainly more difficult. Under the best circumstances, you should determine what you're going to evaluate and how you're going to evaluate it upfront during the program design. For instance, many, if not most, evaluations require that data be collected during the life of the project. So if the plan is to ask clients to evaluate the services they receive, you should be ready to hand over a questionnaire to the first person who walks in the door.

Planning for evaluation also helps you to set program goals and objectives. Just ask yourself: Can it be measured? Here are some other questions to ask yourself when planning for evaluation:

- **For what purpose is the evaluation being done?**
- **Which of the following people will read the evaluation?**
  - Foundation program officers
  - Board of directors
  - Managers and supervisors
  - Professional colleagues
  - Yourself
  - The public
- **What is the method of evaluation?** Evaluations can be done in several ways. Decide which of the following methods or combinations of methods is best for your purposes:
  - Questionnaires and surveys
  - Review of project documentation
  - Interviews/focus groups with users of the program
  - Program observations
  - Pretesting and post-testing

Choosing evaluators: Inside or outside?

Some projects require an *outside evaluator* — someone who's familiar with the program area, has experience as an evaluator, and isn't associated with your organization. In other words, you're looking for a person who has nothing at stake in the results of the evaluation. Projects that need this in-depth analysis are usually large and complex. If a funding agency requests an outside evaluator, expect the agency to pay for the evaluation as part of the project expenses.

Internal staff members do most evaluations. Though not as expensive as outside evaluations, even internal evaluations involve costs. Project budgets should reflect the staff and materials costs that result from evaluations.

Telling the truth

Honesty and forthrightness are important in evaluations. You may be tempted to fudge the results of attendance figures or the number of clients the program has served, but in more cases than not, the truth comes out in the end. An organization can damage its reputation among its peers and funders if someone discovers that evaluations have been falsified.

Programs do fall short of their goals. We wish these letdowns didn't happen, but they do. Remember, you're evaluating against a set of goals and objectives that were projections, maybe as long as three years earlier. The best approach is to provide honest numbers and explain why or how the results are different than those results you expected at the beginning of the project.

Chapter 8

Getting the Work Done with Volunteers

*V*olunteers are the lifeblood of the nonprofit sector. The Bureau of Labor Statistics reports that more than 25 percent of the population over age 16 performed some kind of volunteer work in the United States during the 12-month period ending in September 2008. That's a lot of people — almost 62 million!

Just about every nonprofit charitable organization uses volunteers in some capacity. For example, in most cases, board members serve without compensation. And for many nonprofit organizations in the United States, volunteers do all the work, from planting the trees to paying the bills. Even if your organization employs paid staff, volunteers still provide valuable service. Organizations depend on volunteers to staff telephone hotlines, lead scout troops, provide tutoring, coach youth sports teams, serve hot meals, organize fundraising events, and stuff envelopes. So if you're going to manage a nonprofit organization, you need to know how to work with volunteers.

Of course, you may be sitting in your office asking, "Where are these millions of volunteers?" This chapter offers suggestions to help you decide what kind of volunteers you need, how to find them, and how to keep them happy after they arrive.

Understanding Why People Volunteer

The classic stereotype of a volunteer is someone who has lots of time to spare and is looking for something to do. Although this perception may have been true in the past when many women stayed out of the workplace and gave their free time to charity, that stereotype no longer fits. It's true that more women volunteer than men, but people between the ages of 35 and 44 are the likeliest to volunteer. This is the age range when men and women are probably balancing careers with raising families, not to mention taking care of aging parents, going to the gym, and keeping up with e-mail.

Why is it that people, even very busy ones, volunteer their time? We think it's because they have recognized the benefits of volunteering time to a favorite organization and because nonprofit organizations have become smarter about asking them.

Understanding why people volunteer makes it easier for you to find volunteers, organize their work, and recognize their contributions. However, keep in mind that not everyone is motivated by the same factors. People volunteer for a variety of reasons, including their desire to

- ✔ **Help the community and others.** Helping others usually comes to mind first when people think of the reasons that people volunteer. But as you see when you read deeper into this list, their motives aren't always this simple.

- ✔ **Increase their self-esteem.** Volunteering makes people feel better about themselves. Giving a few hours a week, or even a month, to an organization creates good feelings.

- ✔ **Help out their friends.** Friends are often the first people we turn to when we need help. Volunteering also can make for a great way to get together with friends on a regular basis.

- ✔ **Make new friends.** Volunteering is usually a social activity. People use this opportunity to meet interesting people who share their interests and values.

- ✔ **Try out a job.** People considering a job in the nonprofit sector often discover that volunteering is a good way to get a peek at what happens on the inside.

- ✔ **Polish their résumés.** Adding volunteer experience to a résumé shows a commitment to helping others or to working in a particular field.

- ✔ **Develop new skills.** A volunteer job often gives people an opportunity to learn how to do something they didn't already know how to do.

- ✔ **Enjoy something they love.** Many volunteer jobs come with intrinsic benefits for their participants. Ushers at the symphony get to hear the music. Gardeners removing invasive plants from a native plant preserve get to spend a day in a beautiful natural setting.

Keep this list in mind, and you'll realize that you don't have to focus your recruitment efforts exclusively on retired people or others who have a lot of leisure time. If you can provide an environment in which volunteers can bring their friends, meet others who share their interests, and learn new skills, you can lure even the busiest people into helping. Remember that you have no reason to be apologetic about asking for help: Volunteering benefits those people who step forward to assist you.

Designing a Volunteer Program

Most start-up organizations depend on volunteers because money to pay staff is unavailable. But a lack of resources isn't the only thing that drives a nonprofit to run with an all-volunteer staff. Some nonprofits make a deliberate decision to operate solely with volunteers to contain their costs and to achieve results with a collective effort among people who care deeply enough to contribute their time and effort.

Considering a volunteer coordinator

Although volunteers don't expect to be paid every two weeks, that doesn't mean they come without costs. Recruiting, training, managing, retaining, and thanking volunteers require effort from someone in the organization. We recommend assigning to someone the job of *volunteer coordinator,* a person responsible for overseeing or performing the following duties:

- ✔ **Recruiting:** Volunteers don't grow on trees. Depending on how many volunteers you need and the turnover rate of current volunteers, recruiting may be a more or less continuous process.

- ✔ **Training:** Volunteers don't come to work knowing everything they need to know. They can do any job for which they're qualified, but don't expect them to know the ropes until they're told what to do and how to do it.

- ✔ **Scheduling:** Volunteers need a schedule. Scheduling is even more important if your organization uses volunteers to staff an office or manage other tasks that require regular hours.

- ✔ **Appreciating:** Volunteers need to know that their work is valuable to the organization. This item is the last on our list, but it may be the most important. You don't have to pass out plaques, but we do recommend heartfelt acknowledgment. Saying thank you on a regular basis is essential to retaining your volunteers.

If your organization depends heavily on or is staffed exclusively by volunteers, consider recruiting your volunteer coordinator from among board members or more-experienced volunteers. You can create committees to take responsibility for many jobs, but some detail-oriented tasks — like scheduling or bill paying — are better managed by a single responsible person.

Determining your need for volunteers

Look around your nonprofit organization and decide how many volunteers you need and what functions they can perform. We recommend creating (or helping your volunteer coordinator to create) a schedule of tasks to be completed — planning what needs to be done and how many people it will take to do the work. Table 8-1 lists the kinds of volunteer assignments you may jot down. By having such a list and prioritizing the tasks, you know what to do when an unexpected volunteer walks in the door.

Table 8-1	Sample Volunteer Task List	
Task	*Number of People*	*Time*
Data entry – donor list	1 person	3 hours per week
Bulk mailing	4 people	5 hours per month
Lawn cleanup	1 person	2 hours per week
Childcare	2 people	3 hours on Saturdays
Filing	1 person	2 hours per week

It's possible to have too many volunteers. Almost nothing is worse than asking people to help and then finding out that you have nothing for them to do. You may want to have both your chart of immediate tasks (like in Table 8-1) and a few back-burner projects — like organizing press clippings in a scrapbook or taking inventory in the supply cabinet — in case you end up with more people than you need on a given day.

In the beginning, you may have to experiment before you know exactly how many volunteers you need for a particular job. For example, you may eventually discover that a 2,000-piece mailing takes about five hours for four people to complete. You also may find that hand-addressing envelopes takes longer than using labels and that preparing bulk mail takes longer than doing a first-class mailing.

Writing volunteer job descriptions

Volunteers perform better if they know what they're supposed to do. Preparing job descriptions for volunteer positions also helps you to supervise better and to know what skills you're looking for in volunteers. (Take a look at Chapter 9 for detailed information on writing a job description.)

Volunteer job descriptions should be even more complete than paid-employee job descriptions. And if you can break jobs into small tasks, all the better, because volunteers often share the same job. For example, a different person may answer the office telephone each day of the week. In that case, to bring consistency to the job, you can keep by the telephone a job description that includes a list of telephone procedures, frequently used telephone numbers, and other important information.

ON THE CD

See CD0801 and CD0802 for some sample volunteer job descriptions.

Organizing volunteers

Many nonprofits invite their volunteers to participate in committees. These committees allow the volunteers to step forward and offer their best skills and to learn how to do new things. An advantage of forming committees is that it reinforces the social benefits of volunteering. As committee members get to know one another and figure out how to manage their tasks successfully, you or your volunteer coordinator can step back and let them take full responsibility.

Here's a fictitious example that gives you an idea of how to organize committees: A small nonprofit called the Sunshine and Health Project was organized to provide telephone referral and information sources for people seeking help with weight loss. It was started by three people who had lost weight and decided to help others do the same. A ten-member board of directors provides governance for Sunshine and Health and undertakes key volunteer roles in the organization. The board formed the following committees, which are each chaired by a board member but made up of individuals who provide volunteer services:

> ✔ **Telephone committee:** Sunshine and Health provides most of its services via telephone. The office receives about 60 calls each day from people seeking information about weight loss and referral to health clinics and counselors. The telephones are answered 12 hours a day, from

9 a.m. to 9 p.m., Monday through Friday. Two volunteers share responsibility for the phones in three-hour shifts. The nonprofit needs 40 volunteers each week to answer phones and provide information. Sunshine and Health also needs backup volunteers in case someone is ill or can't make his shift for some other reason.

✔ **Program committee:** This committee researches programs to which callers can be referred, maintains the database containing referral information, and provides training to telephone volunteers. Members of the committee include one physician and two registered nurses, all of whom provide professional oversight.

✔ **Publicity committee:** Sunshine and Health uses several methods to tell the public that its services are available. The publicity committee prepares and mails press releases and records and distributes public service announcements to radio stations. In addition, the committee operates a speakers' bureau of people who have benefited from Sunshine and Health's services. The committee also has developed a Web site and a MySpace page; each of these sites offer basic information about weight loss, maintain a directory of services in various cities, and invite readers to sign up for a monthly e-mail newsletter.

✔ **Fundraising committee:** Sunshine and Health raises funds through several different avenues, including annual family-oriented walk-a-thons, appeal letters sent to people who have used its services, and gifts from businesses promoting a healthy lifestyle. Committee members plan and coordinate the fundraising events, write and send the appeal letters, and make personal calls on the business sponsors. They also call upon all volunteers to make personal gifts, identify possible donors, and provide lists of contacts.

✔ **Administration committee:** Sunshine and Health receives individual donations from people who use its services, grants from foundations, and limited support from the health department in the city in which it's based. The administration committee is responsible for maintaining the organization's financial books, writing thank-you letters to donors, and maintaining a database of past donors.

You may discover other tasks that can be assigned to additional volunteer committees. The kinds of jobs that need to be done vary, depending on the type of service your organization provides. The point to remember is that volunteer work needs to be organized (and supervised) in much the same way that paid work is organized.

In an all-volunteer organization, the responsibility for ensuring that the work is finished appropriately resides with the board of directors. The board must be committed to finding new volunteers and supervising their work. And board members must be ready to step in to do a job if no volunteers can be found.

Board members who also serve as program volunteers must remember to keep their roles as board members (governance and fiduciary) separate from their roles as program volunteers. In the latter case, the volunteers are operating like staff, not board members. Yes, there is a difference. See Chapter 6 for information about understanding and defining board members' roles.

Hunting for Volunteers

Most organizations are always on the lookout for volunteers. After all, volunteers move away, get tired, lose interest, or take new jobs with new hours. If your organization depends on volunteers, you probably need to maintain an ongoing recruitment process. This section shows you how.

Using the tried-and-true methods

To cast a wide net, you want to use more than one method to find volunteers, and you don't want to spend much money on those methods. After all, you're looking for free help. Persistence matters: Good volunteer recruitment is like a healthy habit that you want to repeat. Here are a few of the most common and most successful methods for recruiting volunteers:

- **Placing announcements in the media:** Newspapers and radio and television stations often publish or air public service announcements for nonprofit organizations. Keep your press releases short — less than two pages for print media and less than 30 seconds when you read it aloud for radio and television. (Head to Chapter 11 for more information about writing and distributing press releases.)

- **Hanging posters:** Grocery stores, drugstores, churches, laundromats, schools, and civic buildings often have bulletin boards where you can post announcements. For best results, place them thoughtfully. For instance, put your call for foster homes for kittens at the pet food store and your community garden poster at nurseries and home improvement stores.

- **Taking advantage of word of mouth:** Encourage your current volunteers to recruit others. Have a "bring a friend" day with time for socializing. Ask your volunteers to post your posters in their places of business, and don't forget to invite your own friends and associates.

- **Contacting schools and churches:** Both of these institutions often look for ways for students and members of the congregation to get involved in community service. *Service learning* — through which students learn about a topic by volunteering in their communities and then reflecting on what they have learned in their classrooms — is a growing practice. In fact, many high schools and colleges now have centers for community relations and student volunteering.

Don't forget to reach out to the young people in your area. By doing so, you benefit from their skills and ideas, and you also contribute to training the next generation of volunteers!

✔ **Relying on clubs and fraternal groups:** Many professional and social clubs include serving the community in their missions. From Kiwanis and Elks to the Junior League, Chamber of Commerce, or campus-based sororities and fraternities, clubs and membership groups can be excellent volunteer resources.

✔ **Approaching corporations and businesses:** In some communities, businesses look for volunteer opportunities for their employees. Businesses encourage employee volunteerism in many ways: If they have a community relations, community affairs, or corporate giving department, it's likely to be a good place to begin asking about employee volunteers.

Check with your local United Way affiliate to see whether it operates a loaned-executive program. With this type of program, you may be able to borrow the business expertise of a corporate manager.

Using the Web

Finding volunteers may be as easy as booting up your computer. Besides posting volunteer listings on your organization's Web site, you also can post on other sites. Several organizations maintain databases on the Web where your organization can list its volunteer needs. The databases can be searched by prospective volunteers by zip code and the type of volunteer work available. Here are some sites you can check out:

✔ **Volunteer Match** (www.volunteermatch.org) invites nonprofits to set up accounts identifying the kinds of volunteers they need.

✔ **Idealist** (www.idealist.org) and craigslist (craigslist.org) are other widely used tools for finding volunteers.

✔ **Virtual Volunteering Project** (www.serviceleader.org/vv) is especially helpful if your organization can use volunteers who aren't physically located near your office. Maybe you can use online volunteers to answer questions via e-mail, help write grants and press releases, or get consultation on designing your Web site.

✔ **Youth Service America** (www.ysa.org) helps you involve young volunteers in your work. It organizes an annual National Youth Service Day and other opportunities for volunteers between the ages of 5 and 25. It also operates servenet (www.servenet.org), a database of volunteer jobs for persons of all ages.

Nonprofit organizations also are becoming a growing presence on social networking sites, such as Facebook and MySpace. To get your name out there, you can create a page for your organization. More and more nonprofits are using social networking sites to raise funds and promote events. Chapter 11 provides more information about using the Web to make friends and influence people.

Looking for volunteers at other organizations

No, we don't suggest that you steal volunteers from other nonprofits, but some organizations do exist to provide volunteer help. Volunteer centers, for example, make up a national network of organizations that recruit and place volunteers in nonprofits. You can find the volunteer center nearest you by following the links at the Points of Light Institute Web site (`www.pointsof light.org`).

Similarly, the Corporation for National and Community Service (`www. nationalservice.gov`) was established by Congress in 1993 to operate AmeriCorps (`www.americorps.org`), Senior Corps (`www.seniorcorps. gov`), and Learn and Serve America (`www.learnandserve.gov`). This agency is charged with encouraging national service through volunteering and helping nonprofits and public agencies make the best use of this resource. You can see what programs may benefit your organization by answering a few basic questions on this interactive Web page: `www.national service.gov/for_organizations/programs/selector.asp`.

There's talk of a substantial increase in funding for the programs managed by the Corporation for National and Community Service, leading us to think that existing programs will grow in size and influence over the next few years.

If your organization wants to take advantage of a program offered by the Corporation for National and Community Service, you may need to apply for a federal or state grant, which usually requires sound accounting procedures and extensive reporting of program activities. Turn to Chapters 16 and 17 for information about government grants.

Finding volunteers with special skills

If you're looking for volunteers with special training or experience, spend some time thinking about where you can find them. Limit your recruitment efforts to places where you're most likely to identify the people with the talents you need.

Suppose that your organization is seeking someone with accounting experience to help you maintain your books. Local accounting firms, corporate offices, and public school administration offices may be good recruiting grounds for someone who can assist with bookkeeping. In some states, the professional organization of certified public accountants (CPAs) links its members to nonprofit volunteer assignments.

And don't forget other nonprofit organizations in your community. A more established nonprofit may have staff members who are interested in your cause. You may be able to get some experienced help in setting up your fundraising plan, your computer network, or your publicity materials. Just because someone works at another nonprofit doesn't mean that she won't find it gratifying to apply her skills for you as well.

Sometimes your nonprofit competition won't mind sharing contacts who are loyal to a particular kind of activity. In our city, for example, several organizations put on film festivals once each year, and some volunteers who love to see the films volunteer to work in box offices, press rooms, and other capacities, migrating from one festival to the next. Rather than detracting from their contributions to one organization, their "migrant volunteering" makes these volunteers more knowledgeable and strengthens their public relations skills. When recruiting for short-term volunteer assignments, don't be afraid to ask your "competition" if you can invite some of their great bird watchers, marathon runners, brownie bakers, and scarecrow makers.

Hiring interns

Interns are specialized volunteers who come to you as a part of an education or training program. In most cases, a student intern's goal is to develop practical, hands-on work experience.

Sometimes internship programs require your organization to pay a fee or provide the intern with a modest stipend. You also want to be sure to include interns on your insurance policy. (Refer to the later section "Insuring your volunteers" for more details.)

As with employees and volunteers, you should provide the intern with clear expectations about job duties, attendance, and so on. If you decide to go this route, be ready to spend time supervising and evaluating the intern's job performance. Don't forget that the intern's experience is part of his grade.

Interviewing and Screening Volunteers

If you're placing volunteers in sensitive jobs, such as working with children or providing peer counseling, screen your applicants carefully. Screening, including a fingerprint check, is sometimes required by law, by licensing requirements, or by your insurance carrier. Some states and counties also require a test for tuberculosis. Check with local authorities about the requirements in your area.

A cheat sheet for the FAQs

Be prepared to answer questions when people call to volunteer. If you're already using volunteers to answer the telephone, prepare a list of common questions and their answers, and place that list near the telephone. Here are some sample FAQs that the Sunshine and Health Project, a fictional nonprofit discussed in the section "Organizing volunteers," may need:

What are the hours I would be needed? We answer the phones five days a week from 9 in the morning until 9 at night. We ask people to work a three-hour shift once a week.

How will I know what to say? All volunteers receive one day of training. Training is offered once a month, almost always on Saturdays.

What kind of advice can I give? Our volunteers can't give medical advice or advice on specific diets. Volunteers refer callers to existing services and professionals. We ask volunteers to be positive and to offer general support to all callers.

How do I know where to refer people? We have a complete database of weight loss–related counseling services. It's a simple matter of looking through a loose-leaf notebook or our computer database to find the appropriate phone numbers.

What if I get sick and can't cover my shift? We have volunteers on standby to cover unexpected absences. If you aren't able to volunteer on a regular, weekly basis, you may consider being a backup volunteer.

Are we asked to do any other work? Sometimes we ask volunteers to help with mailings between phone calls.

Will you pay my auto (or public transportation) expenses? We're sorry, but our budget doesn't cover reimbursing volunteers for expenses. Some expenses may be deductible on your income tax, however. You should check with your tax specialist.

Can I deduct the value of my time from my income taxes? No, the IRS doesn't allow tax deductions for volunteer time.

These questions and answers also can be printed in a brochure and mailed to potential volunteers who request more information. Be sure to include background information about your organization in the mailing.

Even though the authorities do the fingerprinting and criminal background checks, you can do some screening of your own as well. Require volunteer applicants to fill out job applications just as if they were applying for paid work. Ask for references and check them. Review résumés and conduct formal interviews. (See Chapter 8 for information about job interviews.) Avoid paranoia, but don't discount your gut feelings, either.

If you're using volunteers in professional roles, such as accounting, check their qualifications just as you would check the qualifications of an applicant for a paid position. It's possible that this process may offend potential volunteers, but it's far better to make sure that the person can do the job, even if she's doing it for free.

See CD0803 for a volunteer intake form.

We realize that screening can be a delicate issue. You're walking a tightrope between the rights of individual privacy and the rights of the organization to be sure that no harm befalls clients. Some potential volunteers may be offended by background checks. Explain to them that the procedures aren't directed at them personally but are in place to ensure that clients are protected. Also, treat all volunteer applicants the same. In other words, don't pass up screening someone just because she's a personal friend.

Managing Your Volunteers

Just like managing paid employees, working with volunteers requires attention to management tasks. Volunteers need training and orientation as well as clear, written lists of responsibilities and expectations. Basic expectations for volunteers are easily outlined in a *volunteer agreement form*. You also want to maintain records of the time and tasks they contribute to your organization, and you should consider whether to include them in your insurance coverage.

See CD0804 for a sample volunteer agreement form.

Providing adequate training

The degree and extent of training volunteers depends on the type of job you're asking them to do. Volunteers who answer telephones, for example, may need more training than those volunteers who stuff envelopes for the publicity committee. To successfully answer phones, these volunteers need to know the background information about the program or service, information about the types of services available, proper telephone etiquette, and emergency procedures, just to name a few.

If you need to provide a full day's training or training over a longer period, we suggest consulting with a professional trainer to either provide the training or help you to design the curriculum. Although you may be concerned about investing too much of volunteers' valuable time in training, remember that key motivations for volunteering include meeting people and enjoying time with friends. Trainings can be great opportunities to introduce volunteers to one another and build camaraderie among them. It's a good idea to schedule refresher training sessions for ongoing volunteers, too.

In addition to on-site training, you should give volunteers written materials that restate the information covered in the training. Include with these materials attendance requirements, whom to telephone in case of illness, and other necessary information that volunteers may need to know when carrying out their tasks.

Larger organizations that use many volunteers sometimes publish a *volunteer handbook.* Such a handbook doesn't need to be an elaborately printed document; it can be several typed pages stapled together or a simple loose-leaf notebook. The more information you provide, the better your volunteers can perform.

Keeping good records

Keep records of your volunteers and how much time they spend doing work for your organization. You may be asked to provide a reference for a volunteer who's working to develop job skills or who's providing a service through an organized volunteer program. You also may need to dismiss a volunteer who's unreliable, and having clear, written records of hours and tasks can justify that difficult act.

If you use professional volunteers to perform tasks that you'd otherwise have to pay for, you can include the value of the volunteer time as an in-kind contribution on your financial statement. Chapter 10 explains more about financial statements.

Insuring your volunteers

Typically, nonprofit organizations carry liability and property insurance. Almost all states require that workers' compensation insurance be in place to cover on-the-job injuries to employees (but not necessarily volunteers). Beyond this basic insurance, coverage depends on the type of services provided and the degree of risk involved. We discuss insurance for nonprofits in greater detail in Chapter 12.

Keep in mind that volunteers usually aren't liable for their actions as long as they work within the scope of the volunteer activity to which they have been assigned, perform as any reasonable person would perform, and avoid engaging in criminal activity. Unfortunately, people these days have become more eager to file lawsuits. If someone sues you or one of your volunteers, you have to legally defend the case even if it's without merit. One advantage of having liability insurance is that your insurance carrier takes on the responsibility of defending the suit.

Workers' compensation may or may not be available to volunteers in your state. If you can include volunteers under your state law, consider doing so, because a workers' comp claim usually precludes the volunteer from filing a suit for damages against your organization. Plus, you want your volunteer to be covered if he sustains an injury.

Insuring volunteers is a subject of debate in the nonprofit sector. Some people take the position that insurance agents and brokers try to convince you to insure anything and everything. Others believe that liability insurance and, in some cases, workers' compensation insurance should be provided. As is the case with all insurance questions, evaluate your risks and decide whether the cost of insuring against risks is a good investment. This process is called *risk management*. To find information about risk management for nonprofit organizations, contact the Nonprofit Risk Management Center (www.nonprofit risk.org).

Eliminating bad volunteers

If you work with lots of volunteers, especially volunteers who perform complex and sensitive jobs, you may discover one or more volunteers who don't have the skills or personalities to perform at an acceptable level. We hope you never face this situation, but if you do — for example, maybe someone is giving bad information or acting rudely — you shouldn't ignore the situation.

Discussing the problem behavior with the volunteer is the first step. Treat this meeting as if you were counseling a paid employee whose job performance was below par. Written job descriptions, written standards for performance, and records of volunteer time and contributed tasks are important when discussing problem behavior.

Exercise caution when meeting with a volunteer about her unacceptable behavior, especially if you don't have clearly written performance guidelines. Volunteers who are released have been known to sue nonprofit agencies. If you have concerns about this possibility, consult an attorney before you do anything.

Talking to someone, volunteer or not, about poor work is never pleasant. However, if someone working for your organization is being disruptive, giving bad information, or otherwise causing potential harm to your program or the people you serve, you have a responsibility to correct the problem.

Saying Thank You to Volunteers

Volunteers give their time and, in many cases, expertise to help your organization succeed. It's only right that you thank them and thank them often. Thank them in the hallway after they've completed their work for the day, and also formally recognize their contributions. Here are some standard ways of recognizing volunteers:

- ✔ **Annual recognition event:** This kind of event is the most formal (and probably the most expensive) way of thanking volunteers. Some organizations have a sit-down dinner or wine and cheese reception once a year to say thanks and give awards to volunteers who have made extraordinary contributions.

- ✔ **Gifts:** Although tokens of appreciation may be much deserved, we recommend caution when giving gifts to volunteers. Don't spend lots of money buying them presents, because you can bet that some of them will ask why you're spending scarce nonprofit money on something that isn't necessary. Getting a local business to donate gift certificates or other items is a better way to go.

- ✔ **Admission to performances or events:** If your organization presents plays, musical performances, lectures, or readings, consider offering free admission to some events.

- ✔ **Public acknowledgment:** You can identify the names of your volunteers in your newsletter or on your Web site. An alternative is an annual newspaper ad that lists the names of your volunteers.

- ✔ **Thank-you letters:** Don't underestimate the power of a simple thank-you note. Unless you have hundreds of volunteers, make sure you write your notes by hand. Most people appreciate a handwritten note more than a form letter or e-mail.

In addition to thank-you letters and recognition events, you can increase volunteer satisfaction (and retention) by treating volunteers well on a day-to-day basis. Here are some easy tips to keep volunteer satisfaction high:

✔ **Don't make volunteers work in isolation if you can avoid it.** Many volunteers give their time because they enjoy socializing with others.

✔ **Vary the job to avoid boredom.** You may need help cleaning the storeroom or hand-addressing 1,000 envelopes, but try to assign jobs that offer more mental stimulation as well.

✔ **Pay attention to the work done by your volunteers.** Your interest in what they're doing adds value to their work and recognizes that many of them are volunteering to develop new skills.

✔ **Help volunteers understand your nonprofit's work.** If they've been answering the telephones in the front office, give them a behind-the-scenes tour or a chance to observe or participate in other activities of the organization.

✔ **Bring in pizza or doughnuts once in a while as an impromptu thank you.** Food can provide a great break from a monotonous job or celebration of a major task's completion.

✔ **Talk to your volunteers.** Get to know them as friends of your organization who are committed to its work.

Chapter 9

Getting the Work Done with Paid Staff

*S*ome nonprofits have paid staff from the very beginning. For example, nonprofits that start out with grant funding to operate a program may have paid staff. Other nonprofits may start more slowly, with the board of directors and other volunteers initially doing all the work and hiring paid employees later. And many nonprofits never have any paid staff. These organizations may use consultants or temporary employees to help raise money or catch up on filing, but they never have the money to support regular full-time employees.

No rules exist about when a nonprofit organization should employ paid staff. You probably aren't going to wake up one morning and say to yourself, "Hey, it's time to hire some staff." The organization must determine whether it has enough work to justify a paid staff and whether it has the resources to pay salaries and associated expenses. New nonprofits often begin by hiring part-time staff or consultants before bringing on full-time employees.

Hiring your first staff member should be cause for celebration. It means that your nonprofit has reached a milestone in its development. But it also means that the organization (and the board of directors) will have more responsibilities to raise funds and ensure that proper personnel policies are in place and followed. This chapter covers the details.

Deciding That You Need Help

Knowing when to take the leap from being an all-volunteer group to being a boss or paid employee isn't easy, and it's not a leap to take without looking at where you're about to land. Hiring employees creates responsibilities for the board, not the least of which is paying a salary every two weeks. You also need to pay payroll taxes and provide a workplace, equipment, and — don't forget — guidance and supervision. Expect to have more bookkeeping duties and more complex financial reports, because you need to keep track of payroll records, vacation time, and sick days and decide which holidays your organization will observe. (The last one should be a snap, right?)

To ease into the transition, a nonprofit may begin by hiring an independent contractor to handle a specific task, such as bookkeeping or grant writing, and then go from there. (We discuss working with independent contractors and consultants later in this chapter.)

A variety of situations, such as the following, may signal that it's time to hire your first employee:

- ✔ The work has been done solely by board members and volunteers, but people are getting tired and the work isn't getting done as well as it should.

- ✔ The demand for your organization's services has increased to the point that volunteers need a consistent point person who can coordinate its complexity or focus on administrative details.

- ✔ The organization's founder has been paid irregularly for work on specific projects. Resources have increased to the point that you can now pay a regular salary.

- ✔ The organization is starting a new activity that requires someone with a specific professional license or degree and no member of the board or volunteer group is appropriately qualified.

- ✔ The nonprofit receives a major grant that both provides more resources and requires significant recordkeeping and program management.

Hiring salaried employees should be a long-term commitment. For this reason, the organization needs to have sufficient cash flow to ensure regular payment of salaries, benefits, and payroll taxes.

A crisis can sometimes take place when a volunteer-run organization hires its first staff member. Knowing that they're now paying someone to be responsible, board members may decide to sit on their hands and let others do the work. Bringing on a first staff member is a good time to honor board and volunteer contributions to the organization (to keep motivation high) and to invest in a board retreat or training that reminds everyone of the work ahead and the board's important role in it.

When you add paid employees to your organization, you assume legal responsibilities that begin with the recruitment process. We recommend that you consult *Human Resources Kit For Dummies,* 2nd Edition, by Max Messmer (Wiley) to be sure that you cover all the bases.

Readying Your Nonprofit for Paid Employees

Before you start writing a job description or placing an ad on craigslist, you need to invest time in some upfront prep work, readying your organization to take on paid employees. This preparation, which we cover in the following sections, includes writing personnel policies, setting up payroll systems, and deciding on benefits.

Developing your personnel policies

Personnel policies and procedures outline how an organization relates to its employees. They're essential for both supervisors and employees because they provide guidelines about what's expected in the workplace and on the job. They lay out expectations for employees, ensure that all employees receive equal treatment, and provide the steps necessary for disciplinary action if it's needed.

Many start-up and small organizations that have only one or two full-time employees give personnel policies a low priority. We suggest, however, that you begin early to formalize your rules with an employee handbook. Doing so really doesn't take much time, and it can save you headaches down the road.

You must follow federal and state labor laws when establishing personnel policies. The U.S. Department of Labor Web site (www.dol.gov) contains the latest information. If you're uncertain about whether you can require certain behavior or work hours from your employees, consult an attorney.

When forming policies, begin with the easy stuff: Decide on your organization's office hours, holidays, vacation policy, and other basic necessities.

Determining work and off time

Most organizations follow the lead of others when setting holiday and vacation policy: Although you find a lot of variation, many nonprofits in the United States grant two weeks' vacation per year to new employees. Employees typically receive more vacation time after a longer period of service, such as three weeks after three years, and four weeks after five to eight years. The most common sick leave policy is ten days per year. While you're at it, you want to give some thought to bereavement and maternity leave policies.

Paid vacation time is a benefit to both employees and employers. Employees return from vacation rested and ready to give their best efforts to the organization. For this reason, you should encourage people to take vacations during the year in which they earn the vacation. Most organizations and businesses don't allow employees to accrue vacation time beyond a certain amount. This policy ensures that employees use vacations for the purpose for which they're intended. Such a policy also limits the need to make large cash payments for unused vacation time if employees resign or are terminated.

See CD0901 for sample personnel policies.

Covering other important items

In addition to vacations and holidays, which are discussed in the preceding section, you have these other basics to cover in your personnel policies:

- ✔ A statement that the board of directors may change the policies
- ✔ A statement of nondiscrimination in employment, usually presented as a policy established by the board of directors — especially important if your organization is seeking government grants or contracts — and other policies established by the board
- ✔ A statement about parental leave and long-term disability policies
- ✔ A statement of hiring procedures and the probationary period (see "Evaluating your new hire's progress" later in this chapter)
- ✔ A statement of employment termination policy, including a grievance procedure

Many organizations also include the following few items to help new employees understand the organization:

- ✔ A statement of the organizational mission
- ✔ A statement outlining the history of the organization
- ✔ A statement of the values held by the organization

Setting up a payroll system

When an organization begins employing workers, it first must establish a payroll system. The organization needs to decide how often to distribute paychecks, for example. You can disburse paychecks on any schedule you choose — weekly, biweekly, semimonthly, or monthly. (*Biweekly* means every two weeks and results in 26 paychecks per year; *semimonthly* means twice a month and results in 24 paychecks per year.) In our experience, semimonthly is the most common schedule for payment, but the decision is up to the organization.

Although in-house staff can handle payroll, contracting with a payroll service is a better option. Most banks either provide payroll services or can recommend a service. Payroll services are inexpensive — they're almost always cheaper than assigning a staff person the job of handling payroll. They make the proper withholding deductions based on income level, number of dependents, and state laws; make tax deposits; and maintain a record of vacation and sick leave. Usually when you contract with such a service, they require that you keep enough funds on deposit with them to cover two or three months of salaries and benefits.

If you decide to handle your own payroll, be sure to make tax deposits on time. Failure to pay federal and state payroll taxes is probably the quickest way to get your organization in serious trouble. Check the Internal Revenue Service, or IRS, Web site (www.irs.gov) for the latest information.

Typical deductions include the following, although state tax laws show much variation:

- Federal income tax withholding
- Social Security and Medicare (must be matched by the organization)
- State income tax withholding
- State unemployment and disability insurance

Providing benefits and perquisites

You make the decisions about some of your employee benefits — such as sick leave, vacation time, and holidays — when writing your personnel policies.

Health insurance is a benefit that your organization may or may not be able to provide to your paid employees. The cost of health insurance decreases based on the size of the group to which you belong. If your organization has only one employee, purchasing health insurance may be costly unless you can join a larger group. Check with state associations for nonprofit organizations or your local United Way office to see whether they have a health insurance program that will cover your employees. For more on insurance, see Chapter 12.

Preparing to Hire

After you write your personnel policies, put your payroll systems in place, and decide on your benefits, you're finished with the groundwork needed to hire 1 or 100 employees. You're probably just hiring one person for now. To set off on that path, you want to clearly describe what that job entails, consider salary levels, and announce the position. This section walks you through those important steps.

First things first: Writing a job description

One of the first things you should do when looking to hire a paid employee is to write a job description for the position you want to fill. Going through this exercise helps you clarify the skills needed for the job and guides you in selecting among applicants. The final description serves as a job blueprint for the new employee.

A job description usually includes the following information:

- A short paragraph describing the job and the work environment
- A list of duties and responsibilities
- A list of skills and abilities needed for the job
- Experience and education required
- Special qualifications required or desired

We include several standard job descriptions on the CD. See CD0902 for an Executive Director job description, CD0903 for a Development Director job description, and CD0904 for an Office Administrator job description.

When writing your job description, keep in mind that work in nonprofit organizations can be split into three broad areas:

- **Services:** Services are the reason the organization exists in the first place. They may include developing protected open space on a coastal mountain range, providing home visits and hot meals to seniors, or organizing after-school activities for children. This list is almost unlimited.

✔ **Administrative functions:** These functions include bookkeeping and accounting, office management, property or building management, marketing, Web design, clerical services, benefits administration, and contract management. You can add to this list as needed.

✔ **Fundraising:** This area falls under various names, including *resource development* and *advancement.* Depending on the size of your organization, one person may be in charge of all aspects of raising money or different people may specialize in writing grants to foundations and government, creating sponsorships with corporations, or raising money from individual donors.

The larger these areas (or departments) are, the greater the specialization within them. But when you're looking to hire your first staff member, that one person may have job responsibilities in more than one area, perhaps even in all three areas. It may seem like too much to describe in a single document, but that complexity and the high level of responsibility this person will have make it particularly important to create a job description that's crystal clear.

Considering necessary qualifications

Some nonprofit jobs require various levels of formal education and special training. If you're hiring someone to provide counseling services, for example, that employee probably needs to meet certain education and licensing requirements in order to provide the services legally. If you're hiring someone to work with children, the applicant may need to pass various background checks, depending on the laws of your state.

Professional and business associations can provide helpful information about job qualifications. For example, if you need specifics about the qualifications that a speech pathologist should have, contact the American Speech-Language-Hearing Association (www.asha.org). The American Society of Association Executives (www.asaenet.org) may help you find appropriate national or local associations.

In addition to any degrees and certifications, you may want to specify that applicants have a certain amount of experience in doing the work you're going to ask them to do. However, if you do so, be prepared to pay a higher salary to fill the position.

You can't, of course, require that an applicant be of a particular ethnic background, race, age, creed, or sexual preference. You can't deny employment to a woman because she's expecting a child. You also can't refuse employment to a person with a disability as long as he can perform the job with reasonable accommodations.

Establishing salary levels

Deciding on a fair salary for your paid employees isn't easy. Compensation levels in nonprofits range from hardly anything to six-figure salaries at large-budget organizations. (Keep in mind, however, that large nonprofits represent only a small percentage of active nonprofits.) We guide you through the process with the following sections.

Considering factors that affect salary

Although exceptions always exist, the following list outlines some factors that determine salary levels:

- **Geographic location:** Salary levels differ from place to place due to the cost of living. If your nonprofit is in a major metropolitan area, expect to pay more to attract qualified staff than if you're located in a rural area.

- **Experience and education:** Someone with ten years of experience can command higher compensation than someone just beginning his career. Education levels also affect salary, as does having specialized knowledge or skills. Jobs requiring a master's degree or a PhD pay more than those jobs that don't.

- **Job duties and responsibilities:** Employees who direct programs and supervise others typically earn more than employees who have fewer responsibilities.

- **Nonprofit type:** Compensation levels vary from one nonprofit to the next. Organizations providing health services, for example, typically have higher salary levels than arts organizations.

- **Union membership:** Labor unions set standards for salaries and benefits in many fields, from classical musicians to nurses and educators.

- **Organizational culture:** This category, which is more difficult to define, is connected to the organization's traditions and values. For instance, nonprofits with boards of directors filled with business and corporate members often offer higher salary levels than organizations with boards that don't have the corporate perspective.

Finding out salaries of comparable positions

A salary survey, which you can conduct by phone or mail, is a good way to assess the current salary levels in your area and for your nonprofit type. Telephone surveys probably should be done from board president to board president because most people are reluctant to reveal their own salaries. Mail surveys can be constructed so that respondents remain anonymous.

The simplest method of finding salaries of comparable positions is to look at other job listings. Not all ads give a salary level, but those ads that do can give you a general idea of what others are paying for similar work.

Some nonprofit management organizations conduct annual or biannual surveys of salary levels in the areas in which they work. More often than not, access to the surveys requires payment, but it's probably a good investment because these surveys tend to be the most complete and up-to-date. A good place to inquire about salary surveys is through your state association of nonprofits (see the National Council of Nonprofit Associations Web site at www.ncna.org).

Using a search firm can be helpful, especially if the position requires a national search. Be prepared to pay a hefty fee, however. Fees are often based on a percentage of the first year's salary.

Announcing the position

After you decide on the qualifications and skills needed for the job you want to fill, advertise its availability. Here's a list of places to publicize your job opening:

- **Professional journals:** If you're hiring for a professional position, professional journals are the place to advertise the job. Search the Web to track down the addresses of appropriate trade-specific journals.

- **Bulletin boards:** Posting job announcements on bulletin boards at colleges, universities, other agencies, job centers, and even grocery stores is an inexpensive approach. In addition, you can put as many details as you want on a small poster at no extra cost.

- **Web sites:** The Web has become a valuable marketplace for job seekers. Search for job listings in the occupation category you hope to fill. Many Web sites charge a fee for posting a job opening. Opportunity Knocks (www.opportunityknocks.org) and Idealist (www.idealist.org) are popular sites.

- **Word of mouth:** This is a tried-and-true method of getting the message out about your job. Spread the word to other nonprofits — especially those in your field — churches, and anywhere else people congregate. Don't forget to e-mail the announcement to colleagues and to appropriate listservs.

Making the Hire

When it comes time to make the big decision, sifting through résumés, conducting interviews, and deciding on an employee can be a daunting task. Sometimes the right choice jumps out at you; other times, you have to choose between 2 or 3 (or 20!) candidates who have equal qualifications. That's when making up your mind becomes difficult.

Looking at résumés

Résumés and cover letters give you the first opportunity to evaluate candidates for a position. Respond quickly with a postcard or an e-mail to tell applicants that their materials have arrived. If possible, give a date by which they can expect to hear from you again. Doing so reduces the number of phone calls you get asking whether you've received the résumé and when you plan to make a decision. It's also the polite thing to do.

Résumés come in various formats, and we don't really have an opinion as to which one is the best. Regardless of how the résumé is organized, here are the questions we ask ourselves when reviewing a résumé:

- ✔ **Is it free of typographical errors and misspellings?** A typo may be excused if everything else appears to be in order, but more than one or two errors implies that the candidate is likely to be careless in her job.

- ✔ **Is the information laid out in a logical, easy-to-follow manner?** The relative clarity of the résumé can give you insight into the applicant's communication skills.

- ✔ **Does the applicant have the proper job experience, education, and licenses, if needed?** We like to give a little slack on experience because sometimes highly motivated and effective employees are people who have to "grow into" the job. Also, nonprofit organizations often receive résumés from people who are changing careers. They may not have the exact experience you're looking for, but maybe what they learned in their previous jobs easily transfers to the position you're trying to fill.

- ✔ **How often has the applicant changed jobs?** You can never be guaranteed that an employee will stay as long as you want him to, but you have to ask yourself, "If I hire this person, will he pack up and move on even before he finishes job training?" At the same time, don't automatically let higher-than-average job switching turn you off to an excellent candidate. Maybe he has an explanation. Ask.

Cover letters also can be good clues to an individual's future job performance. For one thing, you get an idea of the applicant's writing abilities, and you may even get some insight into his personality. Some job announcements state that a cover letter should accompany the résumé, and some even go so far as to ask the applicant to respond to questions such as "Why are you well suited to this job?" or "What do you think are the major issues facing so-and-so?" It's up to you as to whether asking a list of questions enables you to more easily compare applicants to one another.

If good writing skills are required for a job you're posting, ask applicants to include writing samples with their cover letter and résumé.

You'll probably reject at least half the résumés out of hand. We never cease to be amazed by how many people apply for jobs for which they don't have even the minimal qualifications. We understand that searching for a job is difficult and frustrating, but we also wonder whether applicants read our "position available" ads as closely as they should.

Separate your résumés into two piles — one for rejected applications and one for applications that need closer scrutiny. Send the rejected candidates a letter thanking them for their interest. From the other pile, decide how many candidates you want to interview. Reviewing the résumés with one or two board members to bring several perspectives to the choice is often helpful. One technique is to select the top three applicants for interviews. Reserve the other applicants for backup interviews if the first three aren't suitable or if they've already accepted other jobs.

Interviewing candidates

After you've chosen the top three to eight résumés, invite the applicants in for an interview. Interviewing job candidates is a formidable task. Big companies have human resource departments with trained interviewers who spend their days asking questions of prospective employees. We're neither human resource specialists nor trained interviewers, but here are some tricks we've learned over the years:

- ✔ **Prepared lists of three or four standard questions that you ask all applicants enable you to compare answers across applicants.** The interview shouldn't be so formal that it makes both the candidate and you uncomfortable, but standardizing it to some degree is beneficial. Here's a short list of typical questions:

    - Why are you interested in this position?

    - What do you see as your strengths? As your weaknesses?

    - How would you use your previous work experience in this job?

    - What are your long-term goals?

✓ **Group interviews with three or more people can give interviewers good insight into how the applicant will perform in board and community meetings.** Also, different people notice different things about each applicant. Avoid making the candidate face a large group, which can make her unnecessarily nervous.

✓ **If an employee isn't your first and the job to be filled is for a director or supervisor position, arranging for each finalist to meet at least some of the staff he'll be supervising is a good idea.** Giving staff members a chance to meet their potential new boss is courteous, and their impressions are helpful in making the final selection.

WARNING!

You can't ask an applicant personal questions about his age, religious practice, medical history, marital status, sexual preference, or racial background. You can't ask whether he has been arrested or convicted of a felony without proof of necessity for asking. You also can't ask whether he has children. Nor can you ask about any physical or mental conditions that are unrelated to performing the job. For information about interviewing and other human resource matters, see HR ProOnline (www.hrproonline.com/ehome.htm).

Taking notes during the interview is acceptable, and you also may find that preparing a checklist on which you can rate the applicant in different areas to be helpful. If you do, try to rate the applicants discreetly. Job interviews are stressful enough without letting the applicant know that you rated him a 3 on a scale of 1 to 10.

Digging deeper with references

Letters of recommendation can be helpful starting points in evaluating candidates, but we assume that no one would include a negative recommendation in her application packet. Therefore, we do think that checking references by telephone or even in a personal meeting, if possible, is necessary.

But sometimes even talking to references doesn't provide much useful information. A job applicant wants to put her best face forward, so naturally she chooses people with favorable opinions as references. Also, employment laws are such that speaking to a former employer often yields little more than a confirmation that your applicant was employed between certain dates.

If you have the opportunity to have a good conversation with the candidate's former employer, pay close attention to what they're not saying as well as attending to their description of the candidate's abilities. Some typical questions ask what duties the applicant handled in her previous jobs, what her strengths and weaknesses were on the job, whether the candidate had a positive attitude toward work, and whether the reference would rehire the candidate.

If the applicant is working for another organization, don't contact the current employer. You don't want to breach her confidentiality.

We've included a sample reference-checking form on CD0905.

Often, the grapevine is the best way to get information about a candidate. Using the grapevine is easier if the candidate has been working in your community, of course, but even if the applicant hails from another city, you can call other nonprofits to get information. You may be able to find people who have knowledge of the candidate's previous work. (Of course, be wary if you come across an informant who has a personal grudge against the applicant. It's not always easy to know whether this is the case, so don't depend on a single source.)

You can conduct formal background checks of education credentials, criminal history, and other information as long as you get the applicant's permission. If you feel that this type of research is necessary, we suggest hiring a reputable company that specializes in this sort of work.

The degree to which you go to collect information about an applicant depends on the magnitude of the position. If you're hiring someone to lead a large and complex organization, you likely want to dig deeper into a candidate's background than if you're hiring a data entry clerk. We do know of several instances when people were hired for big jobs after less-than-stellar performances in their previous positions. We're not suggesting that people shouldn't be given a second chance; we're simply saying that you should know as much as possible about an individual's previous job performance before hiring her.

Making your decision

We can't tell you how to make the final decision about whom to hire. You have to weigh qualifications, experience, poise, and desire. These decisions can be difficult, and frankly, you may not be certain that you've made the right choice until the new employee has performed on the job. If possible, get more than one opinion.

If qualifications and experience are equal, intangible factors come more into play. Will the candidate fit well into the organizational culture? Will the candidate's style of work fit with the organization's management style? Do the applicant's professional goals fit with the organization's goals? If this employee is going to be your first, is the candidate a self-starter type or does he need active supervision to do a good job?

Be cautious when making a personnel decision based on intangible factors. A candidate who's charming may be a treat to have around the office, but that doesn't always mean that he'll do the job well.

Make sure you document your reasons for making a personnel decision: They should be based primarily on the candidate's performance in previous jobs and experience that's relevant to your position.

Bringing a New Hire Onboard

Much hard work is behind you after you've actually made a hiring decision. But keep in mind that any employee's first days and months are challenging, and you want to give careful attention to helping your new staff member make a good start.

Confirming employment terms in writing

After a new employee accepts a position orally, it's common practice to send a letter to put the details in writing. Enclose a copy of the personnel policies (see the section "Developing your personnel policies" earlier in this chapter) and place a signature line near the lower-right corner of the letter so the new hire can acknowledge receipt of the letter and the personnel policies. Ask the employee to return a copy of the signed letter to you, and keep the letter in the employee's personnel file.

The letter should include the employee's starting date, job title, and salary, as well as other information that you agreed to in the prehire discussions held between the organization and the employee. For example, you may include a brief statement about the employee's responsibilities.

We put a sample hire letter on CD0906 so you can get a better idea of what we're talking about.

Getting your new hire started on the job

In the United States, one of the first things a new employee must do is complete a W-4 form (for income tax withholding) and an I-9 form (to show proof of the employee's legal right to work in the country). These forms are required by law and are available on the IRS Web site (www.irs.gov). Also, be sure to complete any forms required by your state.

After all the necessary paperwork is out of the way, you need to spend some time getting your new hire acclimated to the working environment. New employees don't begin producing at top form on the first day of work. Absorbing the details of the organization and discovering the ins and outs of new job duties take time. This fact is particularly true when the person hired is the organization's first employee and has no model to follow.

Whether you're a board member for an organization that's hired its first employee, or the director of an organization bringing someone new onto the staff, here are some ways to ease an employee's transition to a new job:

- ✔ **Provide good working conditions.** You may think that a reminder to purchase the basic furniture and tools someone needs to perform his work is too basic, but we've heard about new employees who didn't even have a desk on their first day.

- ✔ **Show the new person around.** Provide a tour of the office and programs, and introduce him to volunteers and board members. Review office emergency procedures on day one. Oh yeah, and don't forget to show the new employee where the bathroom is!

- ✔ **Give the employee information about the organization.** Make available the organization's files and records. Reading board minutes, newsletters, solicitation letters, donor records, and grant proposals will steep him in the organization's work.

- ✔ **Answer questions.** Encourage new employees to ask questions, and provide the answers as soon as possible. Particularly if he's the organization's one and only employee, board members should check in regularly, making themselves available as resources. Being a one-person staff can be lonely and overwhelming.

- ✔ **Offer special training.** A new employee may need special training — for example, about a computer software program or laws and regulations specific to your nonprofit — in order to perform his job. Sometimes you may have to send the employee to a workshop; other times, he can be trained by a board member, volunteer, or another staff member.

Evaluating your new hire's progress

Most organizations establish a period, usually three to six months, when new employees are "on probation." During this time, new employees learn their jobs, and managers can observe them at their work. Although we don't especially like the term *probationary* because it conjures an image of misbehavior, this period is important for both the new staff person and her manager. Be honest with yourself and the employee. If it becomes apparent that the person can't do the job, making a personnel change during this period is easier than after she becomes a permanent employee.

Be sure you've included an explanation of your probationary period in your personnel policies and that the new employee is aware of the policy. Consider adding an option in your personnel policies to extend the probationary period in case job performance is below expectations. Also, be sure to indicate that successful completion of the probationary period does guarantee future employment.

Conduct a performance evaluation at the end of the probationary period. The evaluation should be written (and added to the employee's personnel file) and discussed in a meeting with the employee. Rating employees on a number scale on various aspects of the job was once the common format. Today, a narrative evaluation that addresses performance in achieving previously agreed upon goals and objectives is much more helpful.

 Many employees are happier in their jobs if they have ongoing opportunities to learn new things and develop new skills. An annual employee review is an excellent opportunity to review professional development goals with the employee. It's also a good time to review ways — through workshops, training, or trying on new roles — she may continue to grow in the job.

Managing Employees

Much of this chapter focuses on small organizations that are hiring their first staff members. In these organizations, the board oversees the staff member, and someone taking on the coordinator role — either board or staff — oversees the volunteers.

What if your agency has grown more complex? Everyone needs a boss. In nonprofit organizations, the board assumes that role for the executive director who, in turn, provides supervision to other employees, either directly or through a management team. The common way to visualize these relationships is through an *organizational chart,* a schematic drawing showing the hierarchical management relationships in an organization.

A chart such as the one in Figure 9-1 may be overkill for your nonprofit, especially if you're the only employee, but for larger organizations, charts help to delineate management responsibilities and who reports to whom.

Understanding what a manager does

The responsibility of managing employees includes the following aspects:

- **Planning:** Planning occurs at all levels, beginning with the board of directors, which carries out organization planning, and ending with the custodian, who plans how best to complete cleaning and maintenance tasks. It's best if managers work closely with those employees they're managing to develop department and individual goals.

- **Leading and motivating:** You may want to add inspiring to this category. We believe that good management grows out of respect and cooperation. Be sure that staff members are familiar with the organization's goals and that they know how their work helps foster those goals.

✔ **Gathering tools and resources:** Don't ask someone to dig a hole without giving him a spade. In other words, you can't expect employees to do a good job if they don't have the means to do it. Time, equipment, proper training, and access to information are necessary.

✔ **Problem solving:** This is one of the most important aspects of good management. You can bet that problems will arise as you manage your organization and employees. Be understanding and creative in solving these problems. Ask for help in the form of ideas and suggestions from those employees you supervise.

✔ **Evaluation:** Employees should receive formal evaluations once each year. Effective evaluation begins with goal setting, and you want to help subordinates set clear goals and objectives.

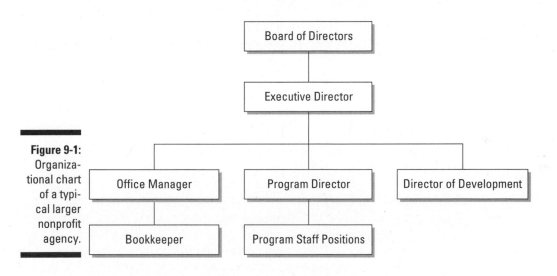

Sample Organizational Chart

Figure 9-1: Organizational chart of a typical larger nonprofit agency.

Communicating with your staff

We can't say enough about the importance of good communication. If your nonprofit has only 1 or 2 staff members, your job is easier than if you need to communicate with 50 or more employees. Either way, good communication is always important.

Of course, confidentiality is important in some matters. For example, if the organization is contemplating a major change, such as a merger with another organization, some information needs to be withheld from the staff. On the other hand, letting rumors circulate about changes that may affect staff can create worse problems than being forthcoming about the details of a potential change. Give people as much information as you can, and be sure they have a chance to tell you how they feel.

Communication is a two-way street. A good manager keeps an open ear and devises ways to ensure that his employees have a way to voice complaints, offer suggestions, and participate in setting goals and objectives.

Holding regular staff meetings

Too many meetings can be a waste of time, but having regularly scheduled staff meetings is a good way to transmit information to employees and give them an opportunity to offer input and feedback and to keep everyone working toward the same goal. Keep these points in mind when arranging staff meetings:

- **Try to schedule the meetings at a specific time on a regular basis.** Hold meetings no more often than once a week and no less often than once a month, depending on the needs of the organization.

- **All meetings should have an agenda.** Nothing is worse than going to a meeting that has no point and no direction.

- **Keep to a schedule.** Unless you have big issues to talk about, one hour is usually long enough to cover everything you need to discuss.

- **Provide time on the agenda for feedback.** Be sure that everyone has a chance to speak.

Writing memos to staff

Use memos to introduce new policies and other important information so you don't have any misunderstandings. By putting the information in writing, you can clearly explain the situation. If the policy is controversial, distribute the memo shortly before a scheduled staff meeting so employees have an opportunity to respond.

Some larger organizations create staff newsletters that cover organizational programs and achievements. People work better if they receive recognition for their work. Stories about client successes, gains made by the organization, and announcements about staff comings and goings help instill feelings of accomplishment and organizational loyalty.

For very large organizations, a dedicated Web site or intranet that's accessible only to employees can transmit information and offer staff the opportunity to provide feedback and communicate with one another.

Talking around the water cooler

Although formal written communication is important, nonprofit leaders also need to communicate informally by being accessible to staff in the hallways and around the water cooler. Some people are able to communicate concerns better in an informal setting than in a staff meeting. Managers who sit behind closed doors all the time often have a difficult time relating with their staff. However, don't force the camaraderie. Let it develop naturally.

Getting away for staff retreats

From time to time, especially if the organization is facing big changes, you may want to arrange a half-day or full-day retreat to address issues, do department or organizational planning, or provide specialized training. A retreat needs an agenda that's flexible and developed with the help of participants. Every retreat should have an objective and be led by a competent group facilitator.

Letting a staff member go

Some people enjoy barking, "You're fired!" We don't. We've spent sleepless nights before and after terminating an employee who wasn't right for a job. Although you may not lose sleep over letting an employee go, it's obviously not something to take lightly.

When do you need to consider cutting ties with an employee? Sometimes the employee isn't producing the quality of work required by the job or isn't producing work in a timely manner. Other times the employee may be fired for inappropriate behavior, such as not following your organization's guidelines for appropriate interaction with clients.

If you're a boss and facing the likelihood or need to terminate an employee, we recommend that you

- ✔ **Review the written personnel policies that you have provided to all employees.** Document in writing the employee's poor performance or inappropriate behavior and make clear the connection between your complaints and those policies.

  Many people deserve an opportunity to improve. Sit down with the employee and speak candidly and firmly about the level of improvement or change in behavior that you expect. Set written goals for an improved performance and a date for a follow-up consultation.

- ✔ **Respect the employee's privacy.** Don't share your complaints with others except, if necessary, your board chair.

> ✔ **Encourage the employee to leave as soon as she's terminated and walk her to the door.** Disgruntled former employees can damage your organization's records and documents in a few days, hours, or even minutes.

Wrongful discharge lawsuits are common and can be very expensive. If you need to terminate an employee and aren't sure how to proceed, consult with a human resources expert or an attorney. The upfront investment may save you much time, expense, and trouble later.

Sometimes organizations have to let employees go because they no longer have sufficient money to pay the employees' salaries. If you're an employee's boss in this situation, try to do the following:

> ✔ **Give her as much warning as possible about the date of her termination.** Don't keep it quiet while pulling out all the stops to raise money to save her position. Surprising employees with the bad news is inconsiderate.

> ✔ **Try to plan ahead and provide some severance pay to help her while she seeks a new job.** Although you may want to keep her on the job until the last possible minute, good employees deserve good treatment. If she leaves your agency with good feelings, you're in a better position to hire her back in the future.

Using Independent Contractors

Maybe your organization isn't quite ready to take the leap into the employment waters just yet. However, if you have work that needs to be done that volunteers can't do, working with an *independent contractor* may be a way to accomplish some organizational goals.

According to employment and tax laws in the United States, you can hire people in two ways: as salaried employees or as independent contractors. Rarely do you say to yourself, "I need an independent contractor to design my Web page," or "I need an independent contractor to write more grants for us." More commonly used terms are *consultant* or *freelancer.* For example, small organizations may contract with an accountant or bookkeeper to maintain financial records and prepare financial reports.

Independent contractors aren't just a resource for small organizations: Large-scale, well-heeled nonprofits also use them. A good organizational consultant, hired as an independent contractor, can bring a fresh perspective to assessing an organization's work, a depth and breadth of experience the organization hasn't yet developed, and focused attention to a project — say the writing of a new strategic plan — that staff can't give while managing day-to-day operations.

Differentiating an independent contractor from an employee

Technical differences between employees and independent contractors are reflected in how you hire, pay, and manage them. Independent contractors almost always are paid a flat fee or hourly rate for their work, ideally on a schedule that's set out in a contract that specifies the work to be done and the fee. Although you don't have to withhold federal and state payroll taxes, you need to file an IRS Form 1099 that records the amount paid over a full year (usually a calendar year) and the contractor's Social Security number or federal tax ID number (EIN).

Proceed with caution, because there's often a thin line between an independent contractor and an employee. Just because someone works a limited number of hours each week doesn't mean that he should be an independent contractor. The IRS doesn't look kindly on trying to pass off employees as independent contractors. Here's a short list of factors that differentiate an independent contractor from an employee:

- ✔ **Independent contractors are just that — independent.** Although setting time parameters for the job is fine, contractors should be free to set their own schedules and work with little direction from the organization. They should provide their own offices and equipment.

- ✔ **If you have to provide extensive training for the contractor to do the job, chances increase that the contractor may be considered an employee.** In hiring an independent contractor, you're supposed to be engaging someone with specific expertise.

- ✔ **If a contractor is working only for your organization and is putting in many hours each week, he may be considered an employee.** If you hire a contractor with the idea that the relationship will continue indefinitely, rather than for a specific project or period; or if that contractor provides services that are a key part of your regular business activity, the IRS believes that you likely have the right to direct and control that worker's activities. To the IRS, this association looks like an employer-employee relationship.

If you think that you may be pushing the envelope on this question, consult an attorney or tax specialist who can give you proper advice. Authorities are giving increasing scrutiny to the distinction between regular employees and independent contractors. The IRS may require employers who pay individuals as contractors, when they're really employees, to pay back payroll taxes and penalties.

The IRS has defined "Common-Law Rules" for determining whether someone is an employee or an independent contractor. Check the IRS Publication 15A: Employer's Supplemental Tax Guide for definition of these rules. The publication is available on the IRS Web site at www.irs.gov.

If you want to hire someone for a short-term assignment or a limited number of hours but if the work is taking place in your offices, using your equipment, and requiring your regular supervision, consider using a temporary employment agency. The agency handles the employee's benefits, including their employment taxes, and reassigns the employee if he's a poor fit for the job. Although using a temp agency may cost more than hiring the person directly, the agency can help you find someone who's qualified.

Seeing what an independent contractor can do for you

Independent contractors can help you with just about any aspect of your organization, from personnel matters to hooking up a computer network. But nonprofits most commonly bring them in to help out with

- ✔ **Fundraising:** Fundraising consultants help with grant writing, planning for fundraising, special events, direct mail, and major gift and capital campaigns, among other methods of raising funds.

- ✔ **Organizational development:** Organizational development consultants may guide your board and staff through a planning process or help you develop tools needed to evaluate your organization's work, to name just two examples.

- ✔ **Marketing and public relations:** Consultants can help you spread the word about your organization's good work by handling a public relations campaign directed at the media, developing your Web site, creating compelling brochures and newsletters, creating short promotional films, and many other strategies.

- ✔ **Evaluation and assessment:** Evaluators can take an in-depth look at an organization's programs, bringing specialized skills to that assessment and the value of an unbiased point of view.

Have a clear idea of what you want to accomplish before you seek help. Sometimes you don't know exactly what you're aiming to accomplish, but you should still try to articulate as clearly as possible what your aim is in hiring a consultant before you go looking for one.

Organizational consultants can't solve all your problems; they don't carry magic beans in their pockets. They make recommendations, but quite likely it's going to be up to you to carry them out and push your agency forward.

Finding a consultant: Ask around

We don't have a single best way to find consultants. You certainly can look in your local yellow pages or search the Web for nonprofit consultants who work in your area, but we think that one of the better ways is to use word of mouth, if possible. A few calls to other nearby nonprofits or funding agencies may provide some leads. You also may be able to find a consultant through a nonprofit support organization.

We prefer consultants who have more than one way of doing things. Not all nonprofits are alike, and what works for one may not work for another. Also, as your project evolves, you may find that you need a different kind of help than you originally imagined. Believe us, changes happen all the time. Ask the consultant whether she's willing to consider revisiting the project goals along the way and adjusting her approach if the need arises.

Some consultants work as sole practitioners; others work in consulting companies. Working with a company or consulting group may give you access to more varied expertise. On the other hand, consultants working alone tend to have lower overhead expenses, so their fees may (and we stress *may*) be lower.

Interviewing consultants

Interviewing a consultant is similar to interviewing a regular job applicant. You want to review the résumé carefully to see whether the candidate's experience and expertise match your needs. Don't be intimidated just because the person sitting across the table from you has more experience than you do. He'll be working for you. Ask any questions that you feel are necessary so that you can be sure you've chosen the right person.

Interview more than one person before you make your decision. As with interviewing for staff positions, having more than one person present at the interview is important because it lets you see how the prospective consultant interacts with a small group and gives you multiple perspectives on the consultant.

You may have the opportunity to use a volunteer consultant supplied by a program that provides free or low-cost assistance to nonprofits. Interview these individuals just as you would paid consultants. Remember that you'll be investing time in working with this person, so you need to be certain that she's right for your organization.

Ask interviewees to describe their method or approach to the problem or project that you're seeking to solve or complete. You shouldn't expect them to give you a full-blown plan in the interview, but you should expect a good picture of the initial steps they will take. Also, if your project culminates with a written report, ask the applicant for writing samples.

Don't expect a consultant to solve your problem before you enter into a contract. Although finding out whether the consultant has the ability to do the job is important, expecting him to give you all the answers before you agree to pay for the work is unreasonable.

Signing the contract

You need to have a signed contract with every consultant with whom you work. These points should be clearly stated in the contract:

- ✔ **The scope of work and expected results:** You can include more or less detail here, depending on the type of project the consultant is performing. If you're hiring the consultant to facilitate a one-day retreat for your board of directors, be sure that the contract includes the preparation time needed. Also, will the consultant be writing a report following the retreat? Try to touch on as many details as possible. The more specific, the better. Sometimes if the scope of work is very detailed, that detail is included as an attachment to the main part of the contract.

- ✔ **Fees, of course:** Some consultants charge an hourly rate plus expenses; others charge a flat rate that may or may not include expenses per project. The contract should state that you must approve expenses over a certain amount. Or you can write into the agreement that expenses are limited to a certain sum each month. Consultant fees vary, just like salaries, from one geographic area to another and depend on the type of work to be done and the experience of the consultant.

  We don't recommend paying fundraising consultants a percentage of money raised. Although some consultants, grant writers, and, in particular, telemarketers work under this arrangement, percentage payment isn't considered good practice by most fundraisers and nonprofit managers. See the Association of Fundraising Professional's Code of Ethics for more information about this issue.

- ✔ **The schedule of when you'll pay the fees:** Some consultants who work on an hourly basis may send you an invoice at the end of the month. Consultants working on a flat-fee basis may require advance payment on a portion of the fee. This is fine. It's protection for the consultant, who probably has as many cash flow problems as you do. The final payment shouldn't come before the project is completed. Be sure to ask the consultant for an estimate of her out-of-pocket expenses and how she plans to bill you for such costs.

- ✔ **Special contingencies:** What if the consultant gets sick? What if your organization faces an unforeseen crisis and you don't have time to work with the consultant? What if you've chosen the wrong consultant? You should include a mutually agreed-upon way to end the contract before the project is completed. A 30-day cancellation notice is common.

✔ **A timetable for completing the work:** You and the consultant need to negotiate the timetable. Have you ever had remodeling work done on your house? You know that contractors can get distracted by other work, right? That's why having a schedule is so important.

✔ **The organization's role in the project:** If the consultant needs access to background materials, records, volunteers, board members, or staff, you must provide this access in a timely manner so that the consultant can complete the job on schedule.

✔ **Required insurance:** What if your consultant injures someone in the course of working on your project? If she's not insured, the liability could become your organization's responsibility. Just to be on the safe side, many consultant contracts include standard language about the consultant's responsibility to carry liability insurance and to pay workers' compensation insurance and other legally required benefits if the consulting company has employees who will be working on your project.

✔ **Ownership of the finished product:** This point doesn't apply to every consulting project, but if yours focuses on developing a study or a report, specify in the contract whether your organization, the consultant, or both have the rights to distribute, quote, and otherwise make use of the results. Often the organization has the right to publish and produce the report if it gives proper credit to the author, and the consultant owns the copyright and has permission to make use of lessons learned in articles or future studies. Sometimes you agree to seek approval from one another before using the work.

We think that having the consultant prepare the contract is a good idea. It's the final chance to make sure that he understands what you want done. You may suggest changes when you see the first draft.

Chapter 10

Showing the Money: Budgets and Financial Reports

● ●

In This Chapter

▶ Preparing a budget for an organization

▶ Constructing additional budgets for specific activities

▶ Using your budget

▶ Anticipating revenue and expenses

▶ Putting your financial statement in order

▶ Understanding financial statements

▶ Adopting good financial practices

● ●

*N*onprofit organizations are expected to spend cautiously and honor the trust placed in them by their donors. As a result, they need to be especially good at budgeting and living within their means.

Designing budgets is a critical part of program planning, grant writing, and evaluation. Maintaining a financially stable organization is one of management's most important tasks. To achieve that stability, a nonprofit needs to keep clear records and base its decisions on accurate financial information. Asking the right questions about financial reports is one of the board's key responsibilities.

The best things in life may be free, and volunteers can accomplish a lot, but frankly, no money equals no program.

Making a Budget = Having a Plan

Because a budget is composed of numbers and because we're taught in grade school that arithmetic problems have right or wrong answers, you may panic when faced with making a budget. What if you don't get it absolutely right? It's true that you need to add and subtract your numbers correctly, but you should relax. It really isn't so bad.

Making a budget is yet another form of organizational planning (the topic of Chapter 7). Often it's done hand in hand with other types of planning. It estimates how you intend to gather and disperse money on behalf of your organization's mission. In the course of a year, the cost of utilities or postage may rise, and the cost of airline flights and computer equipment may fall. You're not expected to employ extrasensory perception in making a budget — just to be reasonable and thoughtful.

If your organization doesn't spend more than it takes in, and if it holds onto a little emergency money at the bank, why does it need a budget? Writing and agreeing upon a budget is an important process for your staff or board because it sets its priorities. Equally important is working with the budget after you've created it. After you've written your budget, make note of all the actual amounts that relate to the income you hoped for and expenditures you planned. It's a discipline that keeps your organization on solid ground.

Beginning with zero

In many businesses, the annual budget is made by looking at what happened in the previous year and adjusting numbers up or down based on the work that lies ahead. When you're starting something new, however, you have no previous year's results to consider. In that case, you start with zero and carefully consider each number you use to build your plan. Zero is a hard place to start, but remember that it's where every new organization begins.

A budget has two key sections — income and expenses. (See Figure 10-1 for typical line items.) Because dreaming up expenses that exceed your organization's means is easy, we suggest that you begin with income, making conservative estimates for what you may earn and what you may attract in contributions. As you work on the contributed income estimates, you also may want to look at Chapter 13, which discusses developing a fundraising plan.

Examining income

It's common to separate your income statement into two general categories, "earned" and "contributed," also called "revenue" (contract or fee income) and "support" (grants and contributions), respectively.

Here are some common questions to ask yourself as you begin developing the income section of your budget:

✔ Will you offer services or products for which you'll charge money? How many services and how often? How many people are likely to use them? What can you reasonably charge?

✔ Can you sell memberships to people and give them premiums or discounts in exchange for paying those fees?

✔ Are the founders and board of your organization able to contribute some start-up funds? Are they willing to talk to their friends and associates about contributing?

✔ Is your organization well positioned to receive a grant or grants?

✔ Are you capable of sponsoring a fundraising event?

✔ Could you provide visibility to a business sponsor in exchange for a contribution?

Evaluating expenses

In anticipating expenses, start with anything concerning payment of people. That list may include the following:

✔ **Salaries for employees, both full time and part time:** On your budget, list each position by title and identify the full-time salary and the percent of full time that person is working for you.

✔ **Benefits for salaried employees:** At a minimum, you need to pay approximately 12.5 percent of salaries to cover federally required benefits, such as Social Security, workers' compensation, and unemployment tax contributions. Some states also require disability insurance and local jurisdictions may require paid sick leave. Many organizations provide paid leave to employees for vacations, illnesses, or jury duty. Your organization also may provide health insurance or a retirement plan to its employees. If so, you want to compute those costs as percentages of your total salaries and include them in your budget as benefits. Benefits come immediately after your salary expenses.

When setting up your employee benefits, check on both federal requirements and rules in your state. The United States Department of Labor Web site, `www.dol.gov`, is a good guide to the federally required employee benefits.

✔ **Fees for services to consultants or service agencies:** You may hire a publicist, grant writer, evaluator, or other consultant to handle important tasks. Such consultants are responsible for paying their own tax and insurance costs. Show fees paid to consultants after salaries and benefits in your budget.

Anatomy of a basic budget

INCOME
Earned Income
      Government contracts
      Product sales
      Memberships
      Interest from investments
         Subtotal
Contributed Income
      Government grants
      Foundation grants
      Corporate contributions
      Individual gifts
      Special events (net income)
         Subtotal
         TOTAL Income
EXPENSES
Personnel Expenses
      Salaries
      Benefits @ _% of salaries
      Independent contractors
         Subtotal
Nonpersonnel Expenses
      Rent
      Utilities & Telephone
      Insurance
      Office supplies
      Program materials
      Local travel
      Printing
         Subtotal
         TOTAL Expenses
         Balance (the difference between Total Income and Total Expenses)

Figure 10-1:
A sample budget showing how line items usually are named.

At this point, compute a subtotal for all your personnel costs.

Next, identify all the nonpersonnel expenses, beginning with ongoing operating costs that allow your organization to offer programs. These expenses may include the following:

- ✔ Rent
- ✔ Utilities

- ✔ Telephone and Internet expenses
- ✔ Office supplies
- ✔ Printing
- ✔ Insurance

New organizations often have special start-up costs for the first year including nonprofit registration and filing fees. For example, you may need to purchase desks and chairs, computers, signs, shelving, office cubicles, and even playground equipment; and you may need to pay for training new staff members, first and last months' rent, the telephone and Internet hookup costs, and a photocopier or postage machine lease. Finally, you may have costs associated with the specific nature of the work of your organization. These expenses range widely but can include diagnostic tests, carpentry tools, classroom supplies, and printed materials.

As much as possible, keep notes in your budget files about the estimates you made while drafting your budget. Keeping a worksheet helps you remember your assumptions and follow your budget.

We present three different organization budgets on the CD with this book — CD1001, CD1002, and CD1003. Two of the examples show how organizations compare budgets to actual costs.

What's a good budget?

In a good budget, the income and expenses are equal to one another, or you have somewhat more income than expenses. That's what people mean when they say that a budget is "balanced."

Having said that, organizations' budgets vary widely, and no one right model exists. As a general rule, your budget looks healthy when you show multiple sources of income. Why? Wouldn't it be easier to keep track of one or two major grants and contracts? Or one annual special event?

The reason is based on the adage "Don't put all your eggs in one basket." What if a power outage strikes on the night of your gala? What if one of your major grant or contract sources changes its guidelines? Your programs could be jeopardized.

Another sound concept is "saving for a rainy day." Many organizations slowly develop a *cash reserve,* money put aside in case unexpected expenses arise. If they need to use their cash reserves, they take care to replace them as soon as possible. Often their board sets a policy for how large a reserve they want to keep and how quickly expended reserve funds must be replaced. Many organizations work to create a cash reserve that is equal to at least three months of their operating costs.

Onward and upward (or downward)

As your first year passes and your organization develops programs, it also develops a financial track record. After you have a financial history, anticipating the future can be easier. You need to analyze every assumption you make, but at least you have a baseline of revenues and expenses from the first year.

Here are some questions to consider when drafting future years' budgets:

- ✔ What are your earned income trends? Are they likely to continue or change? Do you face any new competition or opportunities?

- ✔ How many of your current year's grants or contracts may be renewed and at what levels?

- ✔ What's the current financial environment like? Will it affect your previous donors' abilities to give?

- ✔ How likely are you to increase individual giving or special events revenues in the coming year?

- ✔ What's the duration of all employees' employment periods? Anticipate the timing of possible annual raises.

- ✔ Do you offer benefits that kick in after an employee has worked with you for three months or six months or five years? If so, don't forget to include these increased costs.

- ✔ When does your lease obligate you to pay for rent increases or taxes?

- ✔ Have rate increases been scheduled for utilities, postage, or other services?

Isolating general administrative and fundraising costs

Some of your organization's expenses are defined as being general administrative or fundraising costs and aren't allocated to program expenses. The expense of having an audit, for example, is allocated to general administrative costs, while mailing costs for your end-of-the-year fundraising letter would be identified as fundraising. IRS Form 990 that nonprofits file annually asks organizations to present their expenses to identify which annual costs are for general administration and which are for fundraising. (See Chapter 5 for more about preparing a 990.)

What do you show if you don't have to pay for it?

Some nonprofit organizations benefit from donated goods and services rather than, or in addition to, contributed and earned cash. Suppose, for example, that a local business provides office space for your organization so you don't have to pay rent, 50 volunteers contribute labor to your organization each week, and a major advertising firm sponsors a free marketing campaign to promote your work. These gifts of goods and services are called *in-kind contributions.*

How can you show these valuable resources in your organization's budget? First, we encourage you to make the effort. If you don't show these contributions, you don't truly represent the scope of your agency in your budget and you're underplaying how much the community values its work. On the other hand, mixing the in-kind materials and services with the cash can make following and managing your budget confusing.

So what's the solution? We prefer creating in-kind subheadings within the budget or summarizing all the in-kind contributions at the end of the cash budget in a separate section.

If you choose to use subheadings and include in-kind items alongside the cash in your budget, don't forget that when you receive an in-kind good or service, it's a source of income and when you make use of it, it's an expense.

You'll want to keep records of volunteer time if you're going to include it in your budgets or financial reports. Generally accepted accounting principles say you should show the value of volunteers' time in your financial statements if they improved a financial asset of the organization (for example, if volunteers rebuilt a greenhouse owned by a nonprofit botanical society) or if the organization needed a task to be performed that required a special skill, the volunteer had that skill, and the nonprofit would have paid for that help if it had not been volunteered (for example, if an attorney reviewed the nonprofit's lease pro bono).

Annually, the nonprofit organization Independent Sector computes a standard average value for volunteers' labor, both nationally and by state. (In 2008, the national average was $20.25 per hour.) On the CD, see file CD1015, which you can use to find a link to these charts on the Independent Sector Web site.

Creating Budgets for Programs or Departments

If your organization focuses on a single service, you can skip ahead to read about projecting cash flow, but if you're like many nonprofit organizations, you manage several programs or departments. Each of these programs has a budget that must fit within the overall organizational budget.

Suppose that when your nonprofit organization begins, you offer only one program — an after-school center that provides tutoring and homework assistance for low-income children. The program really clicks, and more and more children begin showing up after school — some because they need tutors, but others because their parents are at work and the kids need a safe place to go. To serve these new participants, you add art classes and a sports program.

So now, instead of one program, you have three. Each has its own budgetary needs. A volunteer coordinator trains and recruits the tutors and purchases books, notebooks, and school supplies. The art program requires an artist's time, supplies, space for art making, and access to a kiln. To offer a sports program, your agency rents the nearby gym, hires four coaches, uses a volunteer coordinator to recruit parents and other assistant coaches, and purchases equipment. The specific costs of a program — books, art supplies, coaches — are called its *direct* costs.

But each of the three programs also depends on materials and services provided by the people who work on behalf of the entire organization, such as the full-time executive director of your agency, the part-time development director, and the bookkeeper.

Each of the three after-school programs also uses the agency offices, utilities, telephones, and printed materials. The costs that the various programs share — such as the executive director's salary, bookkeeping services, rent, and telephone bills — are called *indirect* costs. You can think of these shared costs as the glue that holds the agency together.

When you prepare a program or department budget, you want to include both direct costs and indirect costs.

Direct costs are pretty straightforward. For example, you know what you have to pay your tutors per hour, and you know how many hours they work. But indirect costs can be sticky, and we don't say that because they're the organizational glue. They're sticky to deal with because determining how to divide them accurately among your organization's activities is difficult.

Many grantmakers are reluctant to pay true indirect costs associated with programs and, if your organization depends heavily on grants, that reluctance can put you in the awkward financial position of being able to pay for a famous basketball coach but not to turn on the lights in the gym.

After recognizing that foundations and nonprofits often don't see eye to eye on how to determine indirect costs, a group of foundations commissioned researchers to write a report entitled, "Indirect Costs: A Guide for Foundations and Nonprofit Organizations." You can find a link to it at CD1015.

When your organization is relatively small with just a few programs, you may be able to keep accurate records for how staff members spend their time, how many square feet in a building a program uses, even how many office supplies each staff member checks out of the supply cabinet. Based on those records, you can estimate fairly your indirect costs.

As your organization grows in complexity and number of programs, you may compute indirect costs by using a formula you derive based on your direct costs. We outline sample formulas and steps to derive them in Table 10-1.

Table 10-1	Indirect Cost Formula for After-School Center
First, add all your direct costs:	
Program	*Direct Costs of Each Program*
Tutoring and homework assistance	$46,000
Arts and crafts	$60,000
Athletics	$164,000
Total direct costs:	$270,000
Then compute the percentage of total direct costs that each program represents:	
Tutoring and homework assistance	$46,000 ÷ $270,000 = 17%
Arts and crafts	$60,000 ÷ $270,000 = 22%
Athletics	$164,000 ÷ $270,000 = 61%

In many cases, you can reasonably assume that the indirect costs of a program correlate to its direct costs, or that a program that's more expensive requires more oversight of staff and more use of office space. In the case of the After-School Center, all the indirect costs — which include a salary for the director, a contracted bookkeeper, rent, utilities, telephones, and printing — total $130,500.

Using this figure, we can put together the direct and indirect costs into a true financial picture of each program by dividing the $130,500 in indirect costs according to the formulas we developed for direct costs in Table 10-1. We outline the proposed allocation in Table 10-2.

Table 10-2	Allocating Indirect Costs for After-School Center	
Program	*Formula*	*Indirect Cost Amount*
Tutoring program	$130,500 × 17%	$22,185
Arts and crafts program	$130,500 × 22%	$28,710
Athletics program	$130,500 × 61%	$79,605

Sometimes organizations write a project budget by identifying all the direct costs in detail and then showing the indirect costs as one lump sum at the bottom of the list of expenses. But some funding sources balk at paying for indirect costs when they're presented this way. The funders want to know what actual expenses contribute to those indirect costs. We recommend that you show the specific indirect costs item by item rather than lumping them all together. For the tutoring program, for example, you would show 17 percent of the executive director's salary, 17 percent of the bookkeeper's fees, and so on.

CD1004 shows the tutoring program budget with the indirect costs specified alongside the direct costs. This shows a true picture of the project's needs.

Working with Your Budget

Your budget isn't capable of getting up and walking out of the room, but it needs to be an "active document." If you simply create it once a year to keep in a file folder and submit with grant proposals, it doesn't do you much good. A good budget is crumpled, coffee stained, and much scrutinized. A good budget guides and predicts.

Numbers in your budgets are meant to be compared. One critically important comparison looks at actual income and expenses alongside the original projections you made in your budget. Most organizations create a spreadsheet that includes columns for:

✔ Annual budget

✔ Year-to-date income and expenses

✔ Current month's budget (1/12 of the annual budget)

✔ Current month's income and expenses

Pay close attention to where you're exceeding your budget and where you're falling short. Use your progress as a guide to adjust your fundraising or your expenditures.

The CD accompanying this book demonstrates two ways of tracking actual income and expenses in comparison to budgeted income and expenses. See CD1005 and CD1006. Also, to take a critical, long view of your financial progress, use the Five Year Trend Line on CD1007.

Other useful exercises to make sure your budget is "living and breathing" include the following:

✔ Involve your staff (paid and volunteer) in the early stages of drafting the coming year's budget. If you can't afford all their dreams, involve them in setting priorities.

✔ Three months before the beginning of your new fiscal year, meet with a small committee of board members to review and refine a budget draft. Present the draft with options and recommendations to the entire board for discussion and formal approval.

✔ If your organization's situation changes significantly, prepare and adopt a formal budget revision. Budget revisions are time consuming, but don't try to proceed with a budget that doesn't reflect the size and scope of your organization. You don't want to try to find your way through Maine with a map of Utah.

✔ Provide copies monthly or quarterly to your entire board or board finance committee. Encourage your board treasurer to summarize the organization's financial situation and invite questions and discussion at each meeting.

✔ Keep notes in your budget file about changes you recommend for years ahead.

Check out CD1008, "Monthly Information Every Nonprofit Board Needs to Know," another tool to keep your budget "living and breathing."

Because we know that revenues aren't earned, grants aren't received, and expenses aren't incurred in equal amounts every month throughout the year, along with these practices, we recommend that you project your cash flow (see the following section).

Projecting Cash Flow

A *cash flow projection* is a subdocument of your budget that estimates not just how much money you will receive and spend over the course of a year, but *when* you will receive and spend it. It breaks down your budget into increments of time. Some organizations create quarterly (three-month) projections, some monthly, some weekly. Although grantmaking organizations and major donors are likely to want to see your budget (and may want to see the version that compares projections to actual amounts), your cash flow projection generally is a document for you, your board, and possibly a loan source.

If you think of a budget as the spine of an organization — supporting all its limbs — the cash flow statement is its heart and lungs. A good cash flow statement is in constant motion, anticipating and following your every move. Based on the careful way you developed your budget, you may know that you're likely to have enough revenue to cover your organization's expenses in the coming year. The cash flow helps you figure out whether you'll have that money at hand when you need it. You can map out a cash flow statement at various levels of detail. Our personal preference is to do cash flow planning monthly.

Constructing your cash flow projection

To set up a cash flow projection, begin with a copy of your budget and add details to the names of all the various categories. For instance, under "Foundation Grants," write down the names of every foundation from whom you now receive money and of any from whom you anticipate receiving a grant. Add the same kinds of details for your expense categories. For example, under "Utilities," add separate lines for each bill you receive, such as water, electricity, gas, or sewer service.

We recommend that you project forward by going backward. Sounds contradictory, doesn't it? Create columns for the most recently completed three months of your year. Go through your records. Put any income received into the appropriate periods, and write down all your expenses in the right categories and time periods. If you've forgotten any categories, you have a chance to add them. Having these actual figures for the recent past helps you see patterns of income and expense.

Now, begin projecting: Go back to each line item and write down the estimated amount that's due during each monthly period. Begin with the "easy" items — like the rent that's a constant amount due on a certain day or the employer's share of federal payroll taxes. Then look at the consistent bills that change a little bit over time. If your utility bills are high during winter months because your agency is using the furnace more, don't forget to project that increase. If you hold a phone-a-thon twice a year that causes unusually high usage rates, figure that in.

As you get into the flow of making predictions, it's easy to become too optimistic about your anticipated income. If you've applied for a grant that you're just not sure about, don't put it into your cash flow projection. If your annual fundraising event raises between $25,000 and $32,000 each year, project $25,000 in income. The reason? You won't have any problem knowing what to do when you have more money than anticipated, but you may have a problem making up a shortfall! Your cash flow projection is supposed to warn you if you're about to fall short.

You're almost finished at this point. As a next step, look back at your financial records to see how much money you had at the beginning of the first month of your cash flow projection. Place this figure in a "Balance Forward" row as the first income item for your first month period. Add it to all the income for that month and subtract that month's expenses. The difference gives you the next "Balance Forward" amount that belongs at the top row for the next column of income for the *next* monthly period. And keep going. The balance for each month is steadily carried over to the top.

Table 10-3 shows a highly simplified sample of a cash flow projection.

Table 10-3	Simple Cash Flow Projection		
Income	*1/1–1/31*	*2/1–2/28*	*3/1–3/31*
Balance forward	$21,603	$9,845	$43,445
Government contract		$65,000	
Williams grant	$15,000		
Power company			$2,500
Board giving	$4,000	$750	
Total income and balance forward	$40,603	$75,595	$45,945
Expenses	*1/1–1/31*	*2/1–2/28*	*3/1–3/31*
Payroll	$22,197	$22,197	$22,197
Health benefits	$2,111	$2,111	$2,111
Payroll taxes	$2,775	$2,775	$2,775
Rent	$2,500	$2,500	$2,500
Electric company	$675	$675	$580
Telephone	$435	$450	$475
Office supplies	$65	$120	$120
Travel and transportation		$1,322	$8,700
Total expenses	$30,758	$32,150	$39,458
Balance:	$9,845	$43,445	$6,487

See CD1010 and CD1011 for a detailed sample cash flow projection and for a blank form you can use to begin your own cash flow statement.

Deciding what to do if you don't have enough

You probably won't have more income than expenses in every single one-month period throughout the year. During some periods, you get ahead, and at other times, you fall behind. Your goal is to sustain a generally positive balance over the course of time and to be able to cover your most critical bills — payroll, taxes, insurance, and utilities — in a timely manner.

Some government agencies and foundations pay grants as reimbursements for expenses after you've incurred them. You may need to prepare your cash flow plan accordingly while waiting to be reimbursed.

We want to promise that you'll always have enough resources to sustain your organization's good work. But some times will be lean. Then what? First, your cash flow projection should help you to anticipate when you may fall short. It enables you to plan ahead and solicit board members who have not yet made gifts in the current year, send letters to past donors, cut costs, or delay purchases.

We also recommend being proactive about contacting your creditors. If you think you can't pay a bill on time, call and ask for an extension or explain that you're forced to make a partial payment now with the balance coming in a few weeks. Your ability to do business depends on your earning and sustaining other people's trust. If you can't have perfect credit, being honest and forthright is the next best thing. It's hard to do, but important.

Don't "hide" behind your bills, thinking that if you don't say anything, nobody will notice. If you're facing a period of debt, tell your board. Also, call anyone to whom you owe money and explain the situation and your timeline for paying your bills. Among other things, your honesty helps them with *their* cash flow. And when your expenses are exceeding your income, always try to cover your federal, state, and local tax obligations, because fees and interest on unpaid taxes add up quickly. If covering those obligations isn't possible, don't forget to call those agencies. Setting up a payment plan, both over the phone and in writing, can prevent your assets (or a board member's) from being frozen.

Borrowing to make ends meet

Another route to managing cash shortfalls is to borrow the money you need to cover your bills. Your cash flow statement can help you plan the size and duration of the loan you need. Here are some of your options if you need to borrow money:

- ✓ **Ask a board member for a loan.** If the board member can help, you can probably secure the loan quickly, but borrowing from a board member is only appropriate to do if you act in accordance with your organization's conflict of interest policies, and if the board member can provide the loan at market rates or below market rates. Make sure to sign a promissory note with the lender and record the board's formal approval of accepting the loan in its meeting minutes.

- ✓ **Ask local foundations whether they know of a loan fund for nonprofit organizations.** Some associations of grantmakers and government agencies offer such loans at low interest to their grantees who face cash flow problems. Such a program is likely to be more sympathetic to your needs than a commercial lending institution may be.

✓ **Apply for a small business loan at your bank.** If your organization doesn't have a credit history, getting a bank loan can be challenging. However, foundations sometimes make this process easier by guaranteeing these bank loans for nonprofits.

✓ **Check to see whether you qualify for a line of credit from your bank.** A *line of credit* allows you to borrow up to a certain sum for a specified period of time. When the organization repays the borrowed amount, often it can't borrow from its line of credit again for a designated period of time. Your organization may want to apply for a line of credit even if it doesn't expect immediate cash flow problems. Doing so can provide a safety net for emergencies.

✓ **As a last resort, borrow the money from an organizational credit card.** Do this only if you're positive that you can repay the loan quickly and cover the interest.

Borrowing money requires time and preparation and usually costs your nonprofit in the form of interest payments. However, borrowing is better than damaging your nonprofit's reputation or incurring severe penalties and interest charges — particularly on tax obligations.

Keeping Your Books Organized and Up-to-Date

After you've created a budget, you need to set up a system for keeping consistent, organized records of your financial information. You may choose to do your bookkeeping by hand or with accounting software. If you're interested in bookkeeping by hand, *Bookkeeping For Dummies* by Lita Epstein, MBA (Wiley) can guide you.

You'll encounter two standard systems for compiling and presenting information about your organization's financial history: cash and accrual. Here are some ways they differ:

✓ **A cash system closely resembles the way most people keep their checkbooks.** You enter income into the books when you receive and deposit a check or cash. You enter expenses when you pay a bill. Many find a cash system to be a comfortable approach because it's straightforward. When your books show a positive balance, you have money in hand or in the bank.

✔ **An accrual system recognizes income when it's promised and expenses when they're obligated.** Suppose you receive a grant award letter from a foundation promising your organization $60,000 over a two-year period. This grant is going to be paid in four checks of $15,000 each. In an accrual system, you enter the entire $60,000 as income in your books when that money is promised — when you receive the grant award letter. On the expense side, you enter your bills into your books when you incur them — which may be before they're due.

Each of these approaches has possible disadvantages:

✔ In cash books, your organization may owe money in unpaid bills, but those debts aren't apparent because they aren't on your books until they're paid.

✔ In cash books, your organization may have been awarded a large grant but may look poor because you haven't received the check.

✔ In cash books, it's more difficult to tell whether you owe payroll taxes.

✔ In accrual books, you may have been promised a large contribution but not yet received it. You may have no cash in hand, but your books look as if you have surplus income.

Keeping books by an accrual system is standard accounting practice for non-profits and is recommended by the Financial Accounting Standards Board, so this section of the book assumes you use an accrual system. To be honest, however, small organizations often can get by with a cash system.

If you decide to use software to keep your books, you can purchase types that are designed specifically for nonprofits, which have some different needs and use a few different terms than for-profit businesses. We recommend that you choose one of these products meant for nonprofits, though accountants differ on whether it's necessary. Some accounting software packages that many small nonprofits use include QuickBooks by Intuit, Peachtree by Sage, and Fund E-Z by E-Z Development Corporation.

If more than four or five users at your organization will be using the accounting software, if your budget exceeds $1 million, or if you need to track many programs, you'll likely want to invest in more-complex accounting software.

The online journals TechSoup and Idealware (`home.techsoup.org/pages/ default.aspx` and `idealware.org`) are excellent sources of articles and information about technology. TechSoup also provides discounted technology products for nonprofits. Read their articles and follow their up-to-date leads. We've included an article on CD1009 and a link through CD1015.

When creating your start-up budget, don't forget to include accounting software — the cost of purchasing the package or online service, of setting it up, and of being trained to use it. As your organization grows and you need more sophisticated software, the setup time will be greater.

Preparing Financial Statements and Conducting an Audit

If a budget is a document about the future, a financial statement tells the story of your organization's past. Nonprofit organizations keep and review their financial records throughout the year, and they prepare a financial statement at least once a year, at the end of the fiscal year. (See Chapter 4 for more information on a fiscal year.) Many organizations also prepare monthly or quarterly "in progress" versions of their annual financial statements.

While good nonprofit accounting software can organize your financial information for you, preparing and interpreting financial statements is a special area of expertise that goes beyond the scope of this book. Many nonprofits seek outside professional help for this essential task. If hiring such assistance is beyond your organization's means, we recommend that you become acquainted with *Accounting For Dummies,* 4th Edition, by John A. Tracy, CPA. (Wiley). If you do choose to prepare your own financial statements, you may want to hire an accountant at year's end to review them for accuracy.

The information in your yearly financial statement resembles (but may not be identical to) the 990-EZ or 990 financial report that your organization must submit annually to the IRS. You can find more information about the differences among these types of 990s and filling one out in Chapter 5. You'll also be including your financial statement in your board orientation packets and with requests for funding. Some organizations publish it in an "Annual Report" of activities. You can find a copy of Form 990 at www.irs.gov.

At the year's end, your organization may choose to have its books audited by a certified public accountant (CPA) or firm. This service involves a formal study of the organization's policies and systems for managing its finances, a review of its financial statements, and commentary about the accuracy of those statements. The accountant may issue an *unqualified opinion,* meaning that the statements appear to be accurate. In "auditor talk" the accountant didn't find a *material misstatement* — false or missing information. If the auditors have recommendations to make about how money is managed or how finances are recorded and reported, they may issue a *management letter* to the board about how the organization can improve its practices. These letters can contain a wide array of recommendations. For example, the auditors may tell the board that the organization did not consistently collect original receipts before writing checks to reimburse staff; that staff travel costs increased dramatically without that increase being approved by the board (and recorded in board minutes); or that the organization's employees are owed so many vacation hours that the organization's work could be jeopardized if everyone were to take his or her deserved holiday.

While some nonprofit organizations look upon a "management letter" as a scolding, its point is to help nonprofit organizations safeguard their financial health by strengthening their policies and recordkeeping.

If you hire a CPA to conduct your audit or financial review, make sure the person has knowledge about or expertise in nonprofit organizations. Nonprofits use some accounting terms and bookkeeping methods that differ from profit-making businesses.

When do you need to conduct an audit? Use the following guidelines to help you determine:

- ✔ **Many states require nonprofits that receive contributions over a specified amount to conduct audits.** This varies by state. Check the offices that regulate nonprofits in your state (usually the Attorney General's office) to see whether they have created specific audit guidelines.

- ✔ **Nonprofits that directly spend $500,000 or more in federal funds in a fiscal year are required to conduct an A-133 audit.** It has a fancy name because it's based on the Office of Management and Budget Circular A-133, and it takes a particularly close look at how government funds are tracked within the organization.

- ✔ **Some government programs also require audits of specific grants or contracts.** Other funders also may require audited statements from applicants.

Even if it isn't required, your board may decide that it's a good idea to have the books examined by an outside CPA. Doing so provides reassurance that financial systems are healthy and that the organization is working with accurate financial information.

If your organization is required to have an audit, your board should form an audit committee. The board president, board treasurer, and paid staff members may *not* serve on this committee, however. The committee selects the audit firm, reviews a draft of the audit and any recommendations from the auditors, and, if necessary, investigates any practices that should be changed.

Although your organization can learn a great deal from an audit, the practice isn't appropriate or necessary for every nonprofit. The process is expensive and time consuming. A rigorous but less-expensive option is having a formal financial review conducted by a CPA firm.

Many nonprofits wonder whether they should seek pro bono audits from accounting firms or ask a board member's firm to audit their books. Although we're big fans of contributed services, a pro bono audit is a bad idea and asking a board member for assistance is a very bad idea. An audit should be prepared independently of the organization's staff and board. It loses its value as the voice of unbiased, outside validation when provided as a gift.

Reading Your Financial Statements

Audited or not, prepared by you or by a bookkeeper or accountant, your organization needs to produce financial statements, and it's critically important for you to understand how to interpret them. So in this section, we show you everything you need to know, including how to identify the two parts of a statement and how to arm yourself with the right information.

Getting to know parts of a standard financial statement

Nonprofit financial statements include two important substatements:

- ✔ **The *statement of position* (also called a balance sheet) provides an overview of what an organization is worth.** It outlines how much money is available in bank accounts and other investments; the value of property, furniture, and equipment; immediate bills; and other debts and liabilities.

- ✔ **The *statement of activities* outlines "Revenues, Gains, and Supports" and "Expenses and Other Losses," which tell you how much money the organization received in the past year, its sources for that income, and how it spent that income.** Statements of activities divide an organization's income and expenses into three categories:

    - **Unrestricted funds** were available to the organization to spend in the fiscal year covered by the statement.

- **Temporarily restricted funds** were promised or awarded in the year covered by the statement but they were given to the organization for it to spend in the future or for a specific task that isn't yet complete.

- **Permanently restricted funds** were given to the organization for permanent investments — such as endowments. Earnings on such money may be used toward the organization's costs (your board will set a policy about how much of these earnings may be used), but the amounts donated as restricted gifts shouldn't be spent on current activities.

The statement of activities also contains a statement of *functional expense,* which details expenses spent on programs and those expenses that were exclusively for general and administrative costs and for fund-raising costs.

Many staff and board members are drawn to nonprofit organizations because they're knowledgeable about the services they provide, but their eyes glaze over when they're faced with financial statements. This lack of interest in finances is understandable but can be dangerous: The board and staff are stewards of the organization's resources, and they're responsible for its financial health.

We include a sample of an audited financial statement on CD1012 that you can use to become familiar with the terms used and the organization of information.

Asking the right financial questions

At the year's end, when you've completed the financial statement, we suggest reviewing the following points, either as a board or within the board's finance committee. You can ask different questions about the statement of position (or balance sheet) and the statement of activities. The answers will arm you with a clear understanding of your organization's financial health.

Looking at the statement of position, compare some of the numbers, asking:

- ✔ **Do the cash and cash equivalents exceed the accounts payable?** If so, the organization has enough cash in the bank to pay its immediate bills to vendors.

- ✔ **Do the total current assets exceed the current liabilities?** If they do, the organization has enough money readily at hand to cover all its immediate obligations, such as bills and taxes, employee benefits, and loan payments.

✔ **How much of the assets are made up of property, equipment, or other durable goods the organization owns and what is the nature of those assets?** Some organizations can appear to be financially healthy because their total assets are high, but all those assets are made up of things that would be hard for them to sell.

✔ **Does the current liabilities section show a high amount of payroll taxes payable?** If so, the organization may be delinquent in paying its taxes.

✔ **In the liabilities section, do you see an item for a refundable advance or deferred revenue?** If you see this item, it means money paying for a service was given to the organization before the organization provided that service (such as subscription income theatergoers pay in advance of attending performances). Make sure that the organization has sufficient assets — preferably cash — to provide the services it has promised.

✔ **Has the organization borrowed money?** If so, the amount appears in the liabilities section as a loan or line of credit. Compare its total unrestricted net assets to the total amount borrowed. If the numbers are similar, the organization may have cash at hand but all of it must be repaid to a lender.

The financial statement will be dated, and the answers to the questions you have just asked should give you a good picture of the health of your organization over its entire history leading up to that date. Now it's time to look at the statement of activities, which illustrates what happened in the past year. Two simple questions will summarize that story. Look to the bottom of the page to see:

- **Is the change in net assets a negative or positive number?** If it's negative, the organization lost money in the previous year. If the loss is a high number, ask why it took place. If it's a modest amount, ask whether it's part of a downward trend or something that rarely occurs.

- **Is the number shown for total net assets a positive number?** If so, the organization is in a positive financial position (even if it lost money in the past year). That's good news!

Managing Financial Systems

Even in a small organization, you want to establish careful practices about how you handle money and financial documents. If you have a one-person office, creating all the following controls may be impossible, but you should try to implement as many of them as possible:

✔ Store checkbooks, savings passbooks, blank checks, financial records, and cash in a locked, secure place.

✔ Regularly back up financial records that you keep on computers and store a copy off-site in a safe location.

✔ Assign to different people the separate functions of writing checks, signing checks, reconciling bank accounts, and checking the canceled checks that return from the bank. If you can arrange for four different people to perform these tasks, that's great. If not, maybe a board member can double-check canceled checks. Look for accuracy and for anything that looks fishy, such as checks made out to vendors you don't recognize, checks canceled by people or businesses other than those to whom they're written, or canceled checks that are missing from bank statements. Embezzlement is rare but possible, and taking these steps is a way to detect it. Trust us, we've discovered such a case!

✔ Require two signatures on checks or bank transfers over a certain amount, often $1,000. (You can adopt this requirement as an internal policy, and ask your bank whether it monitors larger transactions to make sure that the policy is followed.)

✔ Retain in organized files (subject to a document retention/destruction policy) all paperwork that backs up your banking documents. These documents may include personnel time sheets, box office or other records for tickets sold, receipts, and invoices.

✔ Keep an itemized list of any furniture or equipment you purchase or receive as donations (including computers), noting the date they were purchased or received and their value.

Chapter 11

Marketing: Spreading the Word about Your Good Work

In This Chapter

▶ Attending to everyday basics

▶ Looking at who you are and who you serve

▶ Building your publicity machine through mass media

You may think that marketing has no place in the nonprofit sector. After all, if an organization's work isn't driven by the dollar, and if its focus is on meeting a community need, why does it need to sell its services? If your motivation is to do good, isn't it crass to toot your own horn?

But wait. Marketing — the process of connecting consumers to services and products — is just as critical to the success of nonprofit organizations as it is to commercial enterprises. Both nonprofit and commercial organizations depend on getting the word out, and the message from both is the same: "Here we are, and here's what we can do for you. Come and check us out. Use our services. And, if you're truly inspired, make a contribution."

You can go far if you have the "goods" — good planning, good stories, good services, and good luck. And, of course, persistence.

Taking Care of the Basics

Before you begin tackling client surveys and media releases, you need to spend a little time making sure you have a few basic communication tools in place. These tools help you tell your clients, audiences, donors, and the general public who you are and what you do.

In this section, we provide some tips for the most basic communication tools that every nonprofit — large or small, new or old — should have.

We recommend TechSoup.org, a free resource for technology information, discounted software, and more, as well as Idealware.org, which offers free information about software for nonprofits. Check their articles, which allow you to compare online payment services for selling products and accepting donations and databases for organizing the information you collect about your constituents. We include links on the CD.

Selecting letterhead

Your letterhead should include your organization's name, address, phone number, fax number, and e-mail and Web site addresses. Many organizations also list their board members on the letterhead. Doing so is a great way to highlight the board members' affiliations with your organization, but if your board is rapidly changing and growing, you may be reprinting the letterhead every few weeks. You also may want to include a tag line, briefly identifying what your organization does, like *Feeding the hungry in Tuborville*. Often the tag line is a phrase drawn from your mission statement.

Preparing an organization overview

An *organization overview* is a one-page overview of your organization's mission and programs. You can enclose it with press releases, grant proposals, and fundraising letters. Place copies in your lobby or reception area for visitors to read. Feature it on the home page of your Web site.

As you grow, your organization may want to get a little bit fancier and produce a folded brochure with photographs or drawings. An effective brochure clearly conveys the essence of your organization. You want it to be inviting and readable. Visual elements help to make a more attractive document and often enable you to tell your story in fewer words.

Designing a logo

A logo is a graphic image that suits the tone of your organization. Many people remember pictures more vividly than words, so they may remember your logo more easily than they remember your organization's name. Try not to resort to standard computer font symbols or clip art when designing your logo. Instead, if you need to be frugal, ask around your organization to see whether anyone knows a graphic artist or a printer with a good eye who can help you create something original. If you can't locate anyone, we recommend a simple solution: Choose an attractive typeface in which to present your name. You can get fancier later.

Whether it's complex or simple, as you're creating your logo, produce several drafts, spend time looking at those drafts, and show them to others, asking for feedback. You don't want to grow tired of your logo or have it confused with the logo of another group in your community.

If your organization is small and your resources are limited, don't design a logo that has to be printed in more than one color of ink. Using just one color reduces printing costs.

Creating a Web site

Having a presence on the Web is as important as being listed in the telephone book or printing a brochure. A basic Web site isn't difficult to create either. You want an overview of your agency on the home page and a few additional pages where people find out more about your organization's leaders and programs.

Be sure to include a contact page with phone numbers and e-mail addresses. Not only does a contact page suggest that you're available to provide more information, but it's a means by which your organization can begin gathering e-mail addresses for further communications about events and programs as well as fundraising. And, while we're on the subject of fundraising, you'll also likely want to include a "donate now" feature for collecting contributions. (See Chapter 14 for more information.)

In good time you can add bells and whistles to your Web site: a gallery of photographs or short videos, articles about your field, a blog or discussion board, and much more. But do keep in mind that as you add features to your Web site, you're also increasing the number and types of things that need to be maintained.

If you're looking for assistance with creating a Web site, you may find free or low-cost help at a local college or university. Often students majoring in graphic arts, Web design, educational technology, or technical writing are required to complete internships or culminating projects as part of their degree programs. You may find a talented, eager designer by contacting their department or by reaching out to the campus's community service learning program. Another option is to search online for a graphic artist through VolunteerMatch (www.volunteermatch.org).

An unattended Web site leaves a bad impression. Broken Web links and out-of-date information tell the reader that your organization isn't paying attention to communicating with its constituents. If you're going to have a Web site, assign someone in your organization the task of checking on and updating it regularly. If your budget allows, consider hiring a Web design firm or Web-savvy individual to create and maintain your site.

Producing an annual report

Begin producing an annual report after your first year of operating. The report may be published as a letter, brochure, Web site, or even a book. Usually, the annual report includes a financial statement for the year, along with an overview of recent accomplishments. It may also include introductory letters from the president and executive director of your organization. An annual report conveys the image of an accomplished organization that's transparent in its communications. The messages the report conveys build trust among people seeking the organization's services or considering making contributions.

Issuing a newsletter

A newsletter offers background stories and information about your organization. You can publish it as a feature page on your Web site, as a PDF document linked to your Web site or attached to an e-mail, or as a printed or photocopied document. Issuing a newsletter is a great way to keep in touch with your organization's constituents. It can take them behind the scenes of your organization. You may use a newsletter to profile members of your staff, board, and constituents; alert followers to coming events; summarize research; and announce news about your organization's work.

Taking care of customers — your most important marketing tool

If your constituents, audiences, patients, clients, volunteers, and board members aren't treated well, you can make major investments in advertising and public relations but still struggle to find new customers and keep your old ones. Small adjustments in customer service can make a big difference to your organization's image.

If your agency is likely to receive calls from people requiring counseling or emergency assistance, make sure that everyone answering the phone is thoroughly trained in how to calm a caller and provide a referral.

Making customer service a daily habit

The trick to providing exemplary customer service is to work at it in little ways all the time. Every staff member and volunteer needs to be aware of the importance of customer service. We offer five key areas to address to improve (or maintain) your service levels:

✔ **On the telephone:** Talk to all staff and volunteers about how to answer the phone politely and otherwise use it to maximum effect. Provide a cheat sheet with lists of extensions, instructions on how to forward calls, and any other useful information. Simple additions to a greeting, like, "May I help you?" or telling the caller the receptionist's name can set a friendly, professional tone.

Make a rule for yourself to return all calls within 24 hours or, if that's not possible, within one week. Let callers know, through your voice mail greeting, when they may expect to hear from you. If you're selecting a voice mail system, make sure it's user-friendly for your callers. We prefer a small number of transfers within the system and options for modifying standard recorded announcements with more personal and pertinent messages.

✔ **At the door:** Someone needs to (cheerfully) answer the door. If you're in a small office without a receptionist and the interruptions are frequent, you can rotate this task among staff members or volunteers. If visitors must use a buzzer or pass through a security system, try to balance the coldness of that experience with a friendly intercom greeting and pleasant foyer.

✔ **Before and after a sale or donation:** If you have something to sell, make it easy to buy. Accepting only cash is far too restrictive. The banker managing your business

account can help prepare you to accept credit card orders. Also, consider selling over the Web; a number of Web services assist small businesses and nonprofits with Web sales and online donations. If a customer isn't satisfied with your product or service, invite the customer to give feedback and listen carefully. Offer a partial or complete refund. Doing so wins loyalty.

✔ **With a note:** Keep some nice stationery and a rough draft of a standard message handy so that writing thank-you notes is easy. Handwritten notes are more personal and often make a stronger impression than formal, typed letters or e-mail messages. However expressing your appreciation in a timely way is more important than the form of that appreciation. Use e-mail if you can get to it more quickly. Write a thank-you note for a contribution within a few days of receiving it.

If your organization receives *things* — like a theatre group that receives play manuscripts or a natural history museum that accepts scholarly papers for publication — have an acknowledgement e-mail ready that confirms the item's receipt and states when the person submitting it can expect to hear from you.

✔ **In the details:** An old saying suggests that the devil lurks in the details, but that's also where you find the heart and soul of hospitality and service. Keep notes in a database about the interests, connections, and preferences of your board members, donors, and frequent customers. Find out the names of your board and committee members' significant others and be prepared to greet them personally at events and on the phone.

Discovering Who You Are: First Steps to Marketing

You've put your basic tools in place and your programs are up and running, but you sense that something is wrong. You know that you're addressing a need and that your agency is highly regarded. Why aren't your programs full? How can you engage more people in the important work that you do?

If a marketing program is what you need (and we believe it is), the first step is understanding your current situation — what you do, who you serve, who admires your work, and who is willing to support it. When you know the answers to these questions, you can begin to build marketing strategies that highlight your agency's strengths and are tailored to all your key audiences — the people who walk through your doors every day to receive your services, your board members and staff, your donors and volunteers, and the community at large. Blend in your budget constraints (we all have to do that!), and you're ready to roll.

Defining your current market

If you want to improve the way you reach the public, you first need to know how your current marketing works. Who are your customers? How did they find out about your organization? Why do they make use of your programs? The following sections help you answer these kinds of questions.

Your A to Z references on marketing and public relations

Whole books — hundreds and hundreds of whole books — have been written on the topic of marketing and the related field of public relations. Our job in this chapter is to take you on a quick flyover of marketing for nonprofit organizations so you get the big picture and know where to turn for details. And for all the details on marketing plans, surveys, public relations, press releases, use of electronic media, and related topics, we recommend four other books from Wiley: *Marketing Kit For Dummies,* 3rd Edition, by Alexander Hiam; *Small Business Marketing For Dummies,* 2nd Edition, by Barbara Findlay Schenck; *Press Relations For Dummies,* 2nd Edition, by Eric Yaverbaum and Ilise Benun; and *E-Mail Marketing For Dummies* by John Arnold.

Surveying your customers to gain important info

You may never discover who reads about your organization in the newspaper or sees your sign every day on the bus, but some people — those with whom you directly communicate — can be identified. Start by defining your core group — your most important constituents — and work out from there.

Suppose that your organization is a small historical society that organizes exhibits and panel discussions at three libraries in your town, publishes a quarterly newsletter, and maintains a Web site featuring news and information about its collection. Your current customers (or stakeholders, if you want to use a common nonprofit term), working from the core to the outer boundaries, include the following:

- Your board and staff (and their friends and relations)
- Your docents and volunteers
- Families and organizations that donate materials to your collection
- Local library staff and board members
- Persons attending your panel discussions
- Schools and other groups visiting your exhibits
- Scholars and other archivists writing to ask about your holdings
- Patrons of the three libraries
- Subscribers to your quarterly newsletter
- Persons visiting your organization's Web site

Drawing up this list of interested persons is easy enough. But for marketing purposes, you need to know as much as possible about the characteristics, backgrounds, and interests of each group. Some things you can do to collect this sort of information include

- Creating a database of your supporters by gathering names and addresses from every possible source within your organization — items like checks from donors, subscription forms from newsletter subscribers, sign-up sheets from volunteers, and e-mail messages sent to the "contact us" address on your Web site. Enter these names and addresses in a computer database or word processing program that can sort them by last name, type of contact, and date of entry; and, if you're planning to send traditional mail to them, sort them by zip code. Articles on the Web sites Idealware.org and Techsoup.org can help you choose a database.

TIP

Review the zip codes appearing most frequently on your list. If you're in the United States, you can visit the United States Census Bureau Web site (`www.census.gov`) and get demographic information about residents in those zip code areas.

✔ Asking the three libraries whether they collect demographic data when visitors apply for library cards and whether they can share that information with you. (Some public agencies offer information about their constituents on their Web sites.)

✔ Asking a few standard questions of schools or other groups when they call to sign up for a tour. Don't engage in a lengthy interview, but find out how they heard about your program, why they want to visit it, and whether they have other needs you may be able to address. You can gather similar information when collecting registrations online.

✔ Inserting clearly worded and inviting surveys in the programs at your public events. At the beginning and end of an event, make a brief public pitch explaining why it's so important for people to respond to the surveys. Make pencils or pens available. Create incentives for completing the form, such as a free museum membership for a person whose survey is drawn at random. Include the same survey as part of your mailed newsletter. Provide a return envelope to make it easy for readers to respond. Similarly, make it easy for visitors of your Web site to subscribe to announcements or services, and send a brief survey to them by e-mail. The higher your response rate, the more accurate and useful the survey information will be.

Designing a useful survey

Developing a picture of your current clients is critically important to creating a marketing plan, and a good survey can be your camera. If you're going to go to the effort to conduct a survey, it needs to have a purpose and must be clear and direct. Here are some general guidelines to keep in mind:

✔ If your survey is long, fewer people will complete it.

✔ You probably want to include some multiple-choice questions, but be sure to have one or two open-ended questions as well so people have a chance to speak their minds.

✔ Be careful not to ask *leading questions,* or questions that suggest the answers that you hope to hear.

✔ Explore different kinds of information by asking how convenient and appealing your events and services are and by asking your patrons what other kinds of programs they would enjoy.

✔ Ask your current consumers how they found out about you. The answers tell you which forms of your current marketing are effective and begin to suggest how you may best further spread the word about your programs.

Be aware that there's an art to writing an effective survey: The way questions are worded can influence the answers you get; and you want to receive clear, candid responses. If you want to seek help in developing your survey, check with local colleges and universities for faculty members or graduate students who understand survey techniques and who may be willing to give you some guidance. You also can find survey subscription services and sample surveys on the Web that give you ideas about wording questions. Two such services are Zoomerang (www.zoomerang.com) and SurveyMonkey (www.survey-monkey.com). For a fee, such sources will distribute your surveys by e-mail and tally the results for you.

You can find two sample surveys (CD1101 and CD1102) that may suggest wording for your survey questions on the CD that accompanies this book.

Organizing and interpreting the responses

After you have survey results, you can compile the responses by hand. Or you can use some of the database and word processing programs that we mention earlier in this chapter to create a record for each person who responds or for each event at which surveys are gathered.

You may discover that you serve several distinct groups of people. For example, low-income students may use the library after school and visit your exhibits while they're there. Middle-income mothers from the immediate neighborhood may bring their toddlers to the library for afternoon stories and take advantage of your programs. And wealthy older adults may volunteer as docents, serve on your board, and attend your organization's panel discussions.

With this valuable information, you may be able to recognize ways to reach more people who resemble the ones you're already serving. The more challenging task is to reach and entice new groups of people.

If you discover that your clients like your program offerings but find the times you offer them inconvenient, do you want to experiment with new times and formats? For instance, do consumers find Sunday afternoons (when the library is closed) to be more convenient? What other barriers inhibit their involvement? Maybe mothers with toddlers want to come to your lectures but need childcare. Perhaps you charge a modest admission fee for lectures but students find that charge to be too high.

One of your most difficult marketing tasks is analyzing the very basis of what you do and how you do it. You may feel that your historical society's close working relationship with libraries is its greatest asset, but the surveys may point out that those libraries are cold and musty during winter months. You may do better by taking over a neighborhood restaurant, creating a "warmer" atmosphere — even offering hot gingerbread and beverages.

To succeed at reaching and serving more people, you want to keep an open mind, and be observant.

Using focus groups as additional tools

Surveys are useful for providing you with general information. You read them looking for an overview of what most people think and feel. Focus groups are another common tool for gathering information from constituents. Because they're based in conversations, they often give you more specific, nuanced responses. Perhaps you want to know what small business leaders think of your agency; a focus group of businessmen and women can help you uncover their attitudes and needs.

How market research can open your eyes

A small nonprofit alcoholism treatment center for women was started in San Francisco in the late 1970s in response to studies that demonstrated multiple programs existed to help alcoholic men but few focused specifically on women. No local service of this type focused on helping Spanish-speaking immigrant women.

The program's mission was to provide comprehensive counseling and alcohol treatment services to low-income women, particularly those originally from Mexico or Central America. Four years into the nonprofit's history, its programs were full and effective, and it had won prestigious contracts from the city. The center had even launched a capital campaign to create a permanent home. It appeared to be very successful. With one exception. The women being served were mostly middle class and white. A few were African American. None came from the neighborhood where the program was based.

The board realized that the center needed to change its image and marketing strategy. Through interviews with women from the center's target population, board and staff realized

that the stigma associated with alcoholism was particularly strong among Mexican and Central American families and women from these cultural groups were struggling with alcoholism in private.

The center began a multifaceted campaign to change this situation, beginning with cultural sensitivity training for counselors. When the center hired new staff, an aggressive effort was made to find Chicanas and Latinas to fill positions. The group published all brochures and other informational materials in Spanish and held press conferences for the Spanish-language press. The center hired a Chicana outreach counselor to meet with community groups, churches, and schools and develop connections and a system of referrals to the agency.

Within two years, more than one-third of the women served were low-income women from Mexico and Central America. The marketing aimed at this community was well worth the investment. Fulfilling the organization's mission depended on it.

When producing a focus group, remember to limit the number of questions asked to fewer than ten (five or six is ideal). Feed participants to create a convivial environment. The conversation likely will be more candid if led by a volunteer facilitator, not someone clearly identified with your organization. Seek permission from participants to record their discussions.

Defining who you want to reach and how

Armed with information about the people who already know about your non-profit, you're now ready to extend your reach by defining target groups you want to serve and discovering how best to reach them. In general, it's wisest to begin with your current constituents and work to expand within their demographic group or to others who are similar to them.

As you shift your attention to reaching new groups, be cautious. You may alienate and lose current followers. The more different demographically your new target groups are from the people you now serve, the more difficult and expensive your marketing task may be.

If you run a local history archive and have audiences of low-income students, middle-income mothers of toddlers, and affluent docents and volunteers, logical new target audiences may include the following:

- ✓ Family members and classmates of the students using the libraries
- ✓ Mothers and toddlers from a wider geographic area surrounding the libraries
- ✓ Docents and volunteers who assist other local cultural institutions
- ✓ Friends and acquaintances of the docents

Your marketing plan is then tailored to reach these groups. Attempting to reach these groups may require changes both in how you present your work and in how you spread the message about that work. Consider some of the ideas in this list to reach the following groups:

- ✓ **The students' classmates and friends:**

  - Contact local history teachers and work with them to link their lessons to archival materials in your collection. Invite them to bring their classes to see your exhibits.

  - Offer student internships and then involve your interns as docents for the school tours.

  - Invite the students who currently use the library space to help in planning, researching, and presenting an exhibit. Honor them for their involvement at the exhibit's opening and provide them with invitations for their friends and acquaintances.

✔ **More mothers and toddlers:**

- Advertise or place articles about your organization's work in local newsletters for parents of young children.

- Post fliers about your organization's work at parks, playgrounds, local stores that sell goods for small children, and other cultural institutions with children's events.

- Provide childcare at lectures and weekend programs.

✔ **Docents and volunteers who also help other organizations:**

- Advertise or place articles in your local volunteer center's newsletter.

- Contact local parent-teacher organizations and offer their members special tours or presentations.

- Exchange e-mail lists of docents and volunteers with other local cultural organizations, and then use the new lists to extend invitations to a special get-acquainted-with-us event.

✔ **Friends and acquaintances of your current docents:**

- Hold a volunteer recognition party and provide each of your volunteers with ten or more invitations for friends and acquaintances.

The cost of implementing new programs and spreading the word about them can add up quickly. Consider what resources you have available (including your time) before committing to big changes in your organization.

Marketing on a shoestring

Effective marketing doesn't have to be expensive. It can be based on multiple grassroots efforts that are small in scale and very specifically targeted. *Guerrilla marketing* is the term for marketing that's cheap, creative, and effective. Jay Conrad Levinson's Web site (www.gmarketing.com) is a good place to find out more about guerrilla marketing.

The guerrilla approach may use stickers affixed to parking meters, sandwich boards with provocative messages, cards passed out to people waiting in ticket lines, or provocative online offers. A famous guerrilla marketing example from the business world includes an Internet start-up company that offered families $5,000 if they would name a child after one of its products. The point of guerrilla marketing is to get customers talking about your organization and its products — to develop "word-of-mouth advertising," which is powerful.

Using Mass Media to Reach Your Audience

What if you want to reach all the people all the time? We're sorry, but you can't. You can, however, extend your reach beyond the contacts known by your friends and family by approaching mass media — newspapers, magazines, radio, television, and the Web. Although some nonprofits pay for advertising to spread the word, most organizations rely on free publicity from the media.

Planning for effective publicity

Before contacting the media, first decide what story you want to tell and who you want to reach with that story. What's distinctive and important about your organization's work? Why is it newsworthy? Be honest: Analyze your idea as if you're a news editor who has to choose among many different stories from many sources. How does yours stand up in the competition?

Ask yourself about your proposed story's relevance: Will it affect the lives of its readers? Is it timely? Does it contain conflict or intrigue or prominent people? The journalism column at about.com (`journalism.about.com`) includes useful articles about how to decide whether something is newsworthy and how to structure a story. We include links to two of these on the CD.

Developing a media list

A *media list* is a compilation of names, addresses, e-mail addresses, and phone numbers of contacts at local (and maybe national) newspapers, radio and television stations, magazines, and Web sites.

Your media list will be a valuable tool that you refine and expand over time. Some metropolitan areas have press clubs and service organizations from which you can buy membership lists, providing a basis for your list. Cision (`us.cision.com`) is a comprehensive online media service. Its databases encompass contacts at online, print, radio, and television outlets. A full membership to Cision can be expensive, but one-time searches are reasonable.

The art of shaping a news story

A few years ago we were involved as grant-makers in supporting the creation of a mural on the exterior of a community center next to a small urban park. One of San Francisco's best-regarded mural artists led the project. She spent a great deal of time talking to the park's neighbors and people who used the building about images to use in her mural. Those people she talked to kept mentioning a young couple who had been killed in the park in a random, accidental shooting several years earlier. Although it wasn't her original subject idea, she included the couple's portraits in the painting surrounded by images representing peace and renewal.

The story of the mural's unveiling was presented to the media as a public memorial event for the neighbors and families of the young couple. Front page, color images of the piece appeared in both the morning and evening papers the next day, and five television stations covered the event that evening. An acclaimed artist completing another mural wouldn't have been a story, but a neighborhood mourning two lost teenagers was hot news.

We hope your nonprofit is never thrown into telling the story of a tragedy, but we give this example to show that not all good work is news. Tragedy is news. Drama is news. Breakthroughs are news. Surprises are news. Stories that connect to current trends are news.

For all the nuances of media list development and management, we recommend that you take a look at *Public Relations Kit For Dummies* by Eric Yaverbaum with Bob Bly (Wiley). In general, your objective is to build two working lists, one that you use with practically every press release you send out and the other for specific opportunities for publicity. The latter group may include the following:

✔ Social and entertainment editors to whom you send news of your annual benefit gala

✔ Social and business editors to whom you announce new members and officers of your board

✔ Opinion page editors for letters to the editor

✔ Sunday magazine supplement editors for in-depth profiles of leaders in your field of work

✔ Features columnists for amusing anecdotes or unusual news

✔ Writers of blogs on topics related to your work

✔ Internet chat room hosts to whom you give your organization's perspective and who you use to test public response to news and ideas

Starting to work with media

Here's our advice for getting started with the mass media:

- ✔ Pay attention to the areas of interest of different media outlets, writers, and reporters and match your story to these interests.

- ✔ Write (or record or film) a basic document and vary it to address the different media interests that you appeal to, making use of your multiple story angles.

- ✔ Send your release in an e-mail. We recommend writing a short introductory note and then cutting and pasting the press release into the body of the e-mail so you don't risk the possibility of your recipient being unable to open an attachment.

- ✔ If you don't receive a response to your e-mail within two days, call the press contact. Persist in following up on every item you send to the press, but stop if you hear a firm "no" or if can hear a tone of annoyance in the writer's voice.

- ✔ Keep the press fully informed about any changes in your story. Printing incorrect information makes them look bad and may hurt your chances of future coverage.

- ✔ Invite the press to make a visit to your program or orchestrate other forms of direct interaction.

- ✔ Take rejection graciously if your media contact decides not to use your story. You need to be able to go back to these people in the future.

Different media outlets require different amounts of lead time. In an ideal situation, you want to begin your efforts to reach the media four or five months in advance of that hoped-for coverage. The first two months are spent creating press releases and public service announcements and shooting photographs. Table 11-1 shows the parts of a press release.

 Many organizations create a press section on their Web sites where they post releases, background information, and images with captions. This tool allows your media contact an easy means for expanding upon the information you have sent and choosing among and downloading the photos he or she prefers for publication.

After you've done the initial legwork over the first couple of months, then you start distributing the materials:

- ✔ Most monthly magazines need to receive your press release and photographs at least two — preferably three — months in advance of publication (even earlier if they're published quarterly or bimonthly).

✔ At the same time that you're mailing to magazines, you want to send advance notice to your most important daily and weekly outlets.

✔ We recommend sending public service announcements (see the section "Putting together public service announcements" later in this chapter) two to three months prior to the time when you hope they'll be used. Although most stations have set aside time for broadcasting nonprofits' announcements, they need time to rotate through the many announcement materials they receive.

✔ Press releases to daily or weekly papers should be sent four to six weeks in advance of the event you want covered. You also may send follow-up releases approximately ten days prior to the event. You certainly want to make follow-up phone calls.

✔ Releases inviting members of the press to a press conference or to witness a special event or announcement may be sent three to ten days in advance of the event.

Table 11-1	Presenting Parts of a Press Release
Placement	*Content*
Top left of page	"For immediate release:" followed by the date you're issuing the press release. If you don't want the press to use it immediately because it contains information that will be publicly announced at a later date, note "Embargoed until . . ." and indicate the date when it can be published.
Top right of page	"For further information contact:" followed by the name, phone number, and e-mail address of a person who can answer questions about the announcement.
Centered	Succinct, clear headline that captures the essential news in your story and that an editor may be able to use directly as the story's headline.
Below headline	The story you want to tell. In the opening paragraph, cover the journalism basics of "who," "what," "where," "why," and "when." Be sure that the most important information appears early in the release in case the publication doesn't have room to print the entire story. Use a clear, direct style and short paragraphs.
	At the end of each page of your release, center the word "more" (often repeated), to tell the reader to go on to the next page. At the end of your story, center the hatch sign (#) to signal that the story is complete.

Reaching your media contacts

Each section of a newspaper and each part of a TV or radio program is made up of materials from multiple sources that are competing for time and space. You improve the odds of receiving attention in the media by providing clear, accurate, and provocative materials in time for consideration and possible use by reporters and broadcasters.

We recommend the following steps when you submit material to the media:

1. **Even if you've purchased a reputable media directory, call to confirm the most appropriate contact person for your story at the newspaper, radio station, TV station, or online outlet, and ask about the format that each wants you to use in your submission.**

   Most venues will want your press release, photographs, and recorded materials to be sent via e-mail. We recommend pasting the press release into the body of that e-mail so there's no danger of its recipient being unable to open an attachment.

2. **Submit clear and accurate written materials and labeled, good-quality photographs.**

   The media generally want photographs to be in the form of high-resolution JPEGs, which work well in print.

3. **Call to see whether your materials have been received.**

   Take this opportunity to ask whether more information, further interview contacts, a different format, or additional photography are needed.

4. **If requested, submit additional information immediately and call to confirm its receipt and clarity.**

5. **If you don't receive a clear response (either "Yes, we'll cover it" or "Sorry, I don't see the story here") to your initial release, call again in a few days.**

6. **If a member of the press comes to cover an event you've announced, provide a press packet (generally on a CD).**

   A press packet commonly contains a press release, fact sheet, background information, and photographs. It briefs the reporter about your event and makes it easy for him or her to check facts when writing a story. If a reporter is covering your event, introduce yourself and be available to answer questions or to introduce the reporter to key spokespeople, but don't be a pest. Let a reporter find his or her own story.

7. **If your situation changes and the press release is no longer accurate, immediately call in the change and, if necessary, revise and resubmit your original release.**

A sample press release (CD1103), press alert (CD1104), calendar release (CD1105), photo caption (CD1106), photo permission form (CD1107), and public service announcement (CD1108) are on the CD. They can help you understand the approaches and formats to use.

When making calls and sending e-mails to members of the press, recognize that they're busy and often working to meet deadlines. If you ask brief, clear questions that they can respond to quickly, you'll find it easy to engage them. For example, "How many photographs would you like?" is easier to answer than "What do you want a picture of?"

Getting listed in the calendar

Getting your organization's events listed in newspaper calendars and broadcast on TV and radio can be critically important to attracting a crowd. Readers, viewers, and listeners use these calendars to help decide how they're going to spend their time on, say, a Thursday night. If your event is listed clearly and accurately, you're in the running.

Larger newspapers and many other media outlets assign the preparation of calendar sections to specific editors. When you put together your media contact list, make sure you identify the calendar editors. And to improve your access to this important source of publicity, contact the calendar specialists in advance and ask for instructions about how they prefer calendar listings to be formatted and how long in advance of the event they want to receive your information.

Putting together public service announcements

Many radio and television stations allot a portion of their airtime to broadcasting public service announcements (PSAs) on behalf of nonprofit causes. Although these stations rarely give away their best viewing and listening hours to this free service, sometimes they do tack PSAs onto the end of a newscast or special program during prime time. But even an announcement played during the morning's wee hours can reach many people.

Public service announcements are brief. Most are 15, 30, or 60 seconds long. You may submit them as written text to be read by the stations' announcers, or you may submit them recorded or filmed on a CD or DVD or as an e-mailed podcast for direct broadcast. Many stations are more willing to use PSAs that are already recorded or filmed, but this isn't universally true. If you submit a prerecorded PSA, also include a print version of the text. Some stations string several announcements together in a general public announcement broadcast, and it's easier for them to work from text.

If you choose to submit a prerecorded PSA, make sure that it's of broadcast quality with excellent sound and/or images. If you're the narrator, spit out your gum! If you mumble or if the images are blurry, stations can't use it. Using the voice of a celebrity — even a local luminary — for your prerecorded PSA can be particularly effective.

The challenge to writing public service announcements is to clearly convey a lot of information in a short time. Write your message and test it against the clock. If you're rushing to finish it in time, it's probably too long. Ask someone else to read it back to you and time that person. You don't want to be the only one who can finish it in 15 seconds.

Table 11-2 summarizes an appropriate format for presenting a public service announcement to a media outlet.

Table 11-2	Presenting a Public Service Announcement
Placement	*Content*
Top left of page	"For immediate release to public service directors for use between [identify dates during which the release is timely]." Also clearly indicate the length of the release (15, 30, or 60 seconds).
Top right of page	"For further information contact:" followed by the name, phone number, and e-mail address of a person who can answer questions about the announcement.
Centered	Brief headline that both orients the reader to the subject of your story and that can become part of the reading of the release.
Below headline	The announcement in large print (sometimes all caps), double-spaced. Make sure that your release can be read within the length of time that you specify and that it flows well. If it includes names or words with unfamiliar pronunciations, spell them phonetically in parentheses next to the challenging words.

Making your own news

Even though your organization won't pay a fee to the news media to have its story appear in print, seeking media coverage can take a significant amount of your time or cost you the fees of a public relations consultant. And coverage is never assured. You may do all the right things and still not be covered in the press.

Another choice is to invest your time and energy into Internet-based tools for social marketing. You can self-publish your news in print, through e-mail announcements, as podcasts, or as short videos on your Web site. Then you can send these items to your constituents to read, view, and — if they're compelling — forward to their networks of friends and colleagues. Green for All, a nonprofit organization focused on developing new jobs in "green" industries, has been very successful with spreading its stories through self-produced, short films. One of its films has even been featured on the White House Web site!

Nonprofits also are spreading the word about their work through such social networking tools as Facebook and Twitter. You can announce events, post photos and videos, and build campaigns using these media. Check out the Wiley publications *Facebook For Dummies* by Carolyn Abram and Leah Pearlman, *Facebook Marketing For Dummies* by Paul Dunay and Richard Krueger, and *Twitter For Dummies* by Laura Fitton, Michael Gruen, and Leslie Poston. Or maybe you want an opportunity to present an opinion piece about recent news or pending legislation. You can create a blog and build a readership for it by providing well-considered opinions and building a list of readers by sending it to e-mail lists.

While these tools may take as much (or more) time than a press campaign, they have the advantage of being direct: Through them, you're speaking directly to readers and viewers and controlling the message you want to convey. That's invaluable.

Chapter 12

Creating a Home for Your Nonprofit — and Insuring It

Some nonprofits can travel light. The service they provide can be managed out of a spare bedroom or small commercial office. Others need specialized, technically sophisticated facilities.

Some nonprofits fit easily into a wide variety of locations. Others can fulfill their missions only if they're located in specific neighborhoods or geographic regions.

Some nonprofits pay nothing for their space: A church, a school, or a public agency gives them shelter. Some save money by buying or leasing property with other nonprofits. Still others pay top dollar for highly visible homes that are an important part of their identities.

Lots of options, lots of decisions. This chapter explores the ins and outs of finding a suitable home base for a nonprofit organization and of protecting the entire enterprise — furniture, fixtures, real estate, staff, volunteers, and board — against the risks of everyday life.

Finding a Place to Do Your Work

If your organization is grappling with a move to a new (or to its first) building, you're facing important decisions about how, when, and where to go. This effort is likely to have three phases:

- ✔ Planning for your needs
- ✔ Identifying possible locations
- ✔ Analyzing the feasibility of the locations you find

How much space and of what kind?

Before you go out to seek a location, make a list of your organization's specific needs. If you've ever shopped for an apartment or house, you know that some features are critically important and some are desired but not essential. Breaking down your space needs by function and then including a list of general requirements helps.

To help you anticipate and specify all your organization's facility needs, check out the list of questions to ask yourself in CD1201. On the same track, you also can refer to the Planning Guides and Glossary of Terms to be found on the Nonprofit Finance Fund Web site as well as the sample list of required spaces worksheet.

Location, location, location

Many nonprofit organizations have learned the hard way that having a beautiful new facility doesn't necessarily mean that their students, patients, or audiences will go there. We suggest that an organization conduct a simple marketing test of a location they're considering. This "test" may take the form of a written survey, interviews, or an open house/walk-through at the proposed site followed by a discussion with current constituents. Also, talk to nearby residents, merchants, and the local police; and spend time observing the site at different times of day.

Many organizations move to larger facilities when they want their programs to grow, and they discover the hard way that offering more seats, classes, or therapy sessions doesn't necessarily mean that they'll be used. Do you have clear evidence of growing demand for your services and that your organization's current physical space is inhibiting its growth? When you conduct your marketing test, you need to know whether more people will go to your new location: Reach out to both potential clients and your current followers.

Your ideal location may change over time as the neighborhood changes. Even if your organization has been based in one place for a long time, before signing a new lease, explore whether its location is still meeting its needs.

Owning, leasing, or finding something free

Stability, convenience, and cost — in addition to location — are key factors to consider when selecting your organization's home. In this section, we discuss the implications of ownership, leasing, and receiving donated space and invite you to weigh the pros and cons.

In considering your real estate choices, also consider your context. Is the real estate market changing? Are interest rates rising or falling? How well are tenants' rights protected by law? Is the building that you lease or enjoy for free likely to be sold?

The pros and cons of owning

Because of the tax benefits of private home ownership, many people assume that owning a building is best for a nonprofit organization. Although a non-profit's building can be a valuable asset, remember that a nonprofit is already exempt from paying most business taxes, so any interest it may pay on a mortgage or building loan isn't a deductible expense — it's just an expense.

Two possible advantages of building ownership are

- ✓ **Ownership stabilizes costs.** If your organization is based in a real estate market where prices are rising, purchasing a building may help to prevent steep rent increases or an untimely eviction.

- ✓ **Ownership improves the public image of your organization.** Organizations owning their own buildings appear in the public eye to be stable institutions. This perception may help them raise money.

Major disadvantages of building ownership for nonprofits can be that it increases the staff's workload and requires a continuing investment. If the organization buys a building that's larger than its needs, it may become a landlord to others and must be prepared to advertise the property, negotiate leases, and manage maintenance and repairs. Whether or not it has tenants, it becomes fully responsible for the building's care.

If your nonprofit organization buys its own building, be sure to set aside a cash reserve for building maintenance. Otherwise, if a boiler explodes or the roof leaks, you may have to suspend operations for an extended period of time to fix the problem.

Considering renting

When you rent a home for your nonprofit organization, you're taking on costs that you need to cover month after month. Often these costs increase from year to year. Rent may not be the only such expense. Here are a few things you want to understand fully before signing a lease:

- ✔ What costs are covered? Is your nonprofit responsible for all or some of the utilities?

- ✔ How long is the lease and does it include options for you to renew it at a similar rate?

- ✔ If property or other taxes increase while you're a tenant, do you pay for the increase or does the landlord?

- ✔ Which repairs are the landlord's responsibility and which ones are yours?

- ✔ Who's responsible for routine building maintenance?

- ✔ What will the landlord permit you to change about the building?

We recommend budgeting for your monthly building costs and your one-time move-in costs, and creating a facility contingency fund to cover minor repairs or occasional expenses (from tree trimming to clogged plumbing). We also recommend consulting with an attorney or with someone familiar with reviewing leases before you sign one.

Deciding whether to take a freebie if it's offered

Taking a free ride through the donation of public or private space to your nonprofit sounds wonderful, doesn't it? Indeed, it lowers your operating costs and allows you to use more of your resources for programs. But you must be willing to look a gift horse in the mouth.

A free building is worthwhile only if it's in the right location and is the right size. Doing effective work is very difficult in an inappropriate space. Ask yourself this: If the building wasn't free, would you have chosen it for your nonprofit?

Two possible disadvantages to accepting free space are

- ✔ **Inappropriate connections:** Making use of free space belonging to another public or private entity identifies your organization with the building's history and other uses.

- ✔ **Loss of control:** If someone provides something free to you, you're put in a weak bargaining position. You may not have a lease, ensuring your use of the space for a prescribed period of time. You may not feel that you can complain if building maintenance is sloppy or repairs are postponed.

Estimating costs

Organizations with what seem to be straightforward plans for moving into new facilities often overlook the true costs of making such a move. Some spaces may need to be altered to suit your organization's needs. Even when you fit right into your new offices, you encounter one-time charges such as signs, cleaning deposits, phone and Internet hookup, and fees or deposits for starting up your utilities.

Here we organize those costs into four general categories:

✔ **Moving**

- Moving van rental or moving service
- Boxes and shipping containers
- Thank-you party or recognition gifts for volunteers

✔ **Setting up services**

- Transfer of utilities (garbage, water, and power)
- Transfer of services (phone, cable, and computer lines)

✔ **Making alterations**

- Constructing new workspaces, service spaces, and shelving
- Moving electrical outlets and adding phone and computer lines
- Furniture, computer, and fixture purchases

✔ **Announcing your change**

- Public notices about your move (postcards, newsletters, press releases, Web site revisions, and e-mail announcements)
- Revising basic printed materials (brochures, stationery, and other publications)
- Signs on your new location
- Open house or party for constituents

The most important *things* for you to move are your constituents. You want to make a thoughtful, sustained effort to invite them into your new facility.

We've included links to the Nonprofit Finance Fund's helpful Moving Guide and Moving Schedule in the Web links on the CD — CD1205.

Taking on a capital project

What if no existing building suits your organization's needs? You may just need to move some walls and expand the bathrooms; or you may be in for a major effort to substantially renovate a space or construct a new building. If you're one of these brave and hardy types, you want to read this part of the chapter along with Chapter 18, which addresses planning and raising money for building projects in greater detail.

Even a small organization with the right board and campaign leadership can manage a successful capital campaign if its expectations are reasonable. So can organizations whose projects are happening at the right place and at the right time — such as those organizations qualifying for redevelopment agency funds or for low-interest bank loans for community development.

To determine whether your organization can manage a capital campaign, you should ask yourself some serious questions, including the following:

✔ What will the project cost? Although you can't design an accurate budget until you have approved architectural drawings and contractor bids, an architect or contractor who's friendly to your organization should be willing to look at the space and offer rough cost estimates.

✔ Are your board members in a position to contribute to a capital campaign above and beyond their usual annual gifts to your organization?

✔ Do public or foundation resources in your region support capital projects? Would they be likely contributors? (Include in this inquiry low-interest loans for nonprofits.)

✔ Do you have staff knowledge and time to contribute to this effort?

We include several items on the CD that should help you think through a possible capital project carefully. CD1202, "Planned Change and Facilities" and CD1203, "Organization Capacity Worksheet," can help you assess your organization's readiness, while CD1204, "Your Project's Relative Size," illustrates the impact a capital project is likely to have on your organization.

You can find leads to community loan and development funds for nonprofits on two helpful Web sites: www.communitycapital.org (focused more on investors than those seeking help, but still rich with information) and www.socialinvest.org.

Having examined these preliminary questions, organizations that are considering capital campaigns often go through a process called a *feasibility study* — research most often led by a consultant who interviews people who support the organization and other generous donors in their communities whose grants and gifts are essential to its success. Through these interviews, the consultant estimates how much the organization is likely to raise with a capital campaign. You find more about this practice in Chapter 18.

The costs of renovating a building are likely to increase (at a rate of some 10 percent per year), and major donors may pledge contributions but wait a year or longer before sending a check. So, if reasonable interest rates are available, borrowing money to avoid delays and complete construction can help contain costs while you're conducting a capital campaign and starting construction. In some areas, local government, foundations, community economic development corporations, or banks may consider awarding low-interest loans as an important form of philanthropy.

As new technology changes the needs of working spaces, and building code requirements become more stringent, renovation of existing buildings may be very costly. Sometimes building a brand-new facility to suit your nonprofit's needs may be your cheaper and more-efficient choice.

Insuring against What Can Go Wrong

Many people who start nonprofits hope to improve conditions in the world, and they conduct their work with modest resources. They're not naïve, but they may have little time to dwell on the things that possibly can go wrong. (Okay, okay, we're making a generalization. The nonprofit arena has its share of serious worriers too.)

But things can go wrong. That's why nonprofits need insurance like everyone else. For the eternal optimists and worriers alike, we highly recommend practicing risk management and finding a good insurance broker who can help you make appropriate choices of insurance and find the most reasonable rates.

Managing your risks

Risk management means identifying and analyzing the risks your organization faces in carrying out its daily business. If you're a smart manager, you eliminate as many of these risks as possible. You're financially rewarded for pursuing this course: The more risks you can eliminate, the lower your insurance premiums are.

Here's a simple example to illustrate risk management: The sidewalk in front of the entrance to your office is beginning to crack in two places. The concrete is uneven and may cause someone to trip and fall. Repairing the sidewalk is better than risking the chances of injury to a visitor and the consequent lawsuit, payments, and bad publicity that may result.

Adding smoke alarms, sprinkler systems, and emergency lighting are other ways to practice risk management. Those safety features are wise investments and will probably lower your property insurance. Although no one can think of everything that may go wrong, try to eliminate as many risks as possible. Insurance agents and brokers can be helpful in this exercise. You can find more information about risk management at the Nonprofit Risk Management Center (www.nonprofitrisk.org).

You must be honest on insurance applications, fully stating your agency's risks. If falsehoods are uncovered, your coverage doesn't protect you.

Determining your insurance needs

A nonprofit's insurance needs vary according to the following:

- ✔ Whether it has employees
- ✔ Whether it makes use of volunteers
- ✔ Whether it has direct contact with clients, students, patients, or audiences and the nature of that direct contact
- ✔ Whether it offers services within its own (or a rented) piece of property

Providing health insurance

Beyond the employee benefits required by law, you'll want to provide health coverage for your employees if possible so they can afford medical attention if they're sick or injured. Offering this benefit also helps you recruit better-qualified employees.

In most cases, an organization can secure group health insurance for its employees at a more reasonable cost than what employees would have to pay if they bought it on their own. Generally, health insurance becomes more affordable as your organization grows and the group for which you're buying it becomes larger.

Insuring against workplace injuries

If an employee is injured in the course of performing duties for your non-profit, workers' compensation insurance covers the cost of medical treatment and — in some cases — the cost of retraining the employee for a different profession. The cost of your workers' compensation insurance is calculated according to the number of employees you have, the number of hours they spend on the job, and the nature of the work they do. Rates for office clerks are considerably lower than rates for lion tamers and trapeze artists.

In most states, workers' compensation insurance is required by law. Therefore, as a nonprofit manager, you don't have a choice about whether to buy it. Instead, you simply make the choice to attend to doing it correctly. As you plan, don't forget to consider the following:

✔ **Do you use docents or other consistent volunteers?** We highly recommend including them in your workers' compensation insurance coverage. We've witnessed two instances in which volunteers were seriously hurt in the course of assisting nonprofit organizations but weren't covered by workers' compensation insurance. The results were nearly catastrophic for the agencies.

✔ **If your organization's staff size or the nature of the work your employees do changes during the course of the year, contact your workers' compensation insurance carrier and change your coverage accordingly.** Don't forget to make this change in coverage if you make temporary changes in the nature of your employees' work. For example, do you conduct an annual fundraising event for which employees are working on ladders, stringing lights and garlands? If you plan ahead to change the definition of the type of work they perform, you can be confident that they're covered.

Workers' compensation insurance is a specialized field of law. If you encounter a legal problem about your coverage, seek assistance from an attorney with workers' compensation expertise.

Some nonprofit organizations require volunteers to sign waivers that release the nonprofits from responsibility for insuring them. However, waivers may not stand up in a court of law.

Purchasing liability insurance

Someone carelessly stretches an electrical cord across a hallway, and a client trips and falls. A shingle falls from the roof and hits a visitor on the head. Liability insurance is based on the oops and ouches of daily life and human error. No matter how minor it may seem, if you make a mistake while performing your organization's duties and someone is injured as a result, you can be sued.

By purchasing liability insurance, you have access to a source of revenue for settling a lawsuit if someone sues you for this kind of mistake. Your insurance company also may provide legal defense, if it's needed. Most businesses purchase liability insurance as a matter of course. You may get by without it for a time, but you may be required to get it if you meet any of the following conditions:

> ✔ You accept a contract or grant from a government source.
>
> ✔ You rent offices or other facilities.
>
> ✔ You seek a city or county permit to use public property.
>
> ✔ You seek an operating or construction permit.

You need to purchase specialized kinds of liability insurance if your organization has significant direct client contact that involves a potential risk. Health clinics and therapy programs need such insurance to protect them if a client is hurt or handled inappropriately. So do programs offering activities with possible physical dangers, such as rock climbing, sail boating, or horseback riding.

If your organization occasionally produces events or conducts work in locations other than its central office or building, check to make sure that you're covered for these off-site events. You may want to purchase a rider to your regular liability insurance policy to cover such situations.

Protecting directors and officers from lawsuits

Although corporate laws vary by state and nation, in most contexts, the personal assets of directors and officers of nonprofit organizations are protected from legal proceedings against those nonprofits if the directors are providing reasonable oversight of the organizations. Nevertheless, just to make sure, you can purchase directors' and officers' liability insurance.

What is "reasonable" oversight? Board members usually are protected if they attend meetings, ask questions, and keep well-informed about the organization — in other words, if they're doing a reasonably good job being board members. If they're not doing their jobs, they may be considered personally negligent and become vulnerable.

Board members' personal assets also can be in jeopardy if the nonprofit organization isn't paying its federal employee taxes. However, even in this dire situation, if the nonprofit has contacted the Internal Revenue Service and worked out a payment plan, board members are unlikely to be affected.

So why would you want to pay for directors' and officers' insurance? The biggest advantage is that it covers the cost of your organization's legal defense against lawsuits. It also may be reassuring to board members and potential board members. Some people refuse to serve on a board if the organization doesn't have directors' and officers' insurance.

Here are some examples of situations in which insurance is highly recommended:

✔ Your organization has to lay off or fire employees. The most common type of lawsuit brought against nonprofit organizations is for "wrongful discharge."

✔ Your organization's work is controversial, making the organization a potential target for lawsuits.

✔ Your organization is a hospital, health clinic, or another kind of entity that — because of the intense, professional service it provides — is more liable to malpractice and other kinds of liability lawsuits.

✔ Your organization has weathered a severe financial crisis. In attracting new board members, you want to firmly reassure them that this financial crisis won't come back to haunt them personally.

✔ Your organization has grown and thrived. It has a large endowment and cash reserves, increasing the likelihood of being a target for lawsuits.

✔ You have the good fortune to have wealthy and influential board members. Although their assets should be protected if they're attentive board members, they're natural targets for nuisance lawsuits.

Protecting property and vehicles

If you own a home and your own car, you undoubtedly value those possessions enough to insure them in case of damage, loss, or theft. You need to protect your nonprofit's building and vehicles in the same way. Suppose that the big bad wolf comes by and huffs and puffs and blows your nonprofit down. Say that a tornado swoops past, taking with it more than you and your little dog Toto. You need property insurance, including — if you're lucky enough to find it — coverage against malicious animals and tornadoes.

The cost of your property insurance varies according to the size and value of your property and how the buildings are constructed. In many places, insuring a house of straw is more expensive than insuring a house of bricks. A terrible irony is that the disaster that you're most likely to face is the one for which your insurance will be most expensive. Sometimes you simply can't get insurance for your likeliest disaster.

Ideally, you want your property insurance to cover your organization for damage repairs — both to the building and its holdings — and provide business interruption insurance covering your losses of income if you're forced by a disaster to be closed for a period of time. In some instances, you won't be able to find property insurance that includes coverage for a likely disaster, so you'll have to purchase a separate policy for protection from that potential crisis or do without that protection. Day-to-day drips and clogs, creaks, and rips are both more likely to happen and more affordable to cover with property insurance. And the higher the deductible, the lower the cost of your insurance.

Most property insurance policies cover the contents of a facility in addition to the building itself. Your policy may place a limit on the amount it pays toward replacing those contents if something goes wrong. Make sure that the coverage is adequate to cover the replacement cost of your organization's furniture, fixtures, and equipment.

If your organization owns its building and has tenants, you need a comprehensive and flexible property insurance policy. Insist that your tenants have their own insurance. You can include this condition in the terms of their leases.

Your organization may own or dream of owning a company car, van, bus, truck, or other vehicle. So, of course, vehicle insurance is necessary. If you can't limit the use of this vehicle to one or two drivers, such insurance may be prohibitively expensive.

Maybe your organization doesn't own a building or vehicle. You still need insurance that protects your property. Buy theft insurance to protect your equipment and furniture, and renters' insurance to cover the cost of repairing accidental damage to the property caused by you or others at your organization.

Getting even deeper into insurance

Health, property, and liability insurance are the primary types of insurance that an organization needs to consider, but they're by no means the only types. Here are a few more:

- ✔ **Employee dishonesty insurance or fidelity bonds:** Insurance of this type protects the organization against employee theft or embezzlement.

- ✔ **Umbrella insurance:** This policy covers some types of extraordinary losses. For example, if you have a general liability policy that pays for losses up to $500,000, you may want to get an umbrella policy that kicks in if a settlement is higher than $500,000. Umbrella policies also set an upper limit on coverage but tend to be less expensive than basic liability policies.

- ✔ **Long-term disability insurance:** Although the cost may be prohibitive for small organizations, offering long-term disability insurance is an excellent employee benefit.

Part III

Successful Fundraising

The 5th Wave   By Rich Tennant

"I know you're passionate about your fundraising, but I wish you wouldn't refer to my family as your donor-in-laws."

In this part . . .

We lead you into the realm of grants and annual fund drives, E-fundraising, galas, and golf tournaments, revealing the mindset of people who receive your requests for funds, including charitable foundations, private corporations, individuals, and the government. And we help you to understand the language of fundraising. In the event a fund drive or building project is part of your plans, we give special attention to capital campaigns.

Chapter 13

Crafting a Fundraising Plan

*I*f an organization is going to provide a public service, it needs money. Plain and simple. It may be run by volunteers and need just a little money, or it may need lots of money to pay for employees, office space, and formal research. If it's a brand-spanking-new organization, it needs start-up money, or what's called *seed funding*.

Any nonprofit — whatever its purpose — grows out of someone's idea, someone's passion (maybe yours!) to make the world better. Raising money is inviting others to share in that belief and passion.

Different kinds of causes appeal to different people or institutions. Your organization may get most of its money from the government, grantmaking foundations, businesses, or individuals. Successful fundraising is based on a plan, and a good plan is based on understanding an organization's likeliest sources of funding. A good plan is also balanced. No organization should put all its eggs in one basket or imagine its entire omelet coming from one chicken.

In this chapter, we show you how to create a plan for gathering your funding eggs from a number of nests. If your organization is new, we give some ideas for where to begin.

Recognizing Who Raises Funds

Federal tax codes designate more than a dozen different kinds of nonprofit organizations (which we discuss in Chapter 2). This book focuses on those that are authorized under section 501(c)(3) of that tax code and that qualify as public charities. Such nonprofits are exempt from paying some kinds of taxes, and their donors can take tax deductions for making contributions to them. Because many individual donors, foundations, and corporate foundations are motivated, in part, by that tax deduction, this chapter and the fundraising chapters that follow are written about 501(c)(3) nonprofit organizations with public charity status.

Churches and very small organizations (if their annual gross receipts are less than $5,000) that are performing a public service can receive contributions that are tax-deductible to their donors even though they may not have applied for and received 501(c)(3) status from the Internal Revenue Service (IRS).

Most states require charities to file registration forms before engaging in fundraising solicitations. Thirty-six states and the District of Columbia accept the Unified Registration Statement (www.multistatefiling.org); others have their own forms. Only a handful of states don't regulate charitable fundraising. See CD0402 to link to the state offices that regulate nonprofits.

Naming Your Sources of Funds

Before plunging ahead, we need to introduce some of the terms that we use in this chapter to describe the different kinds of contributions an organization may seek. Here are some of the important terms:

- **Grants:** *Grants* are formal contributions made to an organization by foundations, corporations, or government agencies, often to help the nonprofit address defined goals or manage specific programs. Some grants, which are called *project* or *program grants,* are for trying out new ideas or enhancing existing programs. Others, called *general operating grants,* support the overall work of an organization.

- **Corporate contributions:** Some corporations create their own foundations (that award grants) and some award contributions directly through corporate giving programs — most often out of their public affairs, community relations, or marketing departments. Many corporations give *in-kind gifts* — contributions of goods and services — rather than or in addition to cash contributions.

✓ **Individual contributions:** Gifts to organizations from private individuals represent the largest portion of private money given to nonprofit organizations. Individual donors may support specific activities or the nonprofit's general costs. You may seek these contributions through the mail, over the phone, through your Web site, in face-to-face visits, or at special events. Common types of individual contributions include the following:

- **Annual gifts:** A contribution written once a year to a charity is, appropriately enough, called an *annual gift.* The consistency of such gifts makes them of great value to the recipient.

- **Major gifts:** As suggested in the name, a *major gift* is a large amount of money. For some organizations, a large gift may be $100, and for others it may be $50,000.

- **Memberships:** Similar to an annual gift in some ways, a *membership* is a contribution made once per year. The difference is that you often make a membership gift in exchange for some benefit or service from the nonprofit, such as a discount on tickets or a free tote bag. Some nonprofits are structured so that their members play a role in their governance, but that's a different, more formal relationship than calling a contributor a member because she paid to join. (See Chapter 4 for details on having members in your corporation.)

  If a donor contributes $75 or more to your organization in exchange for a gift or service, your nonprofit must inform that donor in writing about the value of the gift or service she received and the portion of her contribution that she can claim as a federal income tax deduction. Additionally, your nonprofit must acknowledge in writing to a donor any gift of $250 or more.

- **Planned giving/bequests:** These gifts are contributions that donors make to nonprofit organizations through their wills or other legal documents specifying what happens to their money and property after they die. Generally, the donor works with a trust officer at a bank or law firm to design her planned giving. Large organizations often have staff who specialize in providing donors with technical assistance in this area.

- **Special events:** From marathons to chicken dinners to celebrity concerts, fundraising events generate income that supports organizations. Contributors can deduct from their taxes the portion of any event ticket that's above and beyond the cost of producing the event. Individuals, corporations, and small businesses are the likeliest supporters of special events. We talk about special events at greater length in Chapter 15.

Analyzing Your Potential

Different approaches to raising funds work best for different kinds of organizations. When you make a fundraising plan, you have to be both ambitious about your goals and realistic about what's likely to work for you. As you try to figure out how much money you can glean from each possible funding source, answer the following questions:

✔ **How far do your services reach?** Do lots of people understand, care about, and benefit from your organization's cause? Do you focus on a small geographic area or work at a national or international scale? The answer to this question tells you whether your nonprofit should be casting its net close to home or all over the country or world.

✔ **Are you one of a kind?** If you're unique, you may have a more difficult time explaining to potential donors who you are and what you do. But you may have an advantage when you appeal to foundations that like *model programs* — distinctive efforts that may inform of work others are doing in the same field.

✔ **How popular is your cause?** One year everyone is talking about healthcare, another year public education, and still another year climate change or disaster relief. Regardless of what's happening in the world, the focus of your organization's work will go through times of gaining and losing media attention and broad-based donor support.

✔ **Does your cause elicit strong feelings?** Even if it isn't a cause that's backed by large numbers of people, a hot topic that a small number of people strongly believe in can attract major gifts. A limitation faced by organizations that focus on potentially controversial topics — such as abortion, use of pesticides, or incarceration of juveniles — is that corporations and businesses may be uncomfortable with having their names associated with the cause.

✔ **How well-known and highly regarded are your leaders?** Most people feel better about supporting an organization if they believe in its leaders. If an agency is conducting medical research and the doctors with whom it's working are well regarded, widely published, and nationally known, it may be in a stronger position to secure government grants or contracts. Your organization's leaders are equally important in private fundraising.

✔ **How well-known is your organization?** If your organization is a theater group, do critics frequently review its performances? If it's dedicated to helping young mothers, do news stories often feature its services? Or is it the type of agency that works quietly behind the scenes? If it's the behind-the-scenes type, it may be wise to focus on funding sources that know your organization's field well and understand the quality of its work and the key role that it plays.

✔ **Who do you know?** Your nonprofit's contacts are important to its ability to raise money, especially when seeking funds from individuals. Knowing somebody who may write a big check to an organization is great, but knowing a lot of people who may write small checks is just as good.

✔ **What can you give back to a donor?** Many donors appreciate when they benefit from their gifts to you, so look at what your nonprofit can provide. Maybe your organization produces sumptuous musical concerts and can offer contributors the best seats in the house, print their names in the programs, and give them special access. Maybe your organization is based in an attractive building where a corporate donor's banner can be displayed.

Individuals have a wide variety of preferences when it comes to receiving personal recognition for gifts. Some want to give anonymously. Others want to have buildings named after them (sometimes referred to as the *edifice complex*). Corporations (particularly when they give directly out of their marketing budgets) may consider their contributions to be cause-related marketing, so they may want their involvement to be visible to the public.

✔ **Do you have the money you need to cover fundraising costs?** Special events and *direct mail* (fundraising letters sent to large numbers of people) are expensive forms of fundraising. Grant writing takes time, but its cost is relatively low.

✔ **Do you have expertise?** Do staff members, board members, or volunteers have experience with raising money? If not, can your organization afford to hire expert help? Trained experts may be particularly important in the area of planned giving (seeking bequests) because they know about the legal issues and estate taxes. Working with an expert also may be a good idea if you're undertaking direct mail fundraising, telemarketing, and special events. Professional grant writers may help you identify foundations that you haven't considered in the past, or they may be able to strengthen your proposals.

Determine whether your state or county requires registration for participating in charitable solicitation. If you hire an outside consultant to fundraise, both your organization and that consultant may need to register. To find the rules for your state, refer to CD0402 for links to state agencies that regulate nonprofits.

If a staff member is undergoing training in a new area of fundraising, a board member also should try to take the class. This step not only ensures that the knowledge stays with the organization if the staff member leaves, but it also builds a greater understanding of development and commitment to it within the board.

✔ **How does this year's fundraising climate compare to last year's?** Apart from the value and importance of your wonderful organization, donors give money according to their abilities, and those abilities change with the times. Corporate mergers, changing foundation guidelines, natural disasters, and downturns in the economy all can affect how much money your organization can raise. Do you have good reason to believe that your donors are able or willing to give as much or more to you in the coming year as they gave in the past?

Drafting a Fundraising Strategy

Making a fundraising plan is a lot easier when you have a guide to follow. We recommend a process that follows two stages. In the first stage, you brainstorm and then refine your list of ideas, creating a fundraising strategy that defines reasonable goals. In the second stage, you identify the specific activities to address those goals, set a schedule, decide who will do the work, and make sure that you have the tools you need to succeed. This section takes you through the steps necessary for creating such a fundraising strategy.

Create a list of prospects

If your organization is brand-new, brainstorm with your founding board members the names of people and organizations they know who may support your cause. If your organization has been around for a while, begin by listing its previous contributors. Annotate your list by identifying which supporters are likely to support it again. Then stretch your thinking to consider new prospects — people who know you or who support other causes that are related to yours.

After you begin this effort of generating names and ideas, you'll begin to notice prospects all around you. A good sleuth is ever vigilant, collecting names from newspaper stories, athletic event programs, public television credits, donor display walls in buildings, and related organizations' Web sites. You want to make sleuthing a regular habit!

This kind of brainstorming is best for identifying possible individual donors, but don't restrict your thinking at this stage. Go ahead and name all the prospects you've observed and thought of:

- ✔ The foundations and government programs that fund other organizations like yours
- ✔ The corporations where your board members work or make products that are identified with your cause
- ✔ The neighbors, colleagues, and friends you could persuade

Refine your prospect list

Professional fundraisers will tell you that the three keys to raising money are research, research, and research. After you identify specific foundations, corporations, and government agencies on your list, you want to check on their current guidelines and giving priorities. Approximately 13,000 foundations have Web sites that can help you with that task; you can find many more of them by subscribing to The Foundation Center's online directory (visit foundationcenter.org for more details). You also can search for federal government agencies and programs on the Catalog of Federal Domestic Assistance Web site (www.cfda.gov) and at Grants.gov. See Chapter 16 for more information about conducting foundation research.

As you conduct your search, you're likely to uncover other prospects that you didn't think of when brainstorming, and you also may eliminate many that you discover are inappropriate.

Go back through your list of individual donor prospects with board members, volunteers, and trusted associates. Note who knows whom. Try to discover as much as you can about them from media sources, the Internet, and people who know them. Based on their apparent interest in your organization's cause, whether someone you know can contact them personally, and their records for giving to other causes, mark which of your prospects seem to be highly likely, somewhat likely, and not very likely to support your efforts.

Fill in the numbers

Identifying names of possible donors is just the beginning of the puzzle. You also need to estimate the amounts your donor prospects may give. For this estimate, you have to continue to be a sleuth. For example, you may find clues by tracking down the approximate amounts of their contributions to other organizations.

When researching your foundation prospects, if any give grants of $10,000 or more and if you subscribe, you can look them up in the "Grants" section of the Foundation Directory Online (fconline.foundationcenter.org) and see what the foundations have given to similar projects. You can find grant lists for foundations that award smaller amounts by downloading their IRS Form 990 tax reports from the Foundation Center (foundationcenter.org) or GuideStar (www.guidestar.org) Web sites.

Estimating these figures requires research in each of your categories for types of donors. They're also based on overall goals that you set. These goals probably include attracting new donors, sustaining many of the contributors your organization has had in the past, convincing some donors to increase their gifts, and expanding your types of sources.

If your organization is new, estimating how much you'll receive in donations is challenging, and we recommend that you be conservative. Often we look at the prospect list we've created and set goals for the contributions we intend to secure from our different categories: highly likely (maybe one-half will give), somewhat likely (maybe one-fifth will give), and not very likely (don't count on anything and maybe you'll be pleasantly surprised). Setting these donation numbers gets easier in subsequent years. However, donors' interests and circumstances change, so never assume consistency.

Securing funds to save sea creatures

For years, a prominent North American organization has had the mission of rescuing injured marine mammals. Well-regarded scientists manage the organization, and it has received international awards for its contributions to animal welfare and the environment. Recent news stories have drawn public attention to the effect of pollution in the oceans and recreational boating that endanger animals. The organization maintains several facilities where animals can recover before being released back into the ocean, and school groups visit these sites. Staff members do most of the organization's fundraising. It has put aside some money to work with consultants.

The fundraising plan for this organization may include the following:

✔ Government grants for protection of coastal watershed areas, preservation of endangered species, and research

✔ National foundation grants for publication of research that may assist similar centers in other parts of the United States

✔ Grants from local foundations and corporations to go toward internships for teenagers

who are thinking about careers in marine biology, school field trips, a summer institute for local teachers who want new ideas about how to teach biology and ecology to their classes, and building new tanks and facilities to care for rescued animals

✔ Personal visits to high-profile individual donors conducted by the well-known scientists leading its staff

✔ Personalized fundraising letters to families who have visited its facilities

✔ Fundraising letters addressed to individuals and including photographs of rescued animals and dramatic stories about how they were saved (These letters may be mailed to people who live along the coastal area that the organization serves, to those people who give to other animal rescue causes, or to people who subscribe to science and wildlife magazines. Expert consultants probably will design this campaign, test sample letters, and choose the most appropriate mailing lists.)

Getting Down to Business: Moving from Strategy to Action Plan

A good fundraising plan fills in the practical details that move it from being a list of goals and contacts to being a road map for your fundraising's direction. These three steps help you incorporate the details:

1. **Assign tasks, gather tools, and make a calendar.**

   For each of the revenue areas in your plan (government, foundations, corporations, or individuals), indicate who's going to work on raising the money, how many prospective sources you need, and which tools you need to meet your goals (such as fundraising letters, brochures, or membership cards). Then outline a general time frame for how long it will take and research specific deadlines for government, foundation, and corporate grants.

   Before taking action based on your plan, take a second look at it. Is the plan piling too much work onto one person? Are all the major deadlines falling in February? If so, consider rescheduling and reassigning work to adjust and balance these pressures.

2. **Figure out the cost of achieving each fundraising goal.**

   Many people forget that it costs money to raise money. To keep track of those expenses, it's a good idea to estimate costs and create a fundraising cash flow outline that shows when you need upfront money and when you can expect to secure income from your efforts. Look back at your goals and identify the list of tools you need to meet them. Maybe you need to print fundraising brochures, photocopy newspaper clippings for a grant proposal, or buy the fixings to make pancake batter.

3. **Put the fruits of your labor together in one document, and you have your funding plan!**

   Your finished plan likely will be made up of the following elements:

   - Sources sought and fundraising goals (For example: foundation grants, $75,000, and special event revenues, $2,200.)

   - Prospects identified (both current and prospective contributors), along with amounts they may be expected to give

   - The number of prospects you need to achieve your goals in each category

   - List of who's responsible for making particular contacts or contributing other services to raising the funds

   - Estimated costs of pursuing the contributions in each category

   - Timeline and cash flow projection

Many agencies create an optimum fundraising plan and a bare-bones fundraising plan — one based on their hopes and one based on what they must secure to survive. During the course of the year, they rebalance and adjust their plans.

The CD accompanying this book includes two sample fundraising plans (CD1303 and CD1304) and two sample fundraising budgets (CD1305 and CD1306). You'll find one set for a small school music organization and another for a slightly larger neighborhood park improvement organization.

Budgeting for Fundraising

We've said before that raising money costs money. And no organization receives every grant or gift that it seeks. So it needs to be sure upfront that it can afford its potential fundraising costs and that the costs are appropriate in relationship to the possible return for the nonprofit. Fundraising costs should be a modest part of an organization's budget. The costs will be higher when that organization is starting up or when it's launching a major new fundraising effort and lower when its systems have been tested. Recruiting a new donor almost always costs more than securing a second gift from a past supporter.

From the beginning, a nonprofit needs a system allowing it to keep timely records on all its donors. This system may be a handwritten card file or a complex electronic database. This type of system is important because nonprofits need to remember when they receive grants, how much money they receive, when reports are due, and what kind of reporting is required.

Nonprofits also need to keep information up-to-date about individual donors: who in the organization knows or knew them, how and why they gave their gifts, and whether any special recognition or invitations were promised to them when they contributed. Because nonprofits hope to talk to or keep in touch with these people over time, recording their spouse and children's names, their interests, their business affiliations, and any other pertinent personal information is important.

So the first investment in fundraising may be to acquire a recordkeeping system and donor management software. You also may have to budget for the time it takes to keep the system up-to-date. Current information about fundraising and accounting software can be found on the TechSoup (www. techsoup.org) and Idealware Web sites (www.idealware.org). Here are a couple software options:

✔ eBase (`www.ebase.org`) is a good, inexpensive option. This program runs on FileMaker Pro, but you don't need FileMaker unless you want to customize eBase.

✔ Salesforce.com (`www.salesforce.com`) offers a high-end product for free to nonprofits with up to ten users.

✔ eTapestry (`www.etapestry.com`) offers free services for organizations that have up to 500 contacts in their databases. However, keep in mind that eTapestry costs do rise as the number of records in your system grows past 500.

✔ GiftWorks (`www.missionresearch.com`) is a reasonably priced software option with a reputation for being easy to use.

Specialized fundraising software is terrific, but be careful as you choose your program, because it can be quite costly.

Some other fundraising activities and their costs include the following:

✔ **Grants and contracts:** Most of the cost of securing grants and contracts are labor costs for planning and writing the grant proposal. Some proposals may require CDs or DVDs that illustrate your past work, which cost additional money. If you need numerous copies, that too is an expense, as is shipping the proposal. Sometimes you may want to travel to meet in person with the agency awarding the money, and if that foundation is far from your location, you're looking at another expense. As more foundations are creating electronic application systems, you'll save money on postage and copying, but you may need to invest in upgrading your computer systems.

Nonprofits need to pay attention to a grantmaker's requirements for reporting the results of a project and make sure they can afford to complete the report. Some grants require collection and analysis of extensive data. Some require audited financial statements.

✔ **Individual contributions:** Costs related to securing individual contributions stem from time spent by staff or volunteers compiling lists of possible donors, conducting research about those donors, and developing a script for soliciting a gift.

Solicitation letters are a common tool for reaching individual donors. Such letters can be a relatively costly form of fundraising unless you target a small mailing to your best prospects. Some organizations hire companies to handle telephone solicitation campaigns. Be cautious if you take this step: Some of these companies charge a very high percentage of the money raised in exchange for providing this service. Others are reputable and valued by the nonprofits they serve. Another expense that may serve your organization well is adding capacity to your Web site so that donors can make gifts electronically.

✔ **Special events:** Special events can be a great way to introduce new people to your organization, but producing such events can be one of the most expensive ways to raise funds. Spending 50 or 60 percent of the income from an event to pay for costs is common. Printing, advertising, food, and entertainment all cost money. Also, special events are labor intensive. An agency wants to have an experienced volunteer group or detail-oriented staff to work on special events.

✔ **Planned giving:** If a nonprofit isn't familiar with tax laws regarding wills and estates, it should employ or hire on contract (or attract as a board member) a planned giving expert. Bringing this person on board can be expensive in the short term, but doing so can yield important long-term support for the agency.

Planned giving works best for organizations that have been around for a long time and show good prospects for continuing. Universities, museums, and churches come to mind. Small, new groups have a difficult time attracting bequests.

Planting the Seeds for a New Organization

One tried-and-true rule of fundraising is that people give money to people they know. They also give money to causes they care about. However, making a contribution is an expression of trust. That means the likeliest contributors to a new nonprofit organization are people and agencies that know and admire its founders and their work.

Hitting up people you know

We know of people who have launched their organizations with major grants from a government agency or a large, national foundation, but many more of them start close to home with gifts from their founders, their founding board members, and from the people who know them. They then build out from that inner circle of relationships, gradually creating networks of associations with the friends, family members, and business associates of their initial contributors.

We asked some people who founded organizations how and when they got their first sources of income. One invited 20 people to her house and, after a convincing pitch and some good wine, got most of them to write checks. Another started a youth mentoring program out of his dorm room when he was a college student. He talked his campus into paying him a work-study stipend to begin his project, and then he charged his volunteer mentors modest membership fees to cover basic costs. Another noticed a city department's neglect of small city parks after budget cutbacks and, by knocking on local politicians' doors, secured a city grant to involve volunteers in park cleanup days.

Many organizations start up with contributions from individuals, in part because individuals often make up their minds more quickly than businesses or foundations.

Branching out with special events

Although special events are one of the more expensive ways of raising money, you probably can see real advantages to including them in the fundraising plan for a new organization. Events create a way to inform multiple people about your organization at the same time. The best part is that they then begin to spread the word about your good work. And remember that events don't have to be elaborate. A gathering of a dozen people can be a good start.

Considering government grants

Government grants and contracts may provide significant underpinnings for a new effort, but they come with these three distinct disadvantages for new non-profit organizations:

✔ **In general they take longer to secure.** The review and approval process may be slow, and many government agencies have one annual deadline.

✔ **They often require grantees to comply with rules and regulations regarding permits, board policies, hiring practices, and financial reporting.** Although their rules may be good rules, when you're just starting out, your organization may still be working out its systems and policies.

✔ **They sometimes require their funded organizations to spend money upfront and then submit invoices in order to be reimbursed for an agreed-upon amount of money.** If you have few sources of income, you may not have available funds for this upfront spending.

If your organization is applying to the federal government, you must first register with Grants.gov (`www.grants.gov`). This registration ordinarily takes three to five days, but it is a good idea to plan on two weeks for completing it in case questions arise about your organization.

Approaching foundations

When approaching foundations, you may think that you're at a disadvantage because your project doesn't have a track record. On the contrary, some foundations specifically like to support start-up projects and organizations. If your agency is new, when you're using *The Foundation Directory* (either the book, which is available in many libraries, or the online service, which is available through subscription), check the "types of support" listings to see whether the foundation awards *seed funding,* which is specific encouragement to new activities. If the foundation makes grants in your field of interest and geographic area, it may be a good prospect for helping you launch your organization. You can find more information about conducting foundation research in Chapter 16.

Chapter 14

Raising Money from Individuals

*E*veryone has had some experience with asking for money. Maybe you sold cookies for a scout troop when you were a child. Maybe you asked neighbors to sponsor you in a summer read-a-thon for your school library. Maybe you once had to call Mom and Dad when you were stranded at a bus station in Toledo and couldn't get home for Thanksgiving.

These moments can be awkward, but asking for money for yourself and asking for money for an organization you believe in are very different. Organizational fundraising can feel good because it helps you to do something important for a cause you care deeply about. The hard part is finding the right words to say, the means for conveying those words, and the audience who's receptive to those words.

Responding to the right cause, the right message, and the right person, individual donors give to many kinds of organizations. In fact, they represent the largest portion of private contributions in the United States. This chapter shows you how to flex your own fundraising muscles and convince individual donors to give to your organization.

Often when people think of raising large amounts of money for organizations, they think of securing major grants from foundations or sponsorships from corporations. But we recommend that your nonprofit also include individual giving as a part of its fundraising plans. In total, individuals give more to non-profits than foundations or corporations, and most individuals allow you to use the funds contributed for whatever your greatest needs may be. That kind of flexibility adds considerable value to a contribution — even to a contribution of $20.

Knowing Why People Give and Asking Accordingly

The key rule of fundraising is "If you don't ask, you won't get." Taking the step of asking is critical, but so is knowing how to ask. According to marketing experts who study motivations for doing just about everything, people contribute to nonprofit organizations because they want to

- Feel generous
- Change the world
- Exercise compassion
- Have a sense of belonging to a group
- Feel a sense of well-being, of safety
- Be recognized

By understanding these underlying donor motivations, you can phrase your request in the most effective way. Appeals to new donors often ask them to "join" or "become part of" a movement or cause in order to touch upon the desire for belonging. Appeals also call upon donors' compassion and idealism, and they commonly link the needs of particular constituents served by a nonprofit to the well-being and security of an entire community. That's making the most of asking.

Registering to solicit donations

Many states and some local jurisdictions require organizations that solicit charitable contributions to file registration forms before soliciting. This registration is meant to protect the public from being solicited on behalf of illegitimate causes. The regulations differ from state to state. Typically, the rules don't apply unless the nonprofit raises more than a minimum annual amount. Check with your state's attorney general's office to be sure that your nonprofit is in compliance with all laws. If you are raising funds in states other than where you are based, you may also need to register with their attorney general's offices. It's especially important to check local laws when thinking about raising money through bingo games and raffles. Laws regulating these activities often differ from county to county and city to city.

When you find yourself hesitating to ask someone for a contribution, keep in mind that you're not begging, you're offering them an opportunity to be part of something worthwhile. Giving your organization a gift can make them feel good.

Stating Your Case

A *case statement* is a tool often used when asking for a contribution. It's a short, compelling argument for supporting the nonprofit that can be presented as a brochure, a one-page information sheet, or a glossy folder filled with factsheets, photographs, budgets, or charts. It should be professional, factual, and short enough that readers will read it all the way through.

A good case statement can be used in many ways in fundraising:

✔ After talking about the agency with a potential donor, you leave behind a copy of your case statement for her to consider.

✔ If you need to phone a potential donor, you keep the case statement close at hand as a reminder of the key points to make about the agency.

✔ If you mail or e-mail a fundraising letter, you can borrow wording from the case statement to write that letter or include a copy of the case statement with the letter.

Instructions for writing a case statement resemble a recipe for stew or soup. A few basic ingredients make any version of this dish delicious, and the cook can spice it up with whatever other quality ingredients she has at hand. Follow these steps:

1. **Make notes about the following subjects. Be selective; allot no more than 100 words to any of these items:**

    • The history of the organization

    • The services it offers

    • The organization's key accomplishments

    • Affidavits, reviews, or quotes from enthusiasts who have benefited from the organization's work

    • The organization's future plans

2. **Toss in no more than 50 words on each of these topics:**

    • The organization's philosophy or approach to providing service

    • The pressing needs the organization works to address

    • The ways the organization will measure or recognize its success

3. **Stir in whatever else you have on hand, including**

   - Compelling photographs of the organization's work

   - Charts or maps illustrating growth — for example, increasing numbers of clients the organization serves or the increasing geographic area it serves

   - An overview of the organization's budget and finances, particularly if the budget is balanced and the finances are healthy

   - Anything else that shines a light on the agency: publications completed, awards received, testimony given, work it does with other agencies, and so on

4. **State the giving opportunities your nonprofit offers.**

   The giving options must be clear and not too complicated. Donors want to understand how their contributions can make a difference. Sometimes giving opportunities are linked to the cost of providing services, such as the following:

   - The cost of immunizing one child against a deadly disease

   - The cost of replacing one chair in a symphony hall

   - The cost of rescuing and rehabilitating one injured wild burro

   - The cost of college tuition for one year for one student

   - The cost of planting one acre of trees in a reforestation area

Sometimes opportunities are linked to premiums or gifts the donor receives in return. For example:

   - For a gift of up to $50, the donor receives a coffee mug as a token of thanks. A larger gift is acknowledged with a tote bag.

   - For a gift of several hundred dollars, the donor's name appears on a brass plate on the chair the gift has paid to refurbish.

   - For a gift of $1,000, the donor receives quarterly progress reports from the scientist whose research the gift is supporting.

   - For a gift of several thousand dollars, the donor's name is etched on a tile in the lobby of the organization's new building.

   - For a gift of several million dollars, the lobby is named after the donor.

For a contribution of $250 or more, you must acknowledge the gift in writing and specify the date of the contribution and the amount. If you give that donor something of value in exchange for the contribution, you should mention that in your acknowledgement letter (because the donor must deduct the fair market value of that gift if she itemizes her contribution to your organization in her tax filing). Otherwise, you must include a statement that no goods or services were provided by the organization.

Recognizing your donors

Sometimes a donor's gift to your nonprofit is identified in a public document — a newsletter or performance program — as a Supporter, Patron, Guarantor, or Chief Mucky Muck depending on the size of his contribution. Before acknowledging a donor in print, on a donor wall, or in another public manner, always ask him for permission and ask how he wants to be listed.

When choosing how to recognize your donors, you want to consider the cost of the recognition, the nature of the activity supported, and the way the donor recognition advances (or doesn't suit) your organization's purpose and mission. A simple, printed list of names is dignified and inexpensive. Although donor gifts cost money, having your organization's name printed on T-shirts or tote bags that your donors wear or carry throughout the community may be an effective way of promoting your work. However, if you spend too much on gifts, you can annoy donors or leave them wondering how much you really need their contribution.

When writing your case statement, you don't need to follow the exact order in which we list the elements. Lead with the strongest points and leave out the less compelling items. Choose a strong writer to draft the piece and then test it on others — both within and outside your agency — to see whether it tells a clear, impressive story.

When your case statement is written, produce it for distribution and make sure to match its look to your nonprofit and its intended audience. If your nonprofit is a modest, grassroots organization, your case statement should be simple and direct in its presentation. If it's an environmental organization, you want to produce the case statement on paper made from 100 percent post-consumer waste. If it's an internationally known opera company, your case statement should look dramatic and elegant.

Identifying Possible Donors

Your doorbell rings, and you open the door to greet an adorable child you've never met before. The child is selling candy bars to raise funds for band instruments at school. You played in a band when you were young, so you buy a candy bar, wishing the little fundraiser success.

A few minutes later, the doorbell rings again, and you open the door to greet a second adorable child. You know this child because he lives next door.

You remember when his mother brought him home as a newborn, and you watched him ride his first bicycle down the sidewalk. He's selling the same candy bars to benefit the soccer team at his school: They need equipment and uniforms. You buy *five* candy bars.

Rich or poor, most of us have strong personal feelings about money, and making gifts to charitable organizations reflects our values. Even more important when we make charitable giving decisions is our comfort in contributing our money to people we know, either directly or indirectly. Mapping the personal connections of each member of your organization is a key first step in identifying possible donors.

Drawing circles of connections

Figure 14-1 represents a common brainstorming exercise that nonprofit organizations use to identify possible individual donors. This exercise is most effective if both staff and board members participate. Follow these steps:

1. **Identify the people who are closest to the organization — those within the "inner circle."**

   This inner circle includes staff and board members and active volunteers or clients who frequently use the organization's services.

2. **Identify those people who have the second-closest relationship to the organization.**

   This second circle may include family and close friends of those people in the inner circle, former staff and board members, neighbors of the organization and its inner circle, and clients and volunteers who sometimes use its services.

3. **Take one more step backward and identify the people who make up the third circle.**

   These folks may include grandparents or cousins of those people in the inner circle, old friends whom they haven't seen recently, friends of former staff and board members, and former or infrequent users of the organization's services.

4. **Identify the friends, relatives, and other associates of those who make up circles #2 and #3.**

5. **Search for your cause-related friends and associates.**

   Look for people who may not know anyone involved in your organization, but who demonstrate an interest in the subject and the purpose it represents (as indicated by their memberships, their magazine subscriptions, or their contributions to similar organizations). Follow the local media and watch for people who take an interest in your cause because of their personal experiences. For example, maybe their child was born with the congenital disease that your nonprofit is studying, or maybe they come from a forested part of the state and care about the preservation of old-growth trees.

You can continue enlarging your circle of connections, but with every step you take from the center to the outside, the bond between the organization and the potential donors weakens. As that occurs, the cost of raising money from the people who inhabit those circles increases. Eventually, the cost of securing gifts from an outer circle becomes higher than the likely amount of income to be gained, and it's time to stop.

How do you know when it's time to stop and back up? Most organizations try to keep the cost of their overall fundraising at or lower than 20 percent of their organization's budget. However, when you're starting out, particularly with some kinds of fundraising strategies, such as mailings or special events (see Chapter 15), your percentages may be higher in the first few years. These approaches generally begin to bring in significant contributions as they're repeated and donors renew their gifts. If you're still just "breaking even" in year three, it's time to back up and refocus your approach.

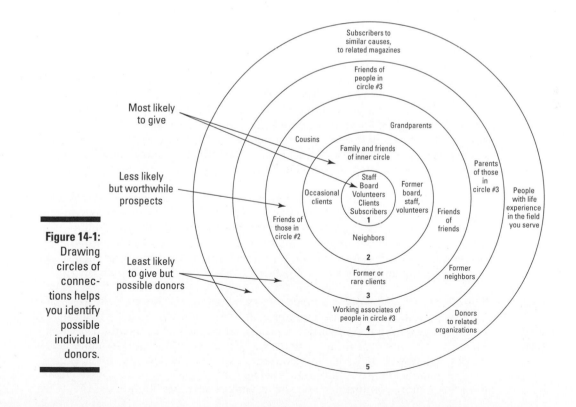

Figure 14-1:
Drawing circles of connections helps you identify possible individual donors.

Getting a list of contacts from your board of directors

Every year, or before you start work on a special event or letter-writing campaign, ask each of your organization's board members to provide the names of ten or more people they know. This exercise is useful for developing a solicitation list.

Most people can sit down and list ten friends and associates off the top of their heads. However, when asked to produce a list in that way, it's unlikely that they will exhaust all their connections and relationships. If you hand board members starter lists of people they may know and then ask them to edit and add to that list, you're likely to get many more names.

To develop this "starter list," think about your board members and their probable networks and connections. Say, for instance, that your nonprofit is lucky enough to have a local business leader on its board of directors. Searching the Web and scouring local business pages to note this leader's affiliations can bring up a variety of connections, such as his business partners and suppliers; members of his professional associations, clubs, or other boards; and his close neighbors. Everyone, no matter how modestly he or she lives, has a web of professional and personal connections.

The next step in developing your organization's network of connections is to address personalized letters from your board members to the people on their lists of ten, providing each of those people with an opportunity to find out more about your organization and to contribute. When asking for their help, make it easy for your contacts to respond: Provide a form for them to fill out and a self-addressed, stamped envelope or link to an online donation service to convey their responses. You may want to save postage by sending your query by e-mail. If you do, make sure the subject line is compelling and the sender is someone the recipient knows.

After you have your list of contacts, you can use it as the basis for a face-to-face individual donor campaign, for mailings, and for event invitations. As you talk to your board members and their friends about their connections, find out as much as you can about how you can best approach these people. Personal preferences vary. Some people prefer to be anonymous donors, while others want to be applauded by a roomful of society leaders when they give.

The cause for which you're seeking money matters, your timing matters, and your organization's reputation matters, but the most important element in raising money from an individual is to have someone he knows and trusts ask for the contribution. This fact is particularly true when it comes to major gift fundraising, where individuals ask other individuals (usually face to face) to make significant contributions, and special events fundraising (because most people are more comfortable socializing with people they know).

Growing a Major Gift

Face-to-face visits are the best way to secure larger contributions, what fund-raising professionals call *major gifts* (see Chapter 13 for more information on major gifts). Rarely does one knock on a door, deliver a short speech, and depart with a check for a large amount. Generally, several contacts must take place before a major donor is ready to make a commitment. This process often is called "cultivation," and the idea of planting the idea, tending a relationship, and harvesting the result when it's fully grown, is an apt one. It takes time. In this section, we break down key steps and tips for growing a major gift.

Before you talk yourself into making a phone call or sending a letter rather than sitting down to talk to a donor face to face, remember that it's more difficult for donors to say no to someone sitting in front of them.

Deciding who should ask

If possible, the board member or staff person who knows the potential donor should make the visit. If that's not possible, the visiting team should be made up of two people who are peers of that person — perhaps a board member who's a local business leader and the executive director. Be careful not to overwhelm a potential donor with a huge SWAT team. Two or three people are plenty.

Preparing to put forth your request

Gulp. It's time to ask someone for money. In preparing for this moment, you need to remember that you're not asking for something for yourself. You're inviting the potential donor to belong, to be a part of something worthwhile. When planning how to describe the reason for the gift, step back for a moment and remember why volunteering for the organization is important to you. How did you become involved? What lives (or lands, or seas) have you seen changed with the organization's work? Sally forth armed with your case statement, which will remind you of the key points you want to mention.

Breaking the ice

Open the conversation with easy material. What did you find out about this person while conducting research, and how do you know her? Maybe your kids attend the same school or you're both baseball fans. Try to use something low key to open the conversation instead of forcing yourself on your "victim" with a heavy sales pitch. The key is creating rapport.

Brief small talk can ease the conversation's start, but don't waste a potential donor's time either. Let her know how you became involved in the organization, and then briefly give an overview of its attributes and current situation. Team members should take up different pieces of the conversation, remembering to let the potential donor talk, too, and paying close attention to the signals she sends. Keeping the meeting comfortable for the prospect is critical.

Adopting the right attitude

When soliciting gifts, be firm and positive, but not pushy. Pay attention to how the potential donor is acting or responding and step back if you discover he isn't feeling well or his business has taken a difficult turn.

Just as you can see signs of when not to press the case, you also may notice signs of readiness when it's going well. The potential donor may express interests in attending an event at the nonprofit. He may begin to tell others good things about the agency. He may display pride in his familiarity with the organization.

Asking someone to contribute to an organization is easier when you've already made a gift yourself. Even if you're a staff member and can't make a large contribution, you'll feel more confident about asking if you've contributed — and the potential donor will find you more credible. In general, it's a good idea for the people in the agency's inner circle to contribute before asking outside individuals to give. (Refer to the earlier section "Drawing circles of connections" for more on those who make up the inner circle.)

Timing the request: An inexact science

Many people don't believe in asking for a specific contribution at the first meeting. They believe in setting the stage — letting a prospective donor know that a campaign or special program is coming up and that the organization will be seeking her help in the future. At a second visit they try to get this person to see a program in action or to meet other board members at an informal gathering. The goal is building a relationship, inviting the potential donor to feel as if she wants to belong with the people leading your agency.

For some major gift campaigns, the fundraisers use a feasibility study. In such a study, someone from outside the organization interviews board members and potential major donors, seeking their impressions of the organization and a suggestion of the size contribution they may make. This process both helps the organization to set realistic goals and warns the "research subjects" that the agency plans to come knocking at their doors.

As with any cultivation, the timing of the harvest is critical. When the time is right, it's like recognizing a piece of fruit that's ready to be picked. Make a date for a follow-up visit. Plan a setting where the conversation can be congenial but focused. Don't rush (a common failing), but don't leave without asking. If the answer is disappointing, ask if you can keep in touch. Sometimes contributors come around at a later time.

Determining what to ask for

Before asking a potential donor for a contribution at one of your follow-up meetings, find out everything you can about the person's gifts to similar causes. (To do so, you can scour donor lists and ask board members who know this person.) This information helps you to ask for an appropriate amount.

Many people believe that you should ask for an amount that's somewhat higher than what you expect to get, because making a request for a generous gift is flattering to the donor. However, you don't want to ask for so much money that the potential donor feels that whatever he gives will be a disappointment. Donors commonly say something like, "I can't do $50,000, but I will consider $25,000 if that would be a help." (Add or subtract zeros as appropriate.)

In most cases, when the donor suggests a level, you don't want to haggle; you may become annoying and cause him to back out of contributing. You may gently push for a higher amount by using the personal associations angle, however: "We were hoping you may become one of our $50,000 donors, along with Joe Schmoe and Sally Smiley, but whatever you can provide would be a big help."

Minding your manners

One of the most important parts of your major gift campaign is thanking your contributors. Do it very soon after the pledge is made or the gift is received. We recommend an immediate phone call and a handwritten note. If you acknowledge a donor thoughtfully and graciously, and follow up that thank-you note with a newsletter or information about the organization's accomplishments, you're strengthening your future relationship with that contributor and can make her feel as if she's part of your organization. That's good manners and smart fundraising.

Raising Money by Mail

We hope that after reading this section of the book you never again refer to the solicitation letters you receive from charities as "junk mail." These letters may not be as welcome as personal letters, but they grow out of a sophisticated and fascinating area of fundraising. Your organization may be much too small to make investing in a direct mail campaign worthwhile, but it can take valuable tips from the "big guys" and develop small-scale letter writing efforts that yield good results.

Taking the direct mail route

If you think you want to try large-scale direct mail fundraising, we strongly recommend that you hire a direct mail consultant or firm to handle your campaign. Direct mail fundraising can be an expensive investment, and you want the best, most up-to-date professional advice available.

Successful direct mail depends on the following:

- ✔ A cause that's meaningful to many thousands of people across your state or the country

- ✔ A clear understanding of what you want to accomplish with a mail campaign (perhaps to reach out to new donors or raise a large number of modest contributions that may be upgraded in the future)

- ✔ A compelling, well-presented letter that makes its reader care about a cause and believe that the nonprofit described can make a difference

- ✔ A well-chosen mailing list, usually purchased from a list broker

- ✔ Nonprofit bulk-rate postage, which can save you a significant amount over commercial mailing rates

- ✔ Easy, clear ways your letter readers can respond to the request by using a return envelope, response card, or Web service

- ✔ Testing your letter and list at a modest scale before sending the letter to hundreds of thousands of names

- ✔ A direct mail schedule through which you solicit donors several times each year

When writing a fundraising letter, remember that many potential donors will read your letter's P.S. before the body of the letter, so include any compelling information there.

To secure a nonprofit bulk mail permit, you must apply to the United States Postal Service, completing PS Form 3624. You can find a link among the Web resources at CD1408.

Successfully raising money through the mail depends on gradual development of a loyal cadre of donors who respond by mail. Less than 1 percent of the people you mail to initially may send contributions, but after they give, you'll add them to your *donor list* — a precious resource you'll develop after an investment of time, effort, and postage stamps. You can send mail to these generous folks in the future and expect a higher rate of return (between 6 and 12 percent).

Donors who make repeat contributions are likely to stick with your organization for several years, making three or four (or more!) contributions in that time, and they'll likely increase the size of their contributions. Adding to this value, you'll uncover prospects for major gifts and planned gifts (contributions from bequests) among these donors.

Before your donor list develops into a significant and loyal resource, a direct mail campaign on your organization's behalf may only break even on the cost of the initial letter writing campaign. You may even recover only half of your cost. That's why direct mail may not be appropriate for a small or start-up organization: the financial risk is high. You need to be able to cover significant upfront costs and not expect a strong return on that investment for several years.

If your organization is newly established, locally focused, too technical for general understanding, or lacking the resources to invest in mailing hundreds of thousands of letters, it still can use letters — both sent through the post office and electronically — to invite people to contribute (see the upcoming section). You can increase your mail response rates by having your staff and board members write to people they know personally.

Succeeding with letters

Your letter isn't just a letter; it also includes a mailing envelope, a reply envelope and card, and sometimes a brochure, a copy of a newspaper clipping, or a photograph. All these pieces should relate to one another and convey a clear, compelling message.

The outer envelope should be inviting to open. For instance, did you use a first-class stamp? Did you handwrite the address and add a special message? The letter itself should give readers enough information that they feel involved in the cause. Most of it should be dedicated to describing the problem that the organization is trying to solve. After that, it discusses how things can be turned around for the better and the organization's specific method or program for doing so. The letter closes with a vision for how things will look if the plan succeeds, and usually includes a combination of short and long paragraphs. Often a key point is underlined or printed in bold for emphasis.

The reply envelope and card should be easy to use, and the reply card should offer a variety of gift levels. Your nonprofit can get a permit from the post office to offer postage-paid envelopes, which make it easier for donors to respond.

Try out your letter at first on your organization's internal lists of board contacts, clients, and donors. Then continually build your potential donor list by making it a habit to collect names, addresses, and e-mails at events you present and meetings and conferences you attend.

Just as important as collecting names for your list is taking care of those names — especially of those who become donors. You want to develop a good database system for recording information about new donors in order to thank them, keep in touch with them, and ask for their support again in the future. You'll find that database programs — usually called fundraising or membership management software — to manage your donor information come in various degrees of complexity and prices. Choose the one that's best for your needs.

On the CD accompanying this book, you'll find a sample donor information record that you can adapt to your needs. See CD1408 for links to eBase, eTapestry, and Salesforce, all of which offer free or low-cost databases for nonprofit organizations.

Just because a donor stops giving for a year or two doesn't mean you should drop him from your list. A lapsed donor is more likely to contribute to your organization than someone who has never given before. However, after five years it's probably wise to drop them from your list.

Treating donors well for great results

Good fundraisers recognize the importance of treating donors well. In fact, the Association of Fundraising Professionals has even developed a thoughtful Donor Bill of Rights that offers standards to follow (www.afpnet.org/Ethics/EnforcementDetail.cfm?ItemNumber=3359).

Good treatment of your donors includes allowing them to tell you if they don't want their addresses shared with other organizations. You can include a check box on your reply card where they can indicate their preference for keeping their information from being traded or sold.

Telemarketing: Dialing for Dollars

In the mid-1980s, direct mail was a wildly successful means of fundraising for many organizations. In the late 1980s, it declined. Households were receiving too much direct mail, making recipients less inclined to read it, and the costs of printing and postage rose. That's when the dinner hour began to be interrupted by incessant telemarketing calls.

Like direct mail, telemarketing is based on a directed message. Telemarketers preselect the recipients for their potential interest in the topic of the call based on their responses to other types of telephone marketing.

The advantages of telemarketing are

- ✔ It's hard to ignore. A human voice engages you in a conversation, and you must respond. It's not like a letter that you can throw into the recycling bin without the author noticing.

- ✔ It can be less costly than a mail campaign. If you use trained volunteers to make the calls (rather than a commercial telemarketing firm), you can manage a campaign at a very reasonable cost.

- ✔ As with direct mail, you can use the elements that shape a large-scale, professional telemarketing project for a modest campaign.

The disadvantages? For donors, the drawback is that no one gets to have a quiet dinner any longer. For the callers conducting the campaigns, the problem is that more and more potential donors use caller ID and won't answer the phone if they don't recognize the caller. And cellphone numbers are relatively difficult to collect for calling purposes. Plus, if you don't have volunteers able to make the calls, commercial telemarketing firms take a very high percentage (as high as 75 percent!) of any funds raised, making it a poor return on investment for donors who want to keep fundraising costs low.

Citizen complaints about intrusive telemarketing have led to the creation of the National Do Not Call Registry, which makes it illegal for businesses to make telemarketing calls to people who register. At present, telemarketing for nonprofit organizations is generally exempt from the federal rules. Check the status of these regulations and applicable state laws before embarking on a telemarketing campaign. Public policy articles on the Association of Fundraising Professionals Web site are a good place to check (www.afpnet.org) or the National Do Not Call Web site (www.donotcall.gov/faq/faq business.aspx#ExemptOrg).

The key steps to beginning telemarketing are writing a script, training volunteers, organizing follow-up calls, and — of course — thanking, cultivating, and upgrading donors over time. We explain everything you need to know in the following sections.

Writing a script

Every call should open with a clear, direct, personal greeting: "Hello, Mr. I'm-Getting-the-Person's-Name-Right, I'm Ms. Call-a-Lot and I wanted to talk to you about the Scenic Overlook Preservation Fund Committee's work."

Having connected with the call recipient, the caller then tries to link that person's interests and behavior to the reason for the call:

- ✔ If she's a past donor, begin with a hearty thank you.
- ✔ If she's been involved in a related cause or effort, mention how important that work is.
- ✔ If she lives near the scenic overlook, mention how beautiful it is and the community's concern for the fragile surrounding environment.

You may notice a tricky moment in the call when you want the potential donor to relax and listen so you can tell your story and not be interrupted. To increase the caller's chances of keeping call recipients on the line, the script should be

- ✔ Engaging and information packed (to hold the listener's attention)
- ✔ Upbeat about the possibility of improvement or change
- ✔ Deeply concerned about the current situation
- ✔ Specific about the time frame in which things need to change
- ✔ Specific about the amount of money the caller hopes the listener can contribute

On the CD accompanying this book, we include a set of telemarketing "do's" and "don'ts" and a sample telemarketing script. See CD1403.

Coaching your callers

Telemarketing can be an excellent board or volunteer group effort. If someone involved with your organization works in an office that has multiple telephone lines, see whether you can borrow the office for an evening. Early evening (6:00 to 8:30 p.m.) on weeknights is generally considered the best time to call, but — as you've probably noticed — telemarketers now frequently call during the day and on weekends as well.

Gather your volunteer team an hour before beginning. Feed them a good meal and give them a pep talk. Building camaraderie among the callers can relax anyone who's nervous. Setting a group goal for the evening and mapping it on a big chart can build morale.

Inform the callers that they must deliver the message in a crisp, clear, and friendly voice. They shouldn't rush, but they also shouldn't leave holes in the conversation that the call recipient can close before the caller can ask for a contribution. They should ask for a specific contribution and confirm the amount. They also should tell the potential donors that they're volunteers; this may make them more likely to pay attention.

Provide your callers with information about each household they're calling, including a recommended gift request. You base your request on the potential donor's past contributions to your organization and others. Sometimes you're just guessing. That's okay if your callers also are good listeners and deftly adjust the amount they're requesting in response to what they hear. If, after a gift is pledged, you feel that you asked for too little money, don't despair. You can ask the donor to upgrade his gift next time.

Collecting the pledge

If a pledge is made, the caller should thank the new donor and try to get her to either provide credit card information over the phone so the gift can be charged immediately or promise to return the contribution within a certain time. Ask the caller to confirm the spelling of the donor's name and address before saying goodbye.

At the end of the evening, everyone present should write brief, personalized thank-you notes. For contacts who promised gifts but didn't charge them over the phone, send the thank-you notes with pledge forms (indicating the specific amount of the promised contribution) and return envelopes.

Every telemarketing campaign suffers from a percentage of unrealized promises, and callers want to keep that percentage as low as possible. You may ask a small number of your volunteers to reconvene for a short follow-up calling session two months after the initial campaign to jar loose any contributions that haven't yet been received.

Raising Money the "E" Way (Easily and Electronically)

Just as your Web site and electronic communications system are tools for serving your constituents and marketing your work, they can be tools for raising money. E-fundraising began to take off after 2001. The Internet can be used as a discrete set of tools or it can be used in combination with traditional mailings and telemarketing.

If electronic systems are so effective, why haven't we all dumped those expensive postage stamps and phone banks and moved our fundraising to the electronic arena, you ask? Well, even though the number of people who make online contributions is increasing and the array of online tools is growing, the Internet isn't working well for all kinds of nonprofits. Online fundraising faces two challenges:

✔ Many people find it relatively impersonal. Organizations must be particularly creative online to cultivate relationships with donors.

✔ Giving is based on trust and not everyone trusts that his money is going where it's supposed to go when contributed online.

However, the numbers of people donating online are growing and online fundraising has worked well in some contexts. It has been an effective tool for disaster and emergency relief campaigns, for which donors want to respond quickly. People also respond well to online fundraising by organizations they already know well, such as their college alumni associations or nonprofit organizations in their immediate communities.

Although you don't use telephones or letters in Internet transactions, e-philanthropy isn't free. The investment in staff time and online services can be significant.

Using e-mail and related tools to build and maintain relationships

Fundraising is about building relationships with people. Individual donors want to feel that they're appreciated, so it's in a nonprofit's best interest to thank donors regularly and keep them informed about what the organization is doing. It can't hurt to get to know the people who give money to your nonprofit, either. Here's where the Internet can be of help.

The most frequently used feature of the Internet is e-mail. It's easy to use, you don't need the latest hotrod computer to use it, and it's cheap and fast. Many nonprofit organizations produce monthly (or more frequent) online newsletters about their work. Distributing these bulletins to donors is a great way to keep them informed about how their contributions are making a difference.

So, you want to obtain an organization e-mail account and address that allows people to contact you (and allows you to build an online mailing list). You can use e-mail messages to compel readers to click through to your Web site where they can find out how to contribute to your organization and read more about it.

Related online tools you want to have at hand include the following:

- ✔ **A Web site:** Your site should have clear, timely information about your organization, a Contact Us option linked to your e-mail address, and a click-through feature that allows Web site visitors to make contributions online. You can read more about creating a Web site in Chapter 11.

- ✔ **A brief electronic newsletter:** This e-newsletter about your organization's work should feature an intriguing subject line and be highly readable. Imagine your typical reader: *If* she opens it, she'll scroll through it quickly. You want to write an inviting sentence or two about each topic, inviting that reader to click through to your organization's Web site and read more about it (noticing the "donate" button while she's there).

- ✔ **An organization blog:** Blogs are great for inviting comments and feedback or group discussion lists (or *listservs*). Both tools are available for free at a number of Web sites.

- ✔ **A social marketing site:** Social marketing options include Facebook, MySpace, and Twitter. These social networking tools remind people of your organization and urge them to take action on your behalf.

E-mail correspondence can be less formal than typed-on-paper business letters, but it shouldn't be overly familiar. Answer questions succinctly — don't ramble on and on. It's a good idea to have a short paragraph description about your organization already written and waiting to be cut and pasted into your e-mails. It can be added to and edited as needed.

CD1404 provides tips for writing an e-fundraising letter, CD1405 provides a sample e-solicitation letter, and CD1406 shows how a nonprofit uses e-mail correspondence to develop a relationship with a potential donor.

Building your e-mail address lists

When corresponding with people who contact you through e-mail or your Web site, consider them prospective donors. If you're e-mailing a new correspondent, ask whether he wants to be added to your mailing list. Make this invitation a habit. However, respect those who decline. Others will accept, and slowly and steadily you'll build your list.

E-mail address lists, like mailing address lists, can be purchased, traded, or borrowed. A nonprofit may be willing to lend or trade its list with another nonprofit with a similar mission. When using a borrowed list, it's important to respect the privacy of the people listed. Don't pass it along to others without permission.

Making your Web site a cultivation tool

A Web site can never replicate a face-to-face encounter with another person, but in designing your site to appeal to possible donors, you can remember that challenge and make it engaging and appealing. Strategies may include

- ✔ Short profiles of clients served and of donors

- ✔ Behind-the-scenes tours of the organization's activities (Our local zoo kept a Web camera on newborn lion cubs so the public could see them before they were on display in an exhibit.)

- ✔ PDFs of studies or research your nonprofit has conducted and links to information and resources about the field in which your agency works

- ✔ E-mail campaigns to political leaders or electronic petitions

- ✔ Bulletin boards and chat rooms on subjects related to your work

- ✔ Clear instructions for how to donate to your organization

The longer a Web site keeps visitors involved, the likelier it is to build their trust and interest.

Most Web sites include a Contact Us page. Make sure this option is user friendly and that someone on your staff is responsible for replying to queries quickly and courteously. Include opportunities for readers of the Web site to sign up for your electronic newsletter or other services and to leave a mailing address and/or telephone number.

You may build the most amazing Web site on the planet, but if readers aren't finding it, it's not fulfilling its role for your organization. One critical question is how to attract the notice of search engines. Some agencies sit back and wait for a Web spider to find their pages; some submit their pages to search engines one by one, which can be time consuming; and some hire a service to submit their information to the leading search engines. See *Search Engine Optimization For Dummies* by Peter Kent for information on getting your site noticed by search engines.

Gathering money online

A key first step to raising money through the Internet is to add a "donate now" button to your organization's Web site. If you have good technology support and a Web site that includes a system for securely collecting money, you can insert your own "donate now" button into your Web site. However, many nonprofits find it easier to take advantage of existing software and services, contracting with a "donate now" service. The number of options available can be daunting. We recommend that you read the online discussions on TechSoup, a nonprofit Web site addressing organizations' technology needs, before you sign up for a service. You can visit TechSoup at www.techsoup.org.

As you shop for the right service for your organization, consider the breadth of the services you're purchasing. Will the agency design your Web site for you? Will it thank your donors? Will it manage a donor database for your online contributions?

Also, look carefully at how and for what an agency charges fees. Most online contribution services charge a setup fee, a monthly fee, and a per-contribution fee. Sometimes you can avoid the monthly fees, but when you do, often you pay a higher fee for each contribution you receive. Some less-expensive nonprofit technology services charge lower fees but send you your contributions in a lump sum, so you only receive the money, not the donor records. On the other hand, some services charge for keeping the donor records or for allowing you to upload them onto your computers.

If your organization is selling goods or services through e-mail, you should know that the Federal CAN-SPAM law makes it unlawful to send unsolicited commercial e-mails unless the e-mails contain a "clear and conspicuous identification that the message is an advertisement or solicitation" (this information doesn't necessarily have to appear in the e-mail subject line); an ability to opt-out electronically from future e-mails; and a valid postal address of the sender.

Distributing your fundraising through volunteers

Technology provides novel ways for your organization's supporters to help raise money. In *distributed fundraising,* an individual supporter creates an online donation account for your organization, and through that account speaks directly to friends and family about your organization's work, urging them to contribute or volunteer. This is a great thing to ask your board members or tech-savvy volunteers to do for you.

As is true with your organization's Web site, a "donate now" button can be added to a distributed fundraising site. However, often the volunteer fundraiser uses an existing Web service to set up the page and collect contributions. Some of these services are Network for Good, Change.org, Changing the Present, Firstgiving, and Facebook Causes. Your volunteer will want to pay attention to the comparable setup fees and percentages of contributions collected by these services.

Other online services invite you to sign up your nonprofit with them. They will make contributions to it when you use their search engines or purchase their products. You can identify and find out more by searching online for "charity portals." Read the fine print about any fees they may charge before registering your nonprofit. Some are fully supported by advertising revenue and are free to their nonprofit participants.

Chapter 15

Making the Most of Special Events

*F*rom glamorous dances under the stars to pancake breakfasts at the local firehouse, most nonprofits include social gatherings as part of the fundraising mix. Special events don't just raise money, however. They're often credited with raising friends along with funds. New donors — who don't know the organization — may come forward because the event itself sounds fun and interesting, because of who invites them, or because someone they admire is being honored. Special events can be a wonderful catalyst for attracting businesses that like to be recognized when they make contributions, or for attracting people who like to socialize and be seen.

At their best, special events raise substantial amounts of money, draw attention to an organization's good work, and attract new volunteers. If fundraising is about cultivation, a special event can be a greenhouse for nurturing growth. You hope to create a special event that becomes an occasion that people look forward to, an annual tradition. Still, a special event can be one of the most expensive ways to raise money. Expenses may eat up half or even more of the gross event income. Putting together a special event draws upon all your nonprofit management skills and can drain staff and board time and energy away from other important activities.

Bottom line? Special events need careful planning. In this chapter, we show you how to plan a successful special event — and steer clear of obstacles.

Thinking through the Whole Event

If you think that a special event is in your future, we recommend sitting down with staff and board members and raising questions like these:

- ✔ What would our organization's followers enjoy doing and how much would they pay to do it?

- ✔ Who does our organization know who can provide event elements — donated goods, celebrity auctioneers, entertainment, or printing services?

- ✔ Who do we know who can be honored at the event or serve on an event committee? The event leadership and volunteer committee are critically important to attracting donors to the occasion.

- ✔ When can we focus attention on a special event? The last six weeks before an event are generally the most labor intensive. Look for a relatively clear six-week block of time in which you don't have grant deadlines or other commitments.

- ✔ When can we hold an event without competing with our other fundraising drives? (If you have an annual fund drive in October, for example, why not plan your special event in the spring?)

We offer some additional advice regarding these questions in the following sections.

Deciding on your event according to your budget

Special events can be produced on bare-bones budgets, for princely prices, or for any amount in between. As with most kinds of investments, event planners expect a higher return in exchange for a higher investment. But don't exceed your means. In this section, we outline some ideas for tailoring an event to your organization's budget.

When deciding on an event, we recommend avoiding anything that can make your guests uncomfortable or deter them from coming, such as:

- ✔ Events that limit your guests' ability to come and go as they want — like a soiree on a boat in the middle of lake.

- ✔ Events at which your intended audience finds the attire, time, or place awkward.

- ✔ Events that are designed to reach an audience that's completely unknown to your organization or its supporters. Do you like to go to a party where you don't know anybody?

After you've sketched out an idea for an event, go to your staff and board members and ask them directly: Would you attend this event? For this price? At this time of year? If your core followers and supporters aren't enthusiastic, the event isn't going to raise money. If the idea excites them and they're willing to play a role in the event planning, you're on your way to success.

Low-budget special events

Most nonprofit organizations have a wealth of talent simply waiting for a showcase. Some of the following suggestions won't work for your organization, but they can get you thinking about similar events that would be perfect for your nonprofit:

- ✓ **Sign up neighborhood children for a summer read-a-thon that benefits the library or an after-school literacy program.** By sending forms home to parents in advance, you can secure their permission and help with collecting pledges. Write to your community newspapers inviting them to help you spread the word as event sponsors.

- ✓ **Offer a bake sale with a distinctive theme celebrating a cultural group or holiday.** Organize your volunteers around three primary activities: setting up and pricing, selling, and taking down the sale. Plan in advance what to do with items that don't sell.

- ✓ **Hold a cocktail party in a board member's home, focused on a theme or honoring a special guest.** Although a cocktail party for 15 people may not raise much money, don't rule this idea out. If every one of your board members signs up to host such a party over the course of a year, the cumulative amount raised may pleasantly surprise you.

Mid-budget special events

If the treasury is a bit fatter and you can afford a few more features in your special event, you may want to do something like one of these ideas:

- ✓ **Identify an up-and-coming performer and ask for a donation of a performance in exchange for the promotion that your event will bring to him or her.** The club or theater rental is likely to be your highest cost. If you choose an unusual site that's donated to you, make sure it can accommodate your performer's needs — acoustics, lighting, electrical outlets, and the like.

- ✓ **Sponsor a daylong cleanup of a coastal area, park, or preserve.** Volunteers can be sponsored by having their friends sign up to pledge a certain gift amount to the organization for each pound or bag of trash that they remove. Offer prizes for the most unusual refuse items found and the largest numbers of sponsorship sign-ups.

- ✓ **Buy out an interesting new restaurant or a beloved community favorite for a night (usually a Monday or Tuesday when it otherwise would be closed) for your guests only.** Work with the restaurant to discount the cost charged to your organization (but not to your guests!) by offering a more limited menu than usual (three to four choices) and by promoting the restaurant through your public relations for the event.

High-priced special events

If money is no object — at the front end, at least — these events may be of interest. All require more upfront cash:

- ✔ **Hire a major speaker or entertainer from a lecture bureau or theatrical agency and use that person as the focus of a dinner party or private concert.** Honor one or more business and community leaders at the event. Form an event committee of people who will invite their friends and people who may want to come for the sake of the honorees.

- ✔ **Present a dance featuring a live band.** Decorate festively. Make sure your crowd likes to dance and that your musicians' repertoire suits the moves that the crowd knows.

- ✔ **Organize a celebrity athletic event.** Celebrity golf, bowling, and ping pong — you name it — are all possible. Create teams pairing professional players with amateurs or local celebrities with donors. If you use professional athletes, liberally handicap the amateurs so that everyone has a chance of winning. Provide trophies or certificates for many kinds of "achievements" — longest drive, bowling ball most often in the gutter, and the quickest victory. Often these events end with celebratory dinners.

- ✔ **Produce a benefit auction, selling contributed restaurant meals, vacations, services, or other valuables your board and committee can secure or donate.** Include a cocktail party or dinner with the live auction as the entertainment. Your guests can bid on smaller items through a silent auction.

Budgeting for an event

The bottom line is very simple: Your total earnings from a special event must exceed your total cost — by a lot, you hope. But how do you get a handle on revenue and expenses? In this section, we offer some thoughts.

If you're staging an event for the first time, it's particularly important *early in the process* to ask your core supporters — board, volunteers, and event leadership — how much they intend to give. Because these people are the most likely to give generously, knowing their intentions helps you forecast the overall results.

Another way to estimate the fundraising potential of an event is to check with organizations that produce similar events. If they have presented a program year after year and yours is a first-time outing, ask them where their income levels began. Try to objectively weigh your event's assets against theirs. Are your boards equally well connected? Is your special guest equally well-known?

The CD accompanying this book includes three sample special event budgets — CD1501 for a tribute dinner, CD1502 for a concert or performance, and CD1503 for a benefit auction.

Figuring the income side

Try to design your event so that it generates income in more than one way. A rummage sale may also include a raffle and the sale of some baked goods. An auction may include advertising in a printed program along with tickets to the event and the income generated from the sale of the auction items. Standard event income categories include:

- Individual ticket sales
- Table or group sales (usually for parties of ten)
- Benefactor, patron, and sponsor donations (for which donors receive special recognition in return for contributing higher amounts than a basic table or seat costs)
- Sponsorships of event participants (for instance, pledging to contribute a particular amount per mile run by a friend)
- Food and/or beverage sales
- Sales of goods and/or services
- Advertising sales (in printed programs, on banners, and so on)
- Purchasing a chance (raffle tickets, door prizes, and so on)

Capturing expenses — expected and unexpected

Unless a wonderful sponsor has offered to cover all your expenses, your event will cost money to produce. The general categories can include the following:

- Building/facility/location (space rental, site use permits, security guards, portable toilets, tents, cleanup costs)
- Advertising and promotion (posters, invitations, publicist costs, postage, Web page development)
- Production (lighting and sound equipment, technical labor, stage managers, auctioneers)
- Travel and per diem (for guest speakers, performers, or special guests)
- Insurance (for example, liability should someone be hurt due to your organization's negligence, or shipping insurance to protect donated goods)
- Food and beverages (including permits for sale or serving of alcohol, if necessary)

- ✔ Décor (flowers, rented tables and chairs, linens, fireworks, banners)

- ✔ Miscellaneous (prizes, awards, talent treatment, name tags, signs, T-shirts)

- ✔ Office expenses (letter writing, mailing list management, detail coordination)

- ✔ All other staff expenses

In spite of your careful planning, certain expenses can appear unexpectedly and cause you to exceed your budget. If you plan to serve food at your event, keep these tips in mind so you can avoid surprise charges:

- ✔ Confirm whether all service and preparation charges are included in the catering budget.

- ✔ If you need to add additional meals at the last minute, find out whether your caterer charges extra. If meals that you ordered aren't eaten, you probably still need to pay for them. Check on your caterer's policy.

- ✔ If some of the wine that you've purchased isn't consumed, is the store willing to buy it back from you?

- ✔ If wine has been donated to your event, find out whether your caterer charges *corkage* fees for opening and serving it.

Soliciting in-kind gifts for your event

When you think about what your event will cost and how you can pay for it, think about the business contacts that your board, staff, and outside supporters have. Often, a business's contribution of *in-kind* (noncash) materials is more generous than any cash contribution to your event. You may need to be flexible about timing and willing to drop things off or pick things up, but don't overlook in-kind gifts. Examples include the following:

- ✔ Businesses in your community that have in-house printing equipment may be able to print your invitations and posters, saving you thousands of dollars.

- ✔ A florist may contribute a roomful of valuable centerpieces in exchange for special recognition in the dinner program.

- ✔ A donor may let you use her beautiful residence as your event site.

You may not want or need all the in-kind gifts that are offered to you. In cases such as these, do look the gift horse in the mouth! Don't accept an in-kind contribution if it's not up to the standards that you need for your event. Also, consider the implications of accepting the gift. For instance, if your agency helps young people recover from drug or alcohol addiction, don't accept a sponsorship from an alcoholic beverage company. If you're afraid of offending the donor or hurting a relationship, you can ask to use the gift in another context and — unless it's inappropriate — acknowledge the donor publicly at your event for his generosity.

Your donors will want to claim tax deductions for their in-kind contributions. They need to be able to substantiate the value of the gifts they give. If they make a contribution of noncash property worth more than $5,000, generally that item must be appraised before a value is assigned to it. The appraisal is not the nonprofit's responsibility. In fact, the charity may *not* serve as the appraiser. However, the nonprofit may have to file IRS form 8282 if it receives and then sells an in-kind donation of more than $500. For more information, see the IRS Web site at www.irs.gov.

Building your event committee

Strong volunteer leadership is the backbone of special events fundraising. Some of the most important work you and your board will do as event organizers is to recruit a chair or co-chairs for an event committee. Choose people who are well connected, and who bring different contacts to their committee work — perhaps one community volunteer, one business executive, and one local athletic hero. Many organizations include a board member on the event committee, but they also use the event as an opportunity to recruit beyond their boards, bringing in new, short-term volunteers.

Your co-chairs' job is to build a network of support for the event. Usually they invite other well-connected people to join them as members of an event committee. Perhaps your board will recruit three co-chairs and those co-chairs will recruit 25 event committee members. Your committee members and co-chairs together then will send personalized letters and invitations and will make phone calls urging people to support and attend the event. If each of them brings 20 people, you'll have quite a crowd!

You'll find two related sample letters on the CD. CD1504 is written by an event co-chair and addressed to someone who's being invited to join an event committee member, and CD1505 is written from a committee member to a potential donor.

Setting a date and location

Check around town to find out whether you're planning to hold your event on the same date as a program by another nonprofit agency. Be as thorough as possible in this date checking. Competing for the same audience on the same date — or even dates that are close to each other — hurts both organizations' results. Also, in general, avoid dates that are too close to holidays, because people want to be with their families.

While the idea may not seem very innovative, good hotels generally are excellent sites for special events. They often have several banquet rooms, and catering, podiums, sound systems, and parking valets are all available at the site. All these extras leave you with fewer details to manage.

Some of the best special events we've attended have been inside the non-profit organizations that they supported or in sites thematically linked to the cause being supported — such as an historic building, a maritime museum, a public park, or an art gallery. Outdoor locations, such as vineyards, formal gardens, and mountaintops can be beautiful but require backup plans for variable weather, and climbing rocky pathways or crossing uneven lawns may make your event inaccessible to some of your hoped-for supporters.

Another creative angle on choosing a location is to match it to an event theme. We've put on a great Halloween party in a former mortuary.

If you're running short on ideas, ask your friends and colleagues about interesting places they've attended events, or hold a brainstorming session with your board.

Starting the Countdown Six Months Out

Although events vary greatly in size and complexity, and although we've pulled off adequately successful events in two or three weeks, we recommend working against a six-month schedule. This section outlines a scheduling checklist for a tribute dinner. It can easily be modified to fit other types of events.

✔ **First three months:**

❑ Develop the plan and pick the event's leadership.

❑ Recruit co-chairs or hosts.

❑ Secure entertainment and a location.

❑ Select a theme and a caterer.

The first three-month period is, not surprisingly, the slowest part of event planning. You can wait for several weeks to hear back from an invited celebrity, and you may need several more weeks to find a replacement if you get turned down.

✔ **Last three months:**

❑ Recruit an event committee or a core group of volunteers.

❑ Visit the site at which the event will be held, checking out all the regulations and recommendations for its use, including required insurance.

❑ Solicit in-kind contributions of materials you need for the event.

❑ If your event is appropriate for a public relations drive, you should be sending out initial press releases and preparing public service announcements (PSAs) at this point too. (See Chapter 11 for PSAs and other parts of a marketing-PR program.)

As you come inside the two-month zone, you pass some additional checkpoints:

✔ **Two months before the event:**

❑ Call all potential committee members and develop your invitation design. All the text on the invitation should be ready for final design and printing by six weeks before the event.

❑ Include a printed list of the final event committee members or core volunteers.

❑ Select your menu and start working on décor ideas.

✔ **Four weeks before the event:**

❑ Mail or e-mail the invitations.

❑ E-mail a second batch of press releases.

❑ Make phone calls to the press and to invitees to confirm coverage and travel plans.

❑ Design the printed program to be passed out at the event.

❑ Assist honorees with their speeches (if necessary).

❑ Gather the elements — baskets, banners, confetti — needed for décor.

✔ **Last week before the event:**

❑ Confirm the number of guests that you expect. A few days before the party occurs, call *everyone* who has made a reservation and confirm whether they're coming. A few people will have had to change plans, increasing or decreasing the number of guests you expect. You don't want to pay for uneaten meals or to run out of food. When ordering food from your caterer, assume that under normal circumstances, 5 percent of your expected guests won't attend. If the event is free, 10 percent of them won't attend.

❑ Plan the seating at the event (if necessary).

❑ Prepare place cards and table cards.

❑ Decorate the site.

Issuing a memorable invitation

Make your invitation something your potential guests will open and remember. Addressing the envelope by hand and using stamps rather than printed postage makes it look more personal, and an intriguing phrase or logo on the outside may lead to its being opened.

What do recipients see first when they open your invitation? Most invitations are made up of an outer folded piece, a reply card, and a reply envelope. Want some more attention? What if a pinch of confetti or glitter falls out of the envelope? Or a small black cat, spider, or bat falls out of your Halloween invitation?

In spite of our recommending these bells and whistles, we are firm believers in clarity. Make sure that the reader of your invitation can easily see who's extending the invitation, what the event is, where and when it's being held, how much it costs, and how to respond to the invitation. If people have to search for these basics, the invitation will land in the recycling bin. And remember that people look forward to your event more if other people they know are going to be there. Make sure the names of the people on your event committees are clearly and prominently presented.

Print the address to which your guest should respond somewhere on the reply card, even though it's also printed on the reply envelope. Sometimes the pieces of an invitation become separated. You want your guests to readily know where to send their reply (and money!).

We include additional event timelines on the CD. See CD1506 for a tribute dinner or luncheon timeline.

You may think that nobody can rain on your parade, but you want to have emergency backup plans anyway. What if your performer is ill, a blizzard shuts down roadways, or your permits aren't approved on time? You need to quickly move, replace, reschedule, or cancel your program. The faster you can communicate any changes, the better your constituents feel about sticking with you and your cause.

Media Coverage: Letting the Public Know

If the mantra of fundraising is "If you don't ask, you won't get," the mantra for special events fundraising is "Nobody will come if they don't know about it."

The advantage of having your event covered in the media is that you reach a large number of people for a relatively modest cost. We emphasize the word *relatively*. Press relations work isn't free.

If your event has a newsworthy angle, send press releases to the media in the hopes of their writing about it or broadcasting the news. (You can find information about writing press releases in Chapter 11.)

Finding a news angle

Think about all the angles you can exploit for publicity. Try to look at it from the point of view of every section of a newspaper or newscast. Modify your basic press release to suit the content of appropriate newspaper and magazine section editors, producers of radio feature shows, and TV newsrooms. Follow up your mailed release with a phone call. A few possibilities include

- **Entertainment section coverage of performers.** You may be able to arrange interviews between your special guests and the local entertainment press that can run on radio, television, or in the newspaper prior to your event.

- **Business section coverage of your event chair or honoree.** Many papers run a column of activities of local business and corporate leaders.

- **Feature stories about the community improvements that your agency has helped to bring about.**

- **Food section coverage of your picnic lunch or outdoor benefit concert.**

- **Health advice connected to your event.** If your organization is sponsoring a 10K run, what's the current advice about dietary preparation for long-distance running? Any medium can be appropriate, but what about a feature in a runners' magazine?

- **Society page coverage of your honorees, event committee members, or other guests at your event.**

- **Radio broadcast of your honoree or guest speaker's speech.**

- **Fashion page or television coverage of attire worn to your gala.**

- **Coverage in a small newspaper.** Many communities have newspapers that are focused on particular neighborhoods, suburbs, or cultural groups. Are any of your honorees, performers, or special guests from those communities?

Printing posters that announce your event or sending personal invitations by mail is more expensive than sending out press releases. But these methods have the advantage of being direct. You can mail invitations to the right individuals and post your posters in high visibility spots in the right neighborhoods.

After the ball is over . . .

Thank-you notes should be written soon after the event and should be as specific and personal as possible. They don't have to be long. Many people find handwritten notes of two or three lines to be much more sincere and memorable than boilerplate letters. Of course, if you have 1,000 donors, you probably can't send personal notes to all of them, but a hand-addressed envelope with a stamp makes your thank-you personal.

We also recommend holding a brief post-event gathering for your key organizers and volunteers a week or two after the event. You can thank them personally again for their effort, but the real purpose is to get their ideas about what worked, what needs to be improved, and what should happen in the future. Good records of this meeting are a jumping-off point for planning the following year's program.

Getting a mention on radio or TV

The mass media need great gobs of news, announcements, and other content every day. You can get some media exposure if you, for example:

- Prepare a prerecorded public service announcement for broadcast by radio stations. (See Chapter 11 for guidelines on PSAs.)

- Donate free tickets to your event to radio stations to use as prizes of various kinds. If a station picks up on the idea, you get a free mention — maybe a number of free mentions.

- Invite live weather or traffic reporters to cover conditions from your location. It can be a novel way to draw attention to your event.

Chapter 16

Finding the Grant Givers

. . . .

. . . .

Great mystique has been woven around the writing of grant proposals. And consulting careers have been made based on that mystique. Don't be fooled by the smoke and mirrors, however! Securing a grant is a competitive effort, but small organizations with volunteer grant writers can succeed if they have good plans and sound organizations.

A classic rule for effective writing of any kind is to know your audience and keep that audience in mind. Grant writing is no different. In shaping a proposal, the grant writer considers the known and likely traits of the people or organizations she's addressing.

This chapter shows you how to find sources of grants and figure out your approach to a grant giver. (Chapter 17 covers writing a grant proposal.)

Planning a Grant Proposal to a Foundation

Grant sources can be grouped into two broad categories: private and public. Private sources are generally foundations and corporations, and public sources are based within some level of the government — city, county, state, or national. We write about public sources later in this chapter, but here we provide the scoop on foundations and corporations.

When you look at the entire nonprofit sector, you'll notice that government support and gifts from individuals provide the largest portion of contributions. Because they play a smaller role, many foundations see their job as being resources for innovation or program improvement. When your nonprofit has a new idea, wants to expand to a new location, or wants to compare and evaluate different methods, foundations often are a good place to turn to for assistance.

It's tricky to generalize, however. Some foundations do provide flexible dollars that can be used for a nonprofit's rent and light bulbs. Others only want to build buildings or provide new computer systems. Grant seeking can resemble putting together pieces of the puzzle that represent an organization's total needs.

Foundation research generally has two phases: Developing a broad list of prospects, and then refining that list until you find the likeliest sources. We discuss both of these phases in this section.

Your time as a grant writer is better spent when you use some of it to study the priorities and behaviors of the foundations you're approaching. *Shotgunning,* or sending the same proposal to a large number of foundations, is a waste of effort. *Targeting,* or focusing your attention on your most likely sources and writing to address their preferences, is much more effective.

Using the Foundation Center to assemble a broad list of prospects

Over the past 60 years, information about funding sources has become increasingly available to the public. One milestone in this movement was the creation of the Foundation Center in 1956. Originally intended to collect information so that foundations could learn about one another, the Foundation Center quickly became a leading source of information for grant seekers. We explain everything you need to know in the following sections.

Understanding the basics about the Foundation Center

The Foundation Center manages five libraries across the United States and a number of official cooperating collections within other libraries and nonprofits. (See Appendix A for more information.) It also publishes several directories in print, on CDs, and through online subscriptions.

If you can't find a nearby Foundation Center branch library or cooperating collection, check with local community foundations, larger public libraries, and college and university libraries. These places often have copies of the Foundation Center's materials. The books and CDs can be expensive for individuals to purchase, so if you can't find them in a nearby library, we recommend that you purchase a short-term subscription to the Foundation Center's online directory.

So what are you looking for when you're using these search tools? You want to determine whether a foundation satisfies the following three criteria:

- **Geography:** Does this foundation award grants in the area where your nonprofit is based?

> ✔ **Fields of Interest:** Does this foundation award grants in the subject area of your organization's work?
>
> ✔ **Type of support:** Does this foundation award the kind of grant that you want?

If you answered yes, good work! You've found an entry for your broad list of prospects. Strive to come up with a list of about 15 or 20 names.

The Foundation Center directories are dense with information, but each of them contains a helpful introduction and annotated sample listing to help you identify where you can find answers to your questions. The foundation's Web site also can guide you. Visit the site at foundationcenter.org.

Discovering the information and sources that the Center provides

The Foundation Center organizes its information in four ways:

✔ Brief profiles of foundations

✔ Brief profiles of companies

✔ Indexes of actual grants of $10,000 or more

✔ Foundations' 990 tax forms

All four are part of the *Foundation Directory Online,* and the first two (the profiles) are presented in published directories. Here are the names of some of the books and materials you may use:

✔ The *Foundation Directory* and the *Foundation Directory, Volume 2,* are books featuring the 20,000 largest foundations in the United States.

✔ The *Guide to U.S. Foundations, Their Trustees, Officers, and Donors* is a three-volume directory of all the foundations in the country.

✔ *FC Search* is a CD containing both brief profiles of all the active foundations (approximately 80,000) and a database of more than 350,000 actual grants awarded of $10,000 or more, and links to many foundations' Web sites.

✔ The *Foundation Directory Online* is an online subscription service that provides all the content that's on *FC Search* as well as profiles of companies that make contributions. You also can search foundations' 990 tax forms.

The information contained in the *Foundation Directory Online* is updated weekly, and the *Foundation Directory* (the book) is published once a year with a midyear supplement. It's great to have access to the most recent information with the online service, but you should use the tools that best serve your research style and are most readily available to you.

The Foundation Center's books aren't your only options. Some regions publish their own guides and some universities have developed excellent databases.

Applying a few tips to effectively search the Center's information

Here are a few pointers to help you as you cast your net using the Foundation Center tools:

- ✔ **Start with the larger foundations first.** Although the United States has more than 80,000 foundations, many of them are very small. As you begin your research, focus on the larger ones by working with the *Foundation Directory*. When you're ready to leave no stone unturned, use the *Guide to U.S. Foundations, Their Trustees, Officers, and Donors*. Or try *FC Search* or the Search 990s feature on the *Foundation Center Online*. These tools allow you to examine every pebble.

- ✔ **Take advantage of indexes and search functions.** If you're using the printed directories, you'll find indexes that allow you to search by geographic focus, type of support, and subject area. The CD and online tools offer search functions that pull out the same information and point you toward foundations that match your project's context, focus, and need.

  Say, for example, that you want a grant for "capacity building" to strengthen your organization. If you want to search for that specific term, turn to the Search 990s feature of the *Foundation Center Online*. Or you can use the keyword search function. The Search 990s feature reviews thousands and thousands (did we say thousands?) of foundations' 990 and 990-PF tax returns.

- ✔ **Determine whether you or your board members have any contacts who serve on foundation boards.** The third volume of the *Guide to U.S. Foundations, Their Trustees, Officers, and Donors* includes an exhaustive index of foundation board members and trustees. You also can gather this information using *FC Search* or the *Foundation Center Online*.

- ✔ **Don't forget that corporations also award grants.** The *National Directory of Corporate Giving* and the "Search Companies" section of the *Foundation Center Online* present corporate foundations and giving programs.

For a step-by-step guide to the foundation research process, see CD1601. Also, for each entry on your broad list, jot down notes and questions on a *foundation prospect evaluation sheet*. You can find a sample evaluation sheet on the CD; check out CD1603. Through cross-checking and deeper study — as we explain later in this section — you narrow your broad list to the five or six best potential sources.

Digging deeper to narrow your prospects

It's time to take your broad list of prospects in hand and find out more about each of them. (Check out the preceding section if you haven't yet compiled your list of prospects.) See what you can discover from the following sources:

✔ **The Foundation 1000:** If one of your prospects is among the 1,000 largest foundations in the United States, turn to *The Foundation 1000,* a book that provides helpful, detailed information. A similarly detailed guide for corporate sources is *Corporate Foundation Profiles.*

✔ **Web sites and annual reports:** Larger foundations (approximately 13,000 of them) produce Web sites with detailed information about their grantmaking guidelines and grantees. Approximately 1,200 foundations publish printed guidelines and annual reports. These Web sites and annual reports can be particularly helpful for grant seekers. They often include brief statements or introductory letters from the foundation's leaders that provide insight into a foundation's philosophy or its current direction. You can find printed annual reports in some libraries, or you can call the foundations and ask to have them sent to you.

✔ **Form 990s:** Foundation 990 or 990-PF forms may be the only place to find a list that shows every single grant a particular foundation has awarded. Foundations are required to make their three most recent 990 reports available to the public. Many of them do so by including them on their Web sites. Other places to find 990s include the Foundation Center (www.fdncenter.org), Nozasearch (www.nozasearch.com), and GuideStar (www.guidestar.org) Web sites. Some state agencies also provide online access to 990s. Finally, you can request a photocopy of a foundation's 990-PF either in writing or in person. The foundation may ask for a reasonable photocopying fee.

Approximately half of the foundations in the United States don't review grant proposals from organizations that are unfamiliar to them and only give to nonprofits that have been chosen by their trustees or staffs. To identify these foundations, watch for the phrases "No unsolicited proposals" or "Gives only to preselected organizations" when reviewing their profiles. If you have been searching through 990-PF documents to find a possible funder, check Part XV, Question 2. Foundations that don't accept unsolicited proposals will check a box here indicating that practice.

A foundation's 990 may be the only place you can see a complete list of grants, but PDF files for the nation's largest foundations are enormous. We recommend against downloading a 990 from one of the larger foundations. Downloading these files is more useful when you're studying small foundations whose grants lists may not otherwise be available.

✔ **The foundation's contact person:** If a foundation listing includes a contact person and phone number — and if it doesn't say you shouldn't call — feel free to call that person to confirm information and ask any questions you may have. However, we recommend that you do so only after you've read as much as you can find about that foundation. This way you can be focused, clear, and knowledgeable as you seek additional information.

Knowing who you're dealing with: Different kinds of foundations

Foundations are formed and governed in different ways. These differences may affect the way you address them as a grant seeker. Four basic kinds of foundations include the following: independent foundations, company-sponsored foundations, community foundations, and operating foundations. In this section, we describe ways you can recognize and understand which is which.

Independent foundations large and small

Most foundations in the United States are classified as *independent* — also called "private" — foundations. Some of the country's largest foundations — such as the Bill and Melinda Gates Foundation, the Ford Foundation, and the Lilly Endowment — are independent foundations, but many small- and medium-sized grantmaking foundations also fall into this category.

When conducting your research, note whether the foundations have paid staff members who can answer your questions: If they do, they're more likely (but not guaranteed) to consider grant proposals from organizations previously unknown to them.

While they vary widely, key characteristics that independent foundations share include the following:

✔ They're established with funds donated by individuals, families, or a small group of people.

✔ Their purposes and modes of grantmaking are set by their boards of trustees, who may be family members (in which case they're called "family foundations"), or their appointed representatives.

✔ Many (approximately 70 percent) of these foundations award grants in the places where they were formed, but they also may award grants in multiple locations.

✔ They must file a 990 or a 990-PF with the Internal Revenue Service (IRS) each year.

Company-sponsored foundations and corporate giving

Corporations and businesses may support nonprofits by creating company-sponsored foundations, or they may award money directly from their company budgets. Some do both!

Whether they manage their giving through a foundation or directly from company coffers, the staff members who coordinate grantmaking also may play other roles within the corporation — such as public affairs director or human resources manager. You may notice that many — both company-sponsored foundations and direct corporate-giving programs — give away goods and services or provide technical assistance, and many of them support educational causes.

Common characteristics of company-sponsored foundations include the following:

- They're established with funds that come from a business or corporation.

- Some of them maintain assets that they invest, and then they award grants from the money they earn on those investments. Many of them add to their grantmaking budgets when their business is having a profitable year. For this reason, their grantmaking budgets can fluctuate dramatically.

- Often they're governed by a board made up of company executives.

- Most of them award grants in the communities where their employees live and work, and they see their grant giving as part of their role as good citizens.

- Sometimes a company's grants support organizations where its employees volunteer or contribute or that its employees recommend.

- Some companies are cautious about supporting causes that could alienate their employees or stockholders.

- They must file a 990-PF with the IRS each year.

Corporations' and businesses' direct-giving programs share characteristics with company-sponsored foundations, but they have a slightly different profile. Consider some of the following characteristics:

- All funds available for grants come directly from company budgets and depend on the business's available resources. In lean years the business may not support charitable causes.

- Like company-sponsored foundations, businesses with direct-giving programs tend to award grants in the communities where their employees live and work.

✔ Many corporate-giving programs want to receive public recognition for their gifts. They justify their charitable giving to their owners or stockholders as "cause-related marketing" and "good public relations."

✔ Gathering information about these programs may be more difficult because the businesses don't need to specify their support of charities in their financial statements.

Many corporate-giving programs match contributions that their employees make to nonprofit organizations. When seeking information about your individual donors, ask whether they work for a company that would match their gift.

In your neck of the woods: Community foundations

The first community foundation, The Cleveland Foundation, was created in 1914. Today more than 700 such foundations exist nationwide. Community foundations have a different, advantageous tax status from other kinds of foundations. The IRS classifies them as "public charities." Other characteristics that they share with one another include the following:

✔ They're started with funds contributed by many sources — trusts and contributions of all sizes from members of the communities they represent. Those communities may be as large as a state (Hawaii and Maine have community foundations), or they may be a county or city (Sonoma, California, or Chicago, Illinois).

✔ Community foundations focus their grantmaking on the geographic areas in which they were established.

✔ They're governed by boards of directors made up of people who represent the communities they serve.

✔ To keep their desirable public charity tax status, they must raise money as well as give it away. For that reason, even a very small community foundation has paid staff members.

✔ Donors to community foundations may contribute to their general grantmaking programs or may create donor-advised funds within their community foundations and play a role in recommending how to award grants derived from their contributions. The number of donor-advised funds in the United States is growing rapidly.

When reviewing a grants list for a community foundation, if you see a grant that doesn't seem to fit within the foundation's published guidelines, it may have been awarded by a donor from an advised fund.

The grantmaking public charity category is broader than the community foundation category, but community foundations are the most common kind. Some public charities focus on addressing specific topics or population groups rather than defined geographic areas. They, too, must raise money as well as give it away. One example is The Global Fund for Women.

Operating foundations: Locked doors for grant seekers

Operating foundations don't award grants. They're formed to engage in their own programmatic activities. When you come across an operating foundation, skip right over it!

Going for a Government Grant

Before you start daydreaming about massive state or federal funding, it pays to compare the pros and cons of private foundation funding to public funding. Table 16-1 sorts things out for you.

Table 16-1	Comparing Private to Public Grant Sources
Private Sources	*Public Sources*
The purpose of the grant-giving entity is set by donors and trustees.	The purpose of the grant-giving agency is set by legislation.
Most funders award grants to 501(c)(3) nonprofit organizations, some give to public agencies, others give fellowships and awards to individuals.	Most agencies award grants, contracts, and loans to nonprofit and for-profit entities, to individuals, and to other government entities.
Most grants are awarded for one year, and, in general, grants are smaller than those awarded by public sources.	Many multiyear grants are awarded for large amounts of money.
The application process requires a limited number of contacts with individuals within the funding agency.	The application process is bureaucratic and may require applicants to work with staff at multiple levels of government.
Grants are sometimes awarded in response to simple two-page letters with backup materials.	Many proposals are lengthy (as long as 40–100 pages).
Agency files are private; applicants may not have access to reviewer comments or successful grants submitted by other agencies. Review panels and board meetings may be closed to the public.	Agency records must be public. Applicants may visit many review panels; reviewer comments and successful proposals submitted by other agencies may be requested.
Foundation priorities may change quickly according to trustees' interests.	Agency priorities may change abruptly when new legislation is passed or budgets are revised.

(continued)

Table 16-1 *(continued)*

Private Sources	Public Sources
Developing personal contacts with trustees or with foundation staff may enhance the applicant's chances of securing a grant.	Developing personal contacts with senate and congressional aides for state or national representatives may enhance your application's chances.
After accepting a grant, in most cases the agency is required to file a brief final narrative and financial report.	After accepting a grant, agencies may be required to follow specified contracting and hiring practices and bookkeeping and auditing procedures. They may have to prove other compliance with federal regulations. Grants can be relatively costly to manage.

If, after reviewing the info in Table 16-1, you decide you're up to the task of seeking government grants, read on.

You may have heard that finding government money is difficult. But remember that one or two major government grants may provide general operating support or may award a grant to your program for as long as five years. The time spent wading through bureaucratic offices and regulations can be worthwhile.

Federal grants

To pursue government funds, you want to study a different set of research guides from those that help you with foundations and corporations. The publication that's most likely to help you is online at www.grants.gov.

Grants.gov only covers federal grant programs. If you're seeking personal financial assistance, follow the links on the For Applicants page of Grants.gov.

Determining the pros and cons of Grants.gov

The bad news about Grants.gov is that it's written in bureaucratic language and the site has so much information that it can be overwhelming. But, the bad news is far outweighed by the good: Grants.gov is the only source you'll need for information about all federal grants. It incorporates more than 1,000 programs representing $500 billion in annual grant awards. After you get past the initial shock of wading through the overwhelming amount of information, the site is relatively easy to search.

Supplementing your search with the CFDA

Federal agencies provide 15 different kinds of funding, from "direct payments for specified use" and "insurance" and "loans" to "program grants." For information about all 15 kinds of federal assistance, turn to another federal publication, the *Catalog of Federal Domestic Assistance* (CFDA), which can be found online at www.cfda.gov.

We steer you to Grants.gov because if grant support is what you're seeking, it will be more tailored to your needs and, perhaps, less cumbersome. However, the CFDA Web site is a powerful tool that you also may want to use. The two use the same catalog numbering system to identify funding opportunities.

Beginning your search with Grants.gov

As you begin your search, you want to pay attention to whether your organization is eligible to apply to a particular program. Some kinds of federal grants are available only to state and local governments, federally recognized Indian tribal governments, and other specified groups — not necessarily nonprofit organizations. So pay attention to applicant eligibility as you read Grants.gov listings.

When opening the home page of Grants.gov, you're invited to search by

- ✔ Agency (which is useful if you know you're interested in reviewing the programs offered by the Institute of Museum and Library Services, the Department of Homeland Security, or another specific agency)
- ✔ Categories (in other words, broad subject areas such as "environment" and "health")
- ✔ Keywords

When you're ready to move beyond browsing, select Grants.gov's Advanced Search page, which allows you to check on coming deadlines, confirm applicant eligibility, and search by funding category. If you happen to know the CFDA number for a specific program, you can enter it and — voilà — the program description will appear.

Grants.gov can tell you which agencies and offices manage the funds for different grant opportunities. After identifying federal programs of interest, experienced grant seekers usually call, write, or e-mail those offices to confirm the information. That's because even though Grants.gov information is updated frequently, it also goes out of date quickly.

We outline more information about searching for federal grants and contracts and suggest further steps to take in your research on CD1602.

Nonfederal government grants

Information about state, county, and municipal grants (which state or local tax dollars generate money for) can be trickier to find than those awarded through federal agencies. That's because the information isn't always compiled in resource guides. Some, but not all, state and city government offices do a good job of informing their constituents about funding opportunities.

Checking the Web site of the state or local agencies related to your project (such as the Department of Education or the Office of Children and Youth) and visiting with local government officials and congressional office staffs are good steps to take in your research.

Chapter 17

Writing a Grant Proposal

*E*ven though grant seeking is highly competitive, writing a good grant proposal isn't particularly mysterious or difficult. First you identify a problem and make it compelling, and then you set goals for solving that problem, and last you propose a possible solution and a way to test the results. In the course of laying out the plan, you also want to assert the special strengths of your organization and a sensible financial plan for the project, both in the near term and later. You present your proposal in a readable form that tells a story and conveys your vision in terms both inspiring and practical.

Some proposals are quite long and elaborate. Some are just a few pages. Some are presented on paper, and others are submitted online. Your research into funding sources (which we describe in Chapter 16) will uncover the preferences of different foundations and government programs, so you can figure out the best mode of presentation, appropriate level of detail, and best method for submitting your proposal. You'll encounter many variations, but this chapter shows you the basics of how to write the grant.

The Windup: Tasks to Complete before the Proposal

Generally, a grant writer develops a proposal by talking with staff members, volunteers, or the board about a project idea. The writer builds the members' enthusiasm and refines the project idea with their knowledge. Before setting fingers to keyboard, the writer should investigate the following:

✔ Who are the constituents who will benefit from the project? (Find out everything you can about them.)

✔ What are others doing in this field?

> ✔ What particular strengths does your nonprofit bring to doing the project?
>
> ✔ Specifically, what do you want to accomplish?
>
> ✔ What will it cost to do this work?

Sometimes a funding source announces a specific initiative for which it's inviting proposals — called a Request for Proposal (an "RFP") or a Program Announcement. In responding to an RFP, the grant writer resembles a job seeker who's convincing a prospective employer (in this case the foundation or government agency) that she (or rather the nonprofit she represents) is the best one for the job.

Asking for permission to ask

Many funding sources want to screen proposal ideas before they receive extensive, detailed documents. This allows them to encourage only truly promising proposals, saving both themselves and grant seekers the time and effort that goes into reviewing and writing longer proposals.

When a grant writer encounters a request for a *letter of inquiry,* he should boil down the essence of the proposal — all eight areas covered in the later section "The Pitch: Writing Your Proposal" — into a readable, compelling letter. The letter doesn't ask for a grant directly, but it asks for permission to submit more detailed information. Most letters of inquiry are two or three pages in length. Follow the foundation's stated preferences.

CD1701 offers a sample letter of inquiry, and CD1702 shows a sample full proposal.

Passing the screening questionnaire

Some funding agencies screen potential applicants by asking them to respond to questionnaires, which are often found on funders' Web sites. Questions may determine specific eligibility — such as whether the non-profit organization provides services in a particular geographic area — while others ask for substantive answers to questions. As with a letter of inquiry, this questionnaire may seem like a barrier to applying but is intended as a tool to keep unlikely applicants from wasting their time and efforts.

A grant seeker shouldn't pass off the letter of inquiry or a questionnaire as an inconsequential hurdle: First impressions can be lasting impressions.

The Pitch: Writing Your Proposal

Deep down, every good proposal is based on a well-considered plan, and designing that plan is a creative, even fun, part of the task. The differences from funder to funder are in how to pitch that plan and the order in which its parts are assembled. But the parts themselves are fairly standard:

- **Cover letter and summary:** Provide a brief overview of the entire project and its costs, linking the project to the interests of the funding source.
- **Introduction or background:** Present the applicant's strengths and qualifications.
- **Problem statement or needs assessment:** Describe the situation that the proposed project will try to improve or eradicate.
- **Goals, objectives, and outcomes:** Outline a vision for success in both broad and pragmatic terms.
- **Methods:** Describe the project activities, who will manage them, and why the proposed approach is the best.
- **Evaluation:** Explain how the organization will measure whether it met its goals, objectives, and outcomes.
- **Budget:** Present the project's costs and sources of income.
- **Sustainability:** Discuss how the balance of funds needed will be raised if a grant is awarded but doesn't cover the entire cost, and, if it's a program expected to continue, how project costs will be covered in the future.

In this section, we cover each of these parts in detail.

CD1703 and CD1704 illustrate two kinds of proposals — a general operating support grant and a project grant.

While you want your proposal to be compelling, it may be a violation of state charitable solicitation laws to make any misrepresentations in a grant application. Tell a true story!

Starting out with the cover letter and summary

Technically, the *cover letter* isn't part of the proposal narrative. It's attached to the top of the proposal where it serves as an introduction to the document's primary points. One of its key roles is to convey how the proposal addresses the foundation's stated priorities. Often a board member signs the letter.

The letter mentions any contact the organization may have had with the funding source before submitting the proposal. For example, you may say, "When I tripped over your umbrella last Tuesday, I couldn't help but notice you were reading a book about frogs. Here at the city park aquarium, we've planned an astounding amphibian exhibition."

Although the cover letter's author always wants to lay out the basics of the request — how much money is needed and for what — she also can use it to say something about her personal connection to the cause. The letter should close with clear, specific information about the contact person to whom the funding source should direct any questions.

The body of the actual grant proposal begins with an executive summary (similar to an abstract for a report) containing a brisk overview of its key ideas. The grant writer usually begins the summary section with a one-sentence overview of the project and how much money is being requested in the proposal. Next she includes key ideas (one or two sentences each) from every section of the proposal. Finally, the grant writer closes the executive summary with the prognosis for future funding for the program.

Don't use the exact same wording to describe your project idea in the cover letter and in the project summary. You don't want to bore your reader.

Introducing your agency

Some proposals contain *introductions*. Others contain *background information* sections. Choose which to use by following the preferences of your funding source or, if no preference is given, by deciding which approach allows you to best present the proposal idea. Whichever you use, this section of a proposal describes the nonprofit organization that's seeking money.

Usually this section begins with a brief history of the nonprofit, its philosophy in approaching its work, and its major accomplishments. Then the writer describes the current programs as well as the constituents served by the programs. After these standard ingredients, the writer draws upon whatever other credentials recommend the organization for the work she's about to propose. Drawing attention to signs of outside validation is helpful. Here are some kinds of things the writer can mention:

- ✔ Media coverage
- ✔ Citations and awards presented to the agency or its leaders
- ✔ Credentials and/or experience of the nonprofit's leadership

> ✔ Other agencies that refer clients to the nonprofit
>
> ✔ Invitations extended to the nonprofit to provide expert advice or testimony
>
> ✔ Major grants received from other sources

Although the writer isn't yet describing the project idea, the items she introduces here should back up the nonprofit's qualifications to do the proposed work. For example, suppose that an after-school program for teenagers offers multiple programs — athletics, arts, and youth-led volunteer work in the community. If the grant request focuses on expanding the community service work, the writer can focus this section on how that volunteer work began and evolved, where the teens have provided services, and who has praised it.

Grant writers often are tempted to write on and on (and on and on and on) (and on and on and on) about an agency's history or its philosophy. Don't drag this section down by including too many details or by using too much eloquent verbiage. One — or at the most, two — paragraphs on these subjects are plenty.

Shaping the problem

A grant writer begins to shape the argument behind the proposal plan in the *problem statement* or a *statement of need*. Generally a writer prepares a problem statement when proposing a new relationship with the constituents who would be served by the project. A statement of need talks about the challenging situations of people (or animals or historic buildings) that the nonprofit already serves.

How do you know whether you need to write a problem statement or a statement of need? Here's an example: If someone notices a decline in the population of a bird species along a lakeshore and writes about that concern, such a discussion would be a problem statement. If a bird conservation organization that has been working to preserve that bird population for several years observes a change in the birds' food source that's affecting their health, that written piece would be a statement of need.

Whichever of these two kinds of statements a writer prepares, this proposal section brings forward the reasons behind the program for which the organization is seeking money. It does so by focusing on needs of constituents the project would serve. It should incorporate some data or statements from experts to back up the needs or problems it describes. And it should capture its reader's attention — making him want to read on.

You shouldn't describe your "problem" as a lack of money but as a situation in the lives of the constituents, whether they're spruce trees, retired adults, or former race horses.

A common mistake made in a problem statement (or statement of need) is identifying the problem's solution. Wait! Hold off! The rest of the proposal is boring for your readers if you propose the solution here. At the most, you may want to plant the beginnings of an idea, or suggest a direction that may be fruitful.

Setting goals, objectives, and outcomes

After the grant writer has described a problem in ways that interest the reader's concerns, the next step is to introduce what the nonprofit can achieve if it takes on the proposed project. The writer hasn't yet described the project activities, but this section jumps ahead to show what could be achieved if the project were a success. Why? First you hope to pique the reader's interest and concern (in the problem statement), next you show him the possibility of a better future (in goals, objectives, and outcomes), and then you explain how to achieve that vision (in the methods section).

Goals, objectives, and outcomes are related but different terms. You find out about them in Chapter 7, which discusses planning. The following points give a brief overview of these terms:

- *Goals* are broad, general results. They may be somewhat lofty.

- *Objectives* should be measurable results. How much do you want to accomplish in what time frame, involving how many people (or trees or salamanders)?

- *Outcomes* are the trickiest to state. An outcome is the answer to the question, "So what?" So what if you provide antismoking classes to high school students, reaching every teen in four school districts? Well, the outcome may be that a lower than average percentage of those specific students begins smoking in high school. Or in college. Or ever.

  The writer wants the outcomes to be significant, measurable, and specific, but he also has to be careful not to overstate how much the project can claim or measure. What if the antismoking classes are one of a series of health classes and others also include antismoking sessions? The question becomes, which program really caused the change?

If a grant says a nonprofit intends to achieve a long-term outcome, the agency better be prepared to conduct the research necessary to find out whether progress is being made toward achieving that outcome.

Presenting (ta-da!) your project idea

At last it's time to explain the project idea. Who will do what to whom over what period of time? If you're writing your proposal for a research project, generally this section is called *procedures*. For most other types of projects, it's called *methods* or *methodology*.

Although this section contains the idea that inspired the organization to seek funding, sometimes the writing is dull. The content is similar to writing a list of instructions, and writers often get wrapped up in describing each step in minute detail.

To avoid the dullness trap, think about constructing an argument from beginning to end. A good methods section opens with an overview of the approach and then leads the reader through key phases in the project's development. It includes enough detail so that the reader can imagine the project clearly but not so much that she sinks into the daily grind. Other techniques to preserve vitality include the use of timelines, charts, or graphs to break up and complement the descriptive text.

Most projects require a few months of preparation before they can be launched. Factor in time for hiring and training staff, purchasing and installing equipment, identifying research subjects, and performing other necessary preliminary steps.

Because this section contains all the project details, you may accidentally leave out or forget important information. Here are two topics that often are overlooked:

- **Hiring:** If you need to hire new staff to do the project work, be sure to discuss the hiring process, job descriptions, and qualifications. See Chapter 9 for ideas on hiring paid staff.

- **Marketing:** Just because you create something great doesn't mean that anyone will show up to take advantage of it. Your proposal must explain how an organization plans to spread the word about this new project and entice the target population into becoming involved. Chapter 11 provides tips on marketing your program to the public.

The proposal must do more than explain what the organization will do. It also must explain why the organization is taking that approach — the rationale. The reason may be that nobody has ever done it this way before. The reason may be that the organization has tested the approach and knows that it works. The reason may be that another organization in another part of the country has tested the approach and the project proposes to try it in a new setting.

Some funding sources ask you to fill out a table with columns in which you describe your goals, the *inputs* (resources you'll put into the project) short-term objectives, long-term outcomes, activities, and intended results. These tables go by several names. Often they're called *logic models*. Sometimes foundations identify them as *theories of change* or *proofs of concept*.

We include a sample logic model on CD1705 along with a link to the W.H. Kellogg Foundation Web site, which provides a helpful free report about logic models and program evaluation.

In an effort to raise as much money as possible to secure a grant, an organization may change its programs to match a particular foundation's interests. The organization's board and management should carefully assess new project ideas to make sure they address the organization's mission. Otherwise, the nonprofit may drift away from addressing the needs of the constituents it was formed to serve or from sustaining previously developed, high-quality programs.

Explaining how results will be measured

If the grant writer has carefully shaped the goals, objectives, and outcomes section of the proposal, the desired project results are clear. The *evaluation* section, then, explains how the organization will measure whether it met those goals, objectives, and outcomes.

This section says who will conduct the evaluation and why that person or organization is right for the job; what information already is known about the situation or population served; what instrument(s) will be used to measure the project's results; and how the finished report will be used.

Different kinds of evaluation are appropriate at different stages of a project. In a project's first year, the most important question may be, "How can we make it run better?" A nonprofit with a brand-new effort may want to spend the first year analyzing its internal efficiency, balance of responsibilities, and general productivity before beginning an intense study measuring outcomes.

Some organizations evaluate all their projects with project staff. Who's better suited to understand the details and nuances of the work? Who else can grasp the purpose and objectives of the project so quickly? Of course, the opposing view is that you get biased results by asking staff members, whose livelihoods may depend on continuation of the project being studied. Yet, outside consultants are more expensive, and they, too, are employed by the nonprofit agency and may have some bias about the report's results.

Evaluation of nonprofit activities has evolved over the past several decades. Here are some common questions addressed in evaluations (progressing from basic to complex):

- ✔ Were project funds spent according to the proposal plan?
- ✔ How many people are being served and by how many units of service (hours of counseling, copies of publications, and so on)?
- ✔ How do consumers of the agency's services rate the quality of those services?
- ✔ How does this agency's work compare to industry standards for effective work of this type?
- ✔ What changes have been affected in the lives of the constituents served?

Surveying the types of evaluation

You do need to report to your funding sources on what you accomplished with their funding, but the most important reason to evaluate your work is to improve your services. In explaining how you'll evaluate a program, you may want to use these standard terms:

✔ **Antecedent evaluation:** Looks at your project's results in the context of the larger environment in which it's operating. Factors may include the nonprofit organization's prior experiences as well as such external factors as the closure of a related program or changes in the economy.

✔ **Formative evaluation:** Assesses the quality of a program during its development phase.

For example, it may be based on gathering feedback about a prototype of a program from the constituents you intend to serve.

✔ **Outcome evaluation:** Measures what changes occurred as the result of services or activities that the nonprofit organization provided.

✔ **Process evaluation:** Describes the steps taken to implement a program.

✔ **Summative evaluation:** Judges the quality of a program at the end of its activities. It compiles data about a program's output, such as how many people were served with how many hours of service.

Often a nonprofit can discover a lot about the effectiveness of its work by analyzing information that it already gathers. For example, some kinds of data an organization may have on file include names and addresses of people participating in public programs, intake and exit interviews with staff and clients, or queries submitted by e-mail via a Web site.

If your agency plans to gather data from new sources (such as through surveys, interviews, and focus groups), the proposal should explain what those sources are, who will design the instruments to be used, who will gather the information, and who will analyze the results.

Talking about the budget

Because a proposal is a request for money, at this point your proposal should present information about project costs and the other funding that's available. If your organization offers only one service for which it's seeking money, the organization's budget is the same as the *project budget.* If the proposal seeks funds for a project that is one of many things the nonprofit does, it's presented as a smaller piece of the overall budget.

Chapter 10 discusses how to compute the indirect costs that all programs within an organization share. Different foundations have different attitudes about covering the indirect costs associated with projects. Check with the foundation to which you're applying to see whether it limits how much can be charged to indirect costs or management and fundraising expenses.

The project budget should be clear, reasonable, and well considered. The grant writer should keep a worksheet of budget assumptions with the grant file in case anyone asks months later how he computed the numbers it contains. Foundations don't want to believe that an organization is inflating the budget, nor do they want to think that the applicant is trying to make his proposal more competitive by requesting less than he really needs. Either approach — budgeting too high or too low in relationship to the cost of a project — can raise a red flag for funders.

Unless the foundation is willing to consider a proposal for 100 percent of the project costs, the proposal budget should include both income and expenses. Some foundations ask for the information in a particular format. For those foundations that don't require a special budget format to be used, here are some general standards that apply to the presentation:

- ✔ Income should head the budget, followed by expenses.

- ✔ If the organization has multiple income sources, contributed sources should be listed apart from earned sources. Within contributed sources, a writer usually lists government grants first, followed by foundation grants, corporate gifts, and contributions from individuals.

- ✔ All expenses related to personnel costs — salaries, benefits, and consulting fees — come first in the expense half of the budget. Usually personnel costs are subtotaled.

- ✔ Non-personnel costs follow the personnel costs and also are subtotaled.

- ✔ Some kinds of project budgets allow for contingency funds of a certain percentage of the project's projected costs. These funds are usually listed last among expenses.

- ✔ Budget footnotes can explain anything that may be difficult for a reader to understand.

The budget is like a spine for the rest of the proposal and supports every aspect of the plan. Costs of every activity in the methods and evaluation sections should be included.

Keep in mind that some project budgets seem simple and straightforward when they really are more complex. Say, for example, an agency wants to purchase a piece of equipment. It researches the cost and writes it down as the one and only budget item. This approach may be foolhardy: Other costs involved may include shipping and installation, insurance, training of staff, and maintenance and supplies.

At some foundations, all project budgets and financial reports are analyzed by staff with expertise in that area. They may be separated from the rest of the proposal for this reading. Therefore, a budget needs to be clear even if it's read on its own — separate from the narrative part of the proposal.

You can find sample foundation budget forms on CD1706. You also can find a sample project budget for a tutoring program within a youth agency on CD1004.

Showing where the rest of the money comes from

In Chapter 13, we introduce the age-old concept of not putting all your eggs in one basket. Between many foundations' reluctance to pay for 100 percent of a project's costs and their preference for offering short-term project support, if you start a new project, you want to know how you can cover the balance of the costs in the present and all the costs when initial project support runs out.

Foundations reviewing grant proposals want to know the same information. What resources, other than the grant that the foundation is considering, are available to the project? And how can the agency sustain the project in the future?

Willingness to cover the full cost of a project varies from foundation to foundation and agency to agency. Some like to "own" a project and have their names strongly associated with it; therefore, they may be willing to cover full costs. Some like to be one of several supporters so that the nonprofit isn't entirely dependent on them. That way, the project can go on even if they can't continue to support it in a future year.

An *additional funding plan* should be clear and reasonable. Because a nonprofit can't assume it will receive every grant for which it applies, a foundation understands if a nonprofit has applied for more grants funding than the full cost of the program. If a nonprofit lists another foundation as a possible source of income for a project, it doesn't necessarily have to have received that grant, but the prospect should be plausible. The size of the grant should be appropriate to others awarded by the agency, and the focus of the foundation should be aligned with the project request.

Foundation staff members talk with colleagues at other foundations. Never lie about having submitted a proposal or having received a grant from another foundation. That lie can undermine your request (and future requests, too)!

Guidelines for future funding are similar to those for additional funding. The plan should be reasonable and well considered. Generally, foundations hope to see agencies growing less dependent on grants over time and are happy to see proposals projecting future increases in earned revenues or individual contributions.

Here are some possible sources for future funding:

- A government contract to sustain a valuable service after it has been developed and tested
- The sale of publications, recordings, or services based on the project
- A membership drive
- A major donor campaign

Some proposals don't need to address these concerns. They seek support for projects that begin and end in short periods of time. For example, a proposal may support the publication of a study of an agency's work and after the agency edits, designs, and posts the report on its Web site, future funding isn't needed. For others, future funding is very important. For example, you wouldn't want to start a recreation center for low-income youths and have to close it after a few years. The lack of program continuity can have a negative effect on the clients.

Having the last word

Not all proposals include a *conclusion*. Some writers feel that a conclusion is repetitive and unnecessary. On the other hand, if the proposal ends with a discussion of future and additional funding, that part of the proposal may seem remote from the passion that fueled the project in the first place.

We recommend taking a bow: A brief concluding section may bring the reader back to the key points of the proposal, leaving a compelling finale as the last thing the reader reads and remembers.

P.S.: The appendix

A proposal always needs an appendix. Five key items are routinely included in the appendix (and often identified by foundations as required enclosures):

- ✔ The project budget (if not placed in the middle of the narrative part of the proposal)
- ✔ Proof of 501(c)(3) status from the IRS
- ✔ List of the board of directors (and of any advisory boards)
- ✔ Current year's organization budget
- ✔ Prior year's financial statement

Other common appendix items include the following:

- ✔ A list of major grants received in recent years
- ✔ An organizational chart outlining staff and board roles
- ✔ A timeline of the organization's history
- ✔ Copies of media clippings about the agency
- ✔ Job descriptions and/or résumés of key staff
- ✔ Samples of evaluations or reports
- ✔ A copy of a long-range plan (or an executive summary if the plan is lengthy)
- ✔ Agency brochures and program announcements
- ✔ Letters of support

On CD1707, we include a checklist for finishing and submitting your proposal.

Throwing Special Pitches for Special Situations

If you prepare a grant proposal following the format we describe in the previous sections, you'll have in hand a very useful document, suitable for submission to many foundations. However, grant writing isn't a field in which one size fits all or even one approach fits all. So in the next sections, we describe some common situations that call for variations on your basic proposal.

If a foundation gives explicit instructions about how to present your proposal, always follow them. You'll notice that example CD1708 is written in the form of answers to a series of questions posed by the funder.

Trolling for corporate funds with a two-page letter

Proposals addressed to corporations and company-sponsored foundations generally are brief. A two-page letter is an excellent approach. If an employee of the corporation is involved with your organization, say so in the first paragraph.

Here's what to do in your letter proposal:

- ✔ Ask for a specific contribution early in the letter. If you've had prior contact with the funder, mention it.
- ✔ Describe the need or problem to be addressed.
- ✔ Explain what your organization plans to do if the grant is awarded.
- ✔ Provide information about your nonprofit organization and its strengths and accomplishments.
- ✔ Include appropriate budget data. If the budget is more than a half-page long, include it as an attachment.
- ✔ Discuss how the project will be sustained in the future.
- ✔ Describe how your organization can acknowledge the gift publicly and provide visibility to the corporation.
- ✔ Make a strong, compelling closing statement.

On the CD accompanying this book, you'll find a sample letter proposal (CD1709) and a sample set of company-sponsored foundation guidelines (CD1710).

Seeking general operating support

If you're seeking funds for general operating support, your proposal needs to make an argument for the work of the entire agency rather than for a specific project. In this type of request, some of the information about current activities, often included in the introduction or background information sections, should be moved to the methods section. The grantmaking organization judges the application based on overall organizational strength and its role in its field. Increasingly, foundations consider the ability of an agency to cooperate or work with others an important criterion.

If you're tailoring a proposal for general operating support, we recommend the following:

- ✔ Prepare an introduction that introduces the problem that the agency was created to solve, the goals it addresses, and its current programs. Give some attention to describing its leadership (board and staff), its history, and how its activities may have evolved over time.

- ✔ In the problem statement, describe current challenges it faces as it works to fulfill its mission.

- ✔ When preparing the section on goals, objectives, and outcomes, address the external goals (how the nonprofit plans to serve its constituents) and internal goals (such as training the board of directors or improving its Web site).

- ✔ Use the methods section to describe the agency's current programs.

- ✔ In the evaluation section, describe various means the agency uses to assess and improve its programs.

- ✔ Include the entire annual budget for the organization in lieu of a project budget.

- ✔ In the section on future and additional funding, briefly describe fundraising or earned income areas the organization is working to increase.

We include a sample general operating support grant on CD1703.

Seed money: Proposing to form a new agency

Some foundations specialize in "seed funding" for new projects and new organizations. A seed proposal has two key ingredients: careful assessment of the problem to be addressed and special qualifications its founders bring to its creation. Here's a quick outline of a proposal for a new endeavor:

- ✔ Background information introduces the people who are creating the organization, their vision, how they identified the idea, and steps they've taken to date to realize their vision.

- ✔ The problem statement thoughtfully presents what the founders have observed and learned about the needs to be addressed.

- ✔ While the goals may be lofty, stated objectives and outcomes should be reasonable considering the developing state of the organization.

 ✔ Methods present plans for the first year or two of activities. They include a discussion of how the organization will be structured and how services will be offered.

 ✔ Evaluation plans may "go easy" during the organization's initial phases. Founders may be testing basic ideas for their feasibility and efficiency for a year or two before studying a program in depth.

 ✔ The budget is likely to be the entire organizational budget. Some seed grant funders are willing to cover such start-up costs as equipment purchases or deposits for renting an office.

 ✔ Future and additional funding should outline basic plans for supporting the nonprofit in the future (unless it addresses a discrete problem that may be solved within a few years).

A foundation may be willing to support a feasibility study for a new idea. Such a grant funds interviews and research into how distinctive the idea is, what the likeliest sources of support are, and how much funding the new organization may expect from such resources. Such a plan arms the seed project in applying for other start-up grants.

Chapter 18

Capital Campaigns: Finding Lasting Resources

*A*s nonprofit organizations mature, their staff and board may grow ambitious to develop resources that can stabilize them. One option they have is to raise *capital* — money to make specific, usually long-term, financial investments.

Some organizations raise capital funds for *ventures* — money they put aside for major program innovations. Some raise capital for *endowments* — money they permanently invest, with the investment returns providing a source of annual income. Still others focus their capital fundraising on buying property or building facilities.

If you're the director of a nonprofit that's taking on a capital campaign, imagine yourself as suddenly having two jobs: leading your organization and its programs and leading its capital project. Can you picture yourself in those two hats? Exhausting thought, isn't it? However, if the campaign project goes well, it can attract new donors and attention to your nonprofit. That benefit, combined with new resources to invest in your work, can make those hats worth wearing.

As varied as their purposes are, most capital campaigns share a set of fundraising activities. Not every organization is positioned to make those strategies work. Read ahead and proceed cautiously before stepping onto the capital campaign trail.

Beginning the Funding Plan

Suppose your adult literacy program wants to share its innovative teaching materials broadly through a series of books, but setting up a publication program requires a substantial initial investment. Maybe your nonprofit school for hearing impaired children balances its budget each year, but it depends heavily on a small number of income sources. Having annual investment returns from an endowment may allow it to provide scholarships for children who can't pay full tuition rates. Or say you've found the building of your organization's dreams. It's just around the corner from where you currently serve clients, and it's bigger and better than your current building. Better yet, it's for sale at a reasonable price. You need money to buy it and money to make repairs.

In each of these cases, you need to raise a significant amount of money that's above and beyond your normal annual fundraising. Where do you begin? Capital fundraising, of course! However, keep in mind that it requires you to analyze your organization's situation and to plan carefully and thoroughly. Not every organization is positioned to succeed at capital fundraising. You need to do the following:

- ✔ **Preplan** by gathering information about technical assistance available to you, reviewing your donor records, and creating a rough campaign budget.

- ✔ **Test** the project's feasibility by meeting with a select group of potential contributors and gauging their possible interest. Consider the timing of your campaign: Will you be competing with other campaigns? How generous are donors in the current economic climate?

- ✔ **Develop** your case by brainstorming with staff and board members.

- ✔ **Analyze** what you find out from the interviews against your initial goal and then refine your goal and plan.

An unsuccessful capital campaign can cost your organization money, hurt its reputation, and exhaust and demoralize your staff and board. If your research suggests that you won't succeed, do *not* be foolhardy and forge ahead anyway.

Preplanning your campaign

After your organization begins thinking that it may want to raise funds for a capital project, we recommend that you seek outside assistance in the form of workshops, classes, or consulting. Convincing yourself that your capital campaign can work is easy, so testing your vision on others is important. Possible resources include the following:

- ✔ A program officer at a local foundation or staff in your city's economic development office or regional community loan fund may be able to suggest other nearby resources.

- ✔ The Nonprofit Finance Fund (www.nonprofitfinancefund.org) may offer programs in your area, including low-cost consultations, small grants for planning, and workshops about understanding and planning capital projects.

- ✔ Colleagues who conducted capital campaigns may be able to guide you to resources they used. Your board may contain members with professional experience in financial lending and investing, architecture, construction, real estate, city government, and law; all can provide valuable assistance. If your board doesn't include such professional skills, its members may know professionals who do.

You need to begin raising funds from individuals and institutions that know your organization and care deeply about its work. Assess your organization's primary sources of contributed income. How detailed and accurate are your donor records? Who's been donating money to your cause and at what level? Critically important in this scan of supporters is identifying a person or a small team of people with resources, dedication, and good connections, who would be willing to lead your campaign.

Begin identifying sources beyond your current supporters. Gather information about major capital resources in your area. For example, which individual donors' names appear on the walls of many nonprofits' buildings? Which foundations and corporations?

When identifying possible resources for your capital campaign, don't overlook loans, which often play an important role in facility projects, both as standard mortgages and in helping organizations complete projects on time. Often donors of large gifts don't write checks for the full amount of their pledges immediately, so organizations borrow some of the money they need to finish construction while waiting to receive those gifts.

If you're interested in loans, find out the following information first: Is your region eligible for federal community development investment funds? (Visit the Coalition of Community Development Financial Institutions Web site at www.cdfi.org to find out more.) Does your area have a community loan fund? Do any local foundations make program-related investments (low-interest loans) to nonprofits? Do any local foundations guarantee bank loans for nonprofits?

Developing a rough budget

Before you test your project to find out whether it's feasible, you need assistance figuring out what it will cost. A common mistake organizations make is forgetting that raising money costs money. They need to dedicate staff time and invest in marketing materials and events. Often they hire outside consultants or new fundraising staff to assist them.

For example, if you want revenues from an endowment to cover five $10,000 scholarships, you need to raise $1 million. Your board may set a different policy, but most nonprofit organizations figure they can expect to earn 5 percent on their endowments and spend at that rate each year without depleting the money they have put aside. If you estimate that meeting that goal will take you a year and a half, you may want to budget for

- ✔ A skilled fundraising consultant who will spend an average of ten hours per week on your project

- ✔ Printed materials describing your organization and campaign

- ✔ Funds to cover the cost of meeting with prospective donors — travel and meals

- ✔ Money to invest in recognizing and thanking donors, including a celebratory event at the culmination of the campaign

We include a sample presentation of capital campaign costs on CD1801.

Budgeting for building projects is complex. If you identify a plot of land or existing building you want to renovate, you need to begin with rough estimates and develop a specific budget later — after you secure architectural drawings, construction permits from your city or county, and bids from contractors.

As you begin developing a budget, find out about the construction rules you need to follow. A local architect or city appraiser/inspector should be able to tell you what enhancements you're required to include in your building. For example, the Americans with Disabilities Act (ADA) establishes an important set of requirements. Buildings for public use must offer ramps and elevators for wheelchair users; appropriately placed plumbing, railings, and equipment; and large-print signs or audible signals. You may think to budget the obvious, more visible modifications needed, but an experienced professional can point out more subtle requirements that you may overlook.

Just because a building is currently in use doesn't mean that you can move right in and begin operating your programs there. Building codes are closely tied to the building's function. Rules for classrooms, for example, sometimes change according to the age of the children. And rooms in which large numbers of people may gather are likely to have stricter safety requirements than those rooms used by individuals as offices. Building codes often change over time, so whenever a building changes hands or its use changes, it then must comply with the most recent requirements.

The CD includes "Capital: Hard and Soft Costs," a checklist from the Nonprofit Finance Fund (CD1802), and three sample capital project budgets (CD1803, CD1804, and CD1805).

Testing feasibility

Remember that tried-and-true method for buying a used car? The one where you circle the vehicle, kicking all the tires? An organization's capital campaign starts with that kind of tire kicking, except that it's called a *feasibility study,* research testing the hypothesis that you can raise the amount of money you need. Four feasibility study test points are

- ✔ **Tire One:** How much money does this organization have the capacity to raise?
- ✔ **Tire Two:** For this particular need?
- ✔ **Tire Three:** At this location and at this time?
- ✔ **Tire Four:** Is that enough money to pay for what the campaign plans to do?

The accuracy of the feasibility study is important to the capital campaign. Whoever conducts it has to have enthusiasm for the project, yet be able to speak honestly about the organization's position and listen carefully to the direct and indirect messages conveyed in the interviews. The person conducting the study must interview key leaders in the organization along with its current supporters and others whose involvement in supporting the project is critical to its success.

Nonprofits often use a consultant for feasibility studies for this reason: She's a step removed from the organization and, therefore, interview subjects are more likely to be frank with her.

Leading the way with the board

Whether or not an organization's board includes wealthy individuals, all its members should contribute to the campaign. The board's willingness to support the campaign is an indication of its being feasible. Also important, potential donors who aren't board members are likely to ask whether you have 100 percent board participation. They're asking whether every board member has given a gift or made a pledge to the campaign.

Board members are expected to lead the way. Their contributions may not be the largest, but they should be made in the campaign's earliest phases.

Why is this step so important? A charismatic executive director may be able to stir up enthusiasm about a capital project, but to succeed, such a project usually requires broad-based support and the assistance of all levels of leadership in the organization. If every member of the board of directors hasn't given to the campaign, it suggests that only a few people really support the idea. Also, people asking other people to make contributions are in a much better position to ask if they, themselves, have given. Board members must be willing to be involved in the campaign fundraising.

In addition, the size of a donor's gift (in relation to what the donor can afford) is some indication of enthusiasm. If a penniless playwright who serves on the board gives $100 toward a capital campaign for a theater, he's making as clear a sign of enthusiasm as a wealthy banker on the board who makes a gift of $1 million. If the wealthy banker makes the $100 gift, it suggests that either the board has one malcontent or that the project is unsupportable.

Going through feasibility study interviews

A typical feasibility study interview opens with an overview of the proposed project, emphasizing why the nonprofit selected the project, and how it can enhance the organization's programs and better serve its constituents. Next, the interviewer describes how much money the project needs and how, in general, the organization plans to raise it. If any major donors are already involved, the interviewer mentions their levels of support. Finally, the interviewer suggests a possible donation to the potential contributor and makes note of whether that person is likely to give to the campaign and how much the contribution may be.

The interview should be a conversation among the parties in the room rather than a one-sided presentation. The more the interviewer can engage the interview subjects in discussion, the more the interviewer finds out about how outsiders view the organization and about the fundraising potential.

In these conversations, most contributors aren't making promises, but they're suggesting their probable levels of support. The study, therefore, is important for two reasons:

- ✔ It gathers information that helps the organization estimate whether its capital campaign goal is feasible.
- ✔ It begins the process of "cultivating" contributions to and leadership for the campaign.

On the CD accompanying this book, you can find an outline of a feasibility study interview (CD1806) and an overview of the parts of a finished study (CD1807).

To continue with the used car metaphor from earlier in the chapter, a feasibility study is like finding out — after talking to your parents, spouse, or the bank — how much you can afford to pay for a car. Your parents may say that they'll give you money for a small sedan but not for a red sports car, and the same is true for a feasibility study. Board members, community leaders, and/or potential donors may tell you that they would support the venture or endowment if it were smaller, or the building if it didn't need a new foundation.

If the feasibility study suggests that you can raise more than you planned, you may consider increasing your capital campaign goal to include more scholarships or a cash reserve for building maintenance.

If the feasibility study suggests that you can't afford a "champagne" version of your plans, you may have to settle for a serviceable "house wine" edition. If your plans already were of the house wine variety, you may want to break the campaign into phases. If yours is a building project, over the first two years, you can make major safety and structural changes or renovate one of several floors. Then maybe three or four years later you can launch the second phase of a capital campaign to cover the balance of the costs.

You also may find out that you need to wait. Perhaps your potential major donors recently gave to another campaign, and although they like your project, they were recently tapped (to borrow a maple syrup metaphor). You may be able to come back to them in two years and receive major contributions. Or maybe potential donors voiced concerns about your organization. Perhaps you don't have good records about past donors. Maybe your board has dwindled in size or your executive director just accepted another job. When you organize, recruit, and hire anew, your campaign can proceed.

And you may find out that undertaking the project isn't a good idea at all. Period. At that point, it's time to start over and plan to address your goals in a different way.

Building the Pyramid of Gifts

You've sketched out your budget. You've set your sights on a reasonable goal. Your next most important need is to identify *campaign leadership* — a team or committee of volunteers who are willing to cheerlead on behalf of the campaign, make personal visits and calls, and sign letters asking for contributions. These leaders may be board members, but we recommend including some people from outside the board if appropriate enthusiasts can be identified. Not only do their efforts ease your board's workload, but their contacts also expand the pool of possible donors, and their involvement illustrates broader community support for the campaign.

Each campaign develops its own strategies and each organization has distinctive strengths to call upon, but most of them use the same diagram, which is based in conventional wisdom. It's called a gift table, and it looks like a pyramid (see Figure 18-1).

Remember the old saying, "A handful of people do most of the work"? A capital campaign works that way. Only a few donors are able to contribute large gifts. They go at the top of the pyramid. Smaller gifts from many other donors fill in the lower levels as the campaign moves forward and the pyramid takes shape.

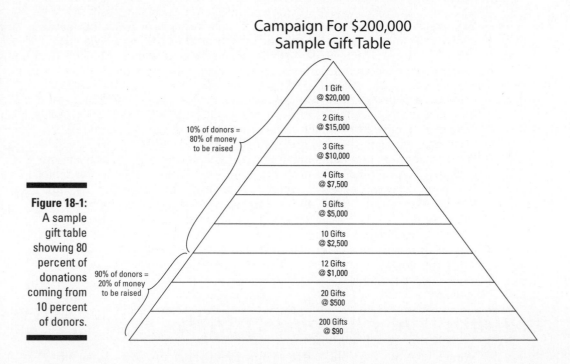

Campaign For $200,000
Sample Gift Table

Figure 18-1:
A sample gift table showing 80 percent of donations coming from 10 percent of donors.

10% of donors = 80% of money to be raised

90% of donors = 20% of money to be raised

1 Gift @ $20,000

2 Gifts @ $15,000

3 Gifts @ $10,000

4 Gifts @ $7,500

5 Gifts @ $5,000

10 Gifts @ $2,500

12 Gifts @ $1,000

20 Gifts @ $500

200 Gifts @ $90

Starting at the top

We know you don't start at the top when building a pyramid, but that's where you begin with a capital campaign. Similarly, we structured the sample gift table in Figure 18-1 starting at the top, using the following scheme:

- ✔ Ten percent or more of the money comes from a single gift, known as the *lead gift*. This large donation crowns the tip of the pyramid.

- ✔ Fifteen percent of the money comes from the next two largest gifts.

- ✔ Fifteen percent of the money comes from the next three largest gifts.

- ✔ Overall, 80 percent of the money comes from 10 percent of the donors. In other words, if you receive 100 contributions, ten of those people will provide 80 percent of the money that you must raise.

Say you're driving across town and pass the Janice Knickerbocker Symphony Hall, the Engin Uralman Medical Center, and the Jerome Kestenberg Museum of Natural History. What do Janice, Engin, and Jerome have in common? Generally, those people whose names adorn buildings made the contribution of 10 percent or more of the campaign total. They're called the *lead donors*.

When you conduct your feasibility study, one thing you're trying to determine is the size of the campaign's largest gift and whether it totals 10 percent or more of the campaign total.

Your lead gift becomes one of your campaign's attractions. Some contributors may support a capital project because they like or admire the person after whom the scholarship fund or building is named, even if they have little connection to the cause or organization.

After the lead gift is in place, your organization begins seeking the other major gifts that make up the first one-third of the funds to be raised. (In our example in Figure 18-1, just six contributions make up 40 percent of the goal.) Individuals usually give these lead gifts that they pledge during personal visits from nonprofit staff and board members. (See Chapter 14 for more about raising money from individuals.)

Continuing down the pyramid's structure to the widening middle, an organization usually moves beyond board members and major donors to seek grants from foundations and corporations.

Ending the quiet phase

Early on, when you're conducting the capital campaign among trustees, close friends of the nonprofit, past donors, and foundations, the campaign is in what's called the "quiet phase." When the organization has raised 75 to 80 percent of the money it needs, the fundraising style changes. The managers are growing confident that the campaign can succeed and announce it to the general public through a press conference, tour, gala party, or cornerstone-setting event.

This is the time to seek smaller donations from lots of people — neighbors, friends of friends, and grandparents. You often can raise these contributions through special events, or mailings, to individuals and smaller foundations and businesses.

Smaller gifts from many people construct the ground-level base of the pyramid. Don't discount these gifts. They're important financially to close out the campaign and also to build a feeling of participation among all your donors.

Annual campaigns and other focused fundraising drives are structured along the gift table pattern. Whether you're raising money for your child's school, an election, or a community fair, a gift table can help to shape your plans.

See CD1808 for another sample capital campaign gift table.

Using a case statement

In Chapter 14 on raising money from individuals, we outline steps for writing a case statement. A capital campaign cries out for a *case statement* — a brief, eloquently stated argument on behalf of the capital project. Sometimes these case statements are fancy brochures with profiles of scholarship recipients, drawings of a planned building, or clients of the future taking advantage of new opportunities. Sometimes they're simple word-processed statements.

A capital campaign case statement should incorporate the following elements:

- Mission and brief history of the organization
- Major accomplishments
- Compelling information about constituents served
- Vision of how the mission can be served better as a result of the capital project
- Vision for the results of the capital investment

✔ The campaign's leadership and goals

✔ Naming and giving opportunities

Shaping a campaign proposal

Grant proposals for capital projects follow the general outline of a standard grant proposal (see Chapter 17) with some variations and additions. The grant writer needs to describe the organization's goals and activities and its constituents' needs, and convincingly describe how a stronger organization with stronger capital assets will better serve the organization's goals and clients. Although your proposal may focus on any kind of capital investment project, we discuss a standard building project in the following outline of a campaign grant proposal:

✔ The introduction includes general information about current facilities and leads up to a discussion of the need for a new or renovated building.

✔ The problem statement describes the needs of clients or potential clients and how the organization's current building (or lack of a building) hinders their satisfaction of those needs.

✔ The goals and outcomes section discusses aspirations that the organization holds for serving its clients and its goals for the capital project (the building's dimensions and amenities).

✔ The methods section briefly touches on how you're delivering services but primarily focuses on how you're conducting the capital campaign, how construction will proceed, and the activities you're undertaking to connect current and future clients to the building. Organizations often include a discussion of the results of the feasibility study in this section as a rationale for how they set goals and how they planned the campaign.

✔ The evaluation section should focus both on whether the building project will meet its goals (such as achieving all city fire and safety code standards) and on how the improved building serves clients.

✔ The budget usually includes two major sections: hard costs (for land or building purchase or construction) and soft costs (for financing, fundraising, and promotion).

✔ The future and additional funding section should discuss how the capital campaign is progressing and where the organization anticipates raising the necessary funds to complete it. This section also should provide information about how the finished project will affect the organization's operating costs and how any additional expenses will be covered in the future.

Realizing the Benefits and Risks of Capital Campaigns

Although you may describe your request for capital support as a one-time need to potential supporters, many campaign donors continue to give after you finish the campaign project. They've been introduced to the agency, they've left their names in its lobby or attached to a scholarship fund, and they want to be sure that it succeeds over time. In the best situations, capital campaigns strengthen the nonprofit organization's programs both by enabling it to improve services and by broadening its donor base. A capital project also can be good for staff morale because it improves working conditions.

But capital campaigns also have their drawbacks:

- ✔ Capital campaigns may detract from organizations' basic fundraising. If you ask a donor to your programs to contribute to a building project, he may or may not contribute to the organization's ongoing programs in the same year.

- ✔ Capital contributions are restricted for a specific purpose and should not be "borrowed" to cover operating costs.

- ✔ Capital campaigns may double, triple, or quadruple an organization's fundraising needs while they're being conducted.

- ✔ Campaigns that don't succeed or that drag on for a long time can damage an organization's reputation. Because buildings tend to be visible entities, the public may be more aware of an organization's slow-moving construction project than of a problem with the programs or services. If you abandon the project, funds contributed to the capital campaign must be returned.

- ✔ Organizations often have turnover in their fundraising staffs after a capital campaign. Employees may stick around to achieve the end of the project, but a heavy workload may cause burnout that leads to quitting soon after they finish the project.

In short, capital projects offer both opportunities and pitfalls, buy-in and burnout, and new donor development and loss of current annual fund donors. But when completed, they often pay for concrete, lasting benefits and are worthy of celebration.

Part IV
The Part of Tens

The 5th Wave   By Rich Tennant

"Concerning the bylaws, Mr. Morganstern's group firmly believes they should be written in iambic pentameter quatrain form, whereas Ms. Ahern's group prefers the couplet form..."

In this part . . .

Here's a place to turn for a quick discussion of some crucial topics. We offer a brief guide to evaluating your work. You also find steps to consider taking if your organization runs into serious problems. And we return to the theme of fundraising, summarizing our experience and advice into easy-to-follow tips.

Chapter 19

Ten Tips for Evaluating Your Organization and Programs

· ·

In This Chapter

▶ Understanding why you should evaluate your programs

▶ Reviewing some tips for assessing program performance

· ·

Assessing the performance of your programs and your organization isn't easy, but evaluating what you do can help you do it better. Besides, if foundation grants help fund your programs, the odds are good that you'll be asked to report whether you achieved your goals and objectives anyway.

You can choose from many different types of evaluations. They can be as basic as counting the number of people who come through your door to as formal as assessments of client behavioral change or changes in public attitudes about international monetary policy.

When you're starting a new program or project, you need to ask yourself how it will be evaluated. You need to find a way to figure out whether you're doing what you say you're doing. Ask yourself these questions: How will I know if the program or project meets its goals? What can I measure or observe in our clients that will signal that we have achieved our objectives? In this chapter, we provide ten tips to help you successfully evaluate your program or project.

Ask Yourself Who You're Doing the Evaluation For

You need to figure out who will want to be updated with the results of your program. It may be your board of directors, your constituents, your contributors, your foundation funders, and, certainly, yourself. Looking at the audience for your evaluation report will help you determine the questions to be asked and the type of data to collect.

If your program was supported by a foundation grant, you probably included the goals and objectives of your program in your grant proposal. When you file your final report to the funder, she'll want to know whether these goals and objectives were met. And, if they weren't, she'll want to know why.

Your board will want to know whether your programs are operating efficiently and effectively and whether they're helping the organization achieve its mission. You'll be interested in knowing whether your program is too expensive for the results it provides and whether you can find a better way to accomplish your goals.

Keep It Simple

If you want to make evaluation a breeze, keep it simple. The most basic sort of evaluation is counting the number of clients served, the number of people in your audience, or the number of media releases distributed to the public. If you proposed that your program would provide after-school art classes to 30 children between the ages of 12 and 15 for an hour each week for 40 weeks, all you need to do is keep attendance records, record the ages of children served, and count the number of weeks the program was in session. Very simple.

This type of evaluation provides basic data about the program, but it won't answer more complex questions like "Did your students learn how to make or understand art?" or "Did learning about art help your students become better math or reading students?" The most challenging question you may ask — that this evaluation won't be able to answer — is this: "Did your after-school program put your students on the right path to become artists or people who appreciate art?"

Use Pre- and Post-Program Assessments

If you want to successfully go beyond simple counting (as described in the preceding section), your best bet is to undertake a pre- and post-program assessment. Yes, this is a nice way of saying "let's give our students some tests." You can create a list of questions that tell you how much your students know about a given topic. Give the test on the first day of class, and then give it again on the final day. You hope that test scores improve and, presumably, the improvement is a result of your program.

"Presumably" is an important word to keep in mind, because it's next to impossible to prove beyond a shadow of doubt that one particular experience or series of experiences caused the improvement that you observe in your students. You probably can assume that if your students increased their understanding of the topic as measured by the pre- and post-program tests, it was because you taught them well. But, as you move to more complex questions, it's not so easy to assume that your program was the single cause of this achievement.

Be Aware of Your Personal Perspective

You don't need to be a trained statistician to undertake basic program evaluation, but you should be cautious in making claims for long-term impacts that can't be tested. You also should understand that your interpretation of the results can be influenced by your biases and your personal stake in the program.

For example, your common sense may tell you that your after-school arts program will help your students do better in school and help them live better lives as adults, but unless you're prepared to present evidence that your program (or others like it) create these outcomes, you should be careful in claiming wide and sweeping effects for your work.

Get Outside Help If Necessary

Avoiding personal bias is one good reason to arrange for a program to be evaluated by an outside evaluator. Sometimes, large project grants from foundations or government agencies require that an independent evaluation be carried out. For most programs, however, outside evaluators are too costly.

If you do decide that an evaluation consultant is needed — either to undertake a complete evaluation of a project or to give you advice on how to do a better job of internally evaluating your program — don't wait until the project is finished to call for the evaluator's help.

Deciding how to evaluate a project should be done at the same time that the program is being designed. By building in your evaluation at the beginning of a project, you can collect baseline data and set up systems for collecting information as you go along. It's much easier to settle on your evaluation approach before you begin than it is to scramble backward to find the information you need.

Monitor Your Progress

Pay attention to the operation of your program while it's in progress. Talk to both clients and staff to ask whether they have suggestions about improving the program. You also can check progress toward reaching the program's objectives and make adjustments, if needed. After all, if problems pop up in the program design or implementation, it's better to fix them as soon as you can.

Ongoing evaluation of a program or project is known as a *formative* evaluation. An evaluation of a program after it's finished is called a *summative* evaluation.

Report What You Discover

When you get ready to report on your program, look at your information carefully. Do you see positive change? Does one group appear to have done better than another group? If so, ask yourself why. Was there a dip in attendance during any part of the program? Did anyone drop out of your classes? If you interviewed program participants, did you discover any information that can be interpreted in your report?

If you like working with charts and graphs, this may be the time to use them. If your evaluation produces numbers — test scores, percentages of participants completing a full course, proportions of the general population reached by your program — showing results in graph form can make a strong point.

Review the goals and objectives of your project and determine whether the information you collected confirms that your objectives were met. If your program fell short of its goals, can you explain why and what you'll do the next time to remedy the situation?

Consider your audience. If you'll be sending a report to a foundation funder or to your board, you'll want to create a more formal report than one you'll share only with your staff.

Tell the Story Without Numbers

While numbers are good, they usually don't tell the whole story. And for many of us, they don't do a good job of conveying the human interest that's present in most nonprofit programs. Sometimes, the best way to communicate the results of your program may be to tell a story about a person or group of people who benefited from your services.

It can be helpful to interview a client and include one or two direct quotations about his experiences as a participant in the program. Be careful to guard your client's confidentiality, however. Use a pseudonym or ask the client's permission before using his name.

Don't go overboard with your prose and don't exaggerate. Your readers will know if your story is unbelievable, so stick to the facts — but do put a human face on them.

Be Honest and Take the Results in Stride

You want everything you do to have a perfect ending, but that isn't always possible. Sometimes plans go awry. Maybe you didn't find the clients you hoped to find, or maybe the audience failed to arrive on opening night.

Honesty is the best policy — for yourself and your funders. If your program failed to meet its objectives, try to figure out why so you can do better next time. Prepare a report that includes accurate data and an analysis of the reasons your program fell short of its goals.

If you do have to submit a less-than-favorable report on your program to your funders, remember that a foundation program officer will appreciate a straightforward and honest appraisal. If you fudge the data, your fibs can come back to bite you.

One purpose of an evaluation is to help you, your staff and board, and your funders discover more about your organization's work. Often, coming away with new knowledge is nearly as important as achieving the results you imagined.

Look at Yourself

Besides looking at your programs, it's important also to evaluate the overall effectiveness of your organization. Is your board of directors providing the guidance and support you need to be successful? Are you making progress toward accomplishing your mission? Are you providing effective leadership?

If your nonprofit has developed an organizational plan, you can assess progress toward the goals and objectives you set for your organization. (See Chapter 7 for information about planning.) Board members often are asked to participate in their own assessment by evaluating themselves. You can find a basic checklist for this purpose at the Free Management Library (www.managementhelp.org).

For leaders of nonprofit organizations, we believe that self-reflection is a valuable tool. Take time to think about your work and consider whether you are on the right path. Don't hesitate to seek out others who are facing similar challenges. Finding a person or persons who can act as a sounding board for your ideas can be a valuable advantage as you manage your organization.

Chapter 20

Ten Tips for Adapting in Hard Times

In This Chapter

▶ Making choices to keep your nonprofit afloat

▶ Closing your doors if it's the best decision

*I*t's likely that you'll come across problems in the course of managing your nonprofit organization. Everyone does. But sometimes those problems are so severe that you must change the way you do your work to address them.

You may face a catastrophe — a natural disaster, the destruction of a venue, or the serious illness or death of a staff or board member. Or shifts in legislation or foundation policies may cause you to lose needed grants or contracts. While some crises are sudden and fierce, others may build gradually. Several modest deficits may add up to significant debt. Needs of your constituents may change. A competitor may win away your clients or staff members.

The choices you make in challenging circumstances depend, in part, on how much time you have to plan. Is the change you're facing sudden or has it been gradual? Is it long-term or temporary? Thinking about a crisis or dry spell when you're currently successful isn't fun, but it's necessary in order to survive. So, in this chapter, we provide ten tips to help you make it through those tough times.

Transforming or even closing a nonprofit in hard times draws on the same courage, leadership, and resourcefulness you used to create it. You need to be clear and decisive, include others in making and executing your plans, ask for help when needed, and base your decisions on clear, accurate information.

Recognize the Need for Change Before It's Too Late

Recognizing a sudden crisis is easy, but often the most difficult aspect of managing a nonprofit is seeing a gradual decline and the need to change. Likely, you work so hard and feel such dedication that you can't believe your organization is floundering.

Financial problems have clear consequences (so be on the lookout for them): When deficits exceed 10 percent of an operating budget, the organization will have trouble paying bills within 30 or 60 days. When the deficit exceeds 20 percent of the budget, the pressure intensifies. The inability to make payroll or timely tax payments signals severe problems.

A loan or an emergency fundraising drive may solve a short-term problem, but an organization must consider whether its programs cost more than its earning and fundraising capacity can provide. It can't keep borrowing funds or crying out for help without alienating its friends and supporters.

Communicate When Making Hard Decisions

A colleague of ours once asked, "What do you mean by 'hard decisions'? Are they hard because they're unpopular? Or are they hard because we must choose among options and the best choice is unclear?" The answer is both.

If you're facing an unpopular decision — laying off staff, for example — it's better to communicate clearly and move forward decisively. The longer you delay, the greater harm you may do to your organization and to those employees.

Take a Break

Sometimes an appropriate first action when you recognize that your organization faces a crisis is to step back and take a breath. You may even consider suspending your programs to give yourself time to plan your next move. Not every nonprofit can do so without harming constituents, but many can. Taking a hiatus can reduce operating costs and allow you to focus full attention on your options.

If you do take a break, communicate your reasons to your members, clients, and funders and keep everyone informed of your progress. Even if you suspend programs, don't stop publishing your online newsletter or quarterly status reports. It's critical to your long-term health as a nonprofit that your supporters know you care about them and — even more important — that you still exist. Also remember that filing and reporting obligations to the IRS and Attorney General's office are not suspended and board elections must be held on schedule.

Revisit Fiscal Sponsorship

We introduce the idea of fiscal sponsorship for new organizations in Chapter 2. If you're facing the need to downsize — even after you're established as a 501(c)(3) organization, a fiscal sponsor may be helpful to you. How? For a percentage of contributed revenues (often 10–20 percent), some sponsors provide check writing and payroll services, access to human resources expertise and insurance, regular financial reports, grants management, and other back-office services — freeing you of those key administrative burdens. Your connection with a well-known fiscal sponsor may reassure a funder that your organization has the capacity to track and manage grant funds.

Collaborate with Others in Your Field

If the field in which you work has seen a decline in funding or an increase in competition for staff or clients, it may be time to identify others who provide similar programs and begin to work together. Who shares your organization's values and approach? Can you serve clients better by combining services?

Forming a collaboration enables you to bring different strengths, resources, and knowledge to a task. It assumes that you can work with greater depth and understanding through a partnership. You also may save some money.

We recommend that you try a temporary, modest project with your partner before launching a large-scale combination of services. Shared goals and values matter and shared fields of interest matter, but personal compatibility is important as well. Also, as you step into a partnership arrangement, make sure that more than one leader in each organization is participating in the conversations and negotiations. Collaborations often falter if the key contact person at one of the two agencies leaves. A team can ensure continuity.

Share a Back Office

Maybe program collaboration won't work for your organization, but other types of collaboration may be successful. For example, why not approach another nonprofit about sharing a staff member? By hiring together, you may be able to offer a stable, full-time job with a competitive salary rather than a part-time gig. In turn, your organizations can engage more experienced and qualified employees. Talk to an employment attourney before sharing a staff member to clarify how the organizations will cover benefits and how the nonprofits will handle conflicting demands on the employee's time.

When sharing an employee, both organizations need to give that person clear direction about setting priorities and balancing attention between them.

Sharing things instead of people also can reduce your operating costs. Consider whether you can save money by purchasing equipment, securing office space, or combining supply orders with others. And don't assume that you can share these things only with organizations that resemble yours. In a recent study of nonprofits in the Puget Sound region, researchers found that some of the best shared-space experiences were among unlike nonprofit organizations, such as a theater school that operated in the late afternoons and evenings and a day-care center that operated early in the day.

Place a Program within Another Agency

One question you should continually ask is how to best meet the needs of the people you serve. Your clients are your reason for existence after all. If your nonprofit is stretched too thin to achieve everything it's trying to do, why not spin off a program, placing it within another reputable agency that shares your values? You may find that another organization, operating at a different scale or involving people with different skills and knowledge, is positioned to do a better job of managing that program.

We understand that it's difficult to give up a piece of your agency's work, but making this choice is the responsible thing to do for your clients. Plus it may allow you to focus on the services that best address your nonprofit's mission. Of course, placing a program with another agency also will likely reduce your costs. We recommend that you consult with an attourney before transferring a program.

Merge with Another Nonprofit

One challenging but responsible choice for your nonprofit may be to merge with another agency. Mergers in nonprofits are similar to those in the business world. Generally, in a merger, one organization dominates the other.

Mergers require thoughtful planning that involves teams of people from both nonprofits. Plan in two phases: First, thoroughly discuss your missions, goals, and program philosophies. If those aren't aligned, the merger won't work. Keep those goals foremost in mind as you move into the second phase of planning, which involves choosing a name, selecting staff, consolidating boards, and arranging a new structure. If problems arise in the second phase of planning, return to the primary conversation and ask whether your missions are aligned and your constituents would be well served by the merger.

When executing a merger, we strongly recommend that you use a facilitator to lead you through the plans and decisions, and work with an attorney to draw up your final agreements. Also be open to the idea of bringing in new staff and board members who will be committed to the merged organization without loyalties to either of the original entities.

Close with Dignity If Necessary

Nonprofit organizations generally resist closure, maybe because they're usually founded by people with a vision and a desire to serve the public. Yet, sometimes closing is the right choice.

If your nonprofit's financial health fails and its program quality declines, it's best if you accept the idea of closure before it's a last-gasp necessity. Shutting down a nonprofit involves several stages — some of them formally defined and some of them merely good practices. We suggest you do the following:

- ✔ **Take care of your employees.** Warn them about the impending closure, and, if possible, provide them with job counseling and severance pay.

- ✔ **Take care of your clients.** Work with other agencies to make sure that client needs will be met in the future. If you have subscribers or members, offer refunds or work with other nonprofits to honor their benefits.

- ✔ **Tell your donors and professional partners.** They should hear about your planned closure from you rather than through rumor or through the press. Clear communication of your story must be presented before rumors begin.

- ✓ **Pay your debts or negotiate settlements of your obligations before closing.** Doing so protects your reputation and the reputation of your board members and also engenders trust in nonprofits as good business partners.

- ✓ **Document your work.** What's your nonprofit's legacy of services to the field? What has it learned? How can your knowledge benefit others? We recommend gathering your information and placing it in a library, school, historical society, or online archive.

- ✓ **Celebrate and recognize your staff, board, and volunteers.** The people who have contributed their time, labor, and expertise to your nonprofit deserve applause and thanks.

Complete the Closing Paperwork

If you decide to close your nonprofit, it isn't enough to lock your doors and put up a Gone Fishin' sign. You also need to take a few formal steps. One of the first is to have a board meeting at which the board votes to dissolve the organization and records that decision in the board minutes. Another is to take an inventory of all your assets — money, furniture, client lists, Web domains, costumes, fish tanks, and so on — and pass them on, sell them, or return them appropriately, honoring your donors' intentions if some things were contributed for specific purposes.

You'll likely want some technical assistance from a consultant or an attorney to complete the paperwork, because you have certain state and federal requirements to meet:

- ✓ **State requirements:** You need to file a formal intent to close with your secretary of state or state licensing department. The form of this document varies by state. Check with the agency through which you incorporated on the appropriate steps to take.

- ✓ **Federal requirements:** Just as you turned to the Internal Revenue Service (IRS) to create your nonprofit, you return to the IRS to shut it down. You must file a final Form 990 tax return (see Chapter 5 for details about the 990) within 4 months and 15 days of your organization's termination. As you do so, check the Termination box on the first page of the return, and answer "yes" to the question you find in Part IV (line 36) about whether the organization liquidated, terminated, dissolved, or substantially contracted.

Chapter 21

Ten Tips for Raising Money

In This Chapter
▶ Applying some tips to raise money for your organization
▶ Being prepared when venturing out to fundraise

*R*aising money is essential to managing a successful nonprofit organization. In fact, nothing is easier than knowing you should be raising money — and nothing is more difficult than asking for it. In this chapter are our ten tips for that all-important task of raising funds.

Ask

One of fundraising's oldest adages is "If you don't ask, you won't get."

Developing fundraising plans, compiling lists of potential donors, and designing invitations are labor intensive. But those tasks aren't the things that slow you down in fundraising. Instead, many people pause when picking up the telephone or ringing the doorbell — in other words, when it comes to asking for money. Then when it's a little too late for the prospective donor to make a decision, write a check, or forward a proposal to a board meeting, these fundraisers make their move and stumble over their own procrastination.

We repeat, "If you don't ask (and ask at the right time), you won't get."

Hit Up People You Know

Some fundraisers believe that the entire money-raising game is in knowing people with money and power and working those contacts — charming them to bend their wills and write those checks. To be honest, if yours is a good cause, that approach isn't bad.

But what if you don't know wealthy people? Does that mean you can't raise money? No, it doesn't. Begin with people you know. Don't be afraid to ask your friends and associates. From a donor's point of view, saying no to someone you know is more difficult than saying no to a stranger.

Tell Your Story

The best way to write an effective fundraising letter or make a successful presentation to potential donors is to tell a story. You don't have to explain how your organization was founded and everything it has done since then (although that history may be worth a brief mention). Instead, the best stories and presentations focus on the constituents you serve and how they benefit from your efforts. These stories are free of jargon, and they're direct in manner. They're hopeful stories that paint a picture of a better future and describe what "better" looks like in clear, specific terms.

Pace the story so it has a bit of drama (but don't stoop to melodrama or hyperbole). Include facts. Recognize and discuss the complexity of the field in which you work, but don't drone on and on about technical matters that will cause your audience to zone out.

Show How You're Improving Lives

In grant writing terms, this piece of advice would be worded as "clearly describe your outcomes." Keep in mind that outcomes are quite different from outputs. *Outputs* is the word used for the quantity of work that a non-profit organization produces — the number of meals served, shelter beds offered, workshops led, miles covered, or acres planted. *Outcomes* is the word for the changes that occur as a result of those outputs. Well-defined outcomes are the hallmark of a good proposal, fundraising letter, or pitch.

In other words, providing training about nutrition to a group of 50 seniors isn't enough if those seniors don't change their eating patterns and live longer, healthier lives. Removing toxins from a lake isn't enough if its fish population and ecosystem aren't revived. Exposing 500 children to formal music lessons isn't enough if none of them can read a simple score later. Don't leave potential donors thinking, "Sounds nice, but so what?"

Make the Numbers Sparklingly Clear

Effective requests for money include information about how much is needed to achieve change or to test an idea. Make sure to present any data you cite in clear terms. In most cases, telling your reader or listener how much a needed change costs — the cost per child to participate in a special classroom for a year, the cost per injured sea mammal rescued, the cost per village to provide emergency food for a week — helps to make your point.

Nothing undermines a well-written proposal or case statement faster or more thoroughly than a confusing budget or a muddled financial statement. Double-check your presentation to make sure every activity in your proposal is represented in the budget and that every item in your budget can be traced easily to the work outlined in your proposal. If some items may be confusing to your reader, include budget notes. In all cases, check your math.

Research, Research, Research

Earlier in this chapter, we told you to ask people you know for money. We're not taking back that advice, but at some point you need to move beyond your immediate circle of acquaintances. That's where doing your homework pays off.

Before you send a fundraising letter, submit a proposal, or visit with a corporate giving director, find out as much as you can about the prospective contributor. Do you have anything in common on a personal level? Maybe the foundation director you're meeting recently published an article. If you read it, you have a conversation topic to break the ice. This advice holds true even when your approach is a direct mail or e-mail appeal: You want to know as much as you can about the people whose names are on the lists you borrow or purchase.

More important, you want to find out as much as you can about your potential donor's giving behavior. Does this person give small amounts of money to a wide array of organizations or generous gifts to a few selected agencies? Does the foundation like to be the only contributor to a given project, or does it prefer to support an activity along with others? Does the corporate giving program prefer a low-key style, or does it like to have the company's involvement highlighted?

You can turn to many sources for this information; just be sure to make research a habit. For instance, you can do any of the following:

- ✔ Refer to the Foundation Center library and its published and online resources (`foundationcenter.org`).

- ✔ Look up the foundation at the Council on Foundations Web site (`www.cof.org`) to see whether it has recently issued a report or has been featured in an article.

- ✔ For personal information about individuals, conduct an Internet search, or check *Who's Who* directories, local newspapers, and college alumni associations.

- ✔ Follow business and social news along with obituaries to keep track of people's families, professional developments, and affiliations.

- ✔ Pay close attention to contributor lists when you attend events at other nonprofit organizations.

Think Like a Trout (Know Your Donors)

Remember the old saying, "To catch a trout, think like a trout"? Well, this saying also applies to raising money for your nonprofit. The point of conducting research is to be able to talk or write about your organization in ways that are compelling to your listener or reader. You don't want to warp your message or change your mission, but you do want to think about it (and talk or write about it) in ways that respect your audience's point of view. To do so, you need to think about your organization as if you were a prospective donor yourself.

All donors have different personal giving styles. So you need to figure out those styles and put yourself in their shoes when deciding how to raise money from particular individuals or companies. You don't want to offer to hold a tribute dinner in honor of someone who contributes anonymously, for instance. And you don't want to downplay a gift from a contributor who relishes public acknowledgment. Some donors prefer the sociability of supporting a cause through a special event, others respond to direct mail appeals, and still others like to see as much of their money as possible going directly to the service being provided. (If possible, let them see that service with their own eyes!)

Many people forget that foundations are nonprofit organizations with mission statements and that their job is to support proposals that further their missions. Your job as a grant seeker is to measure how your goals align with their purposes. For example, many corporate giving programs and company-sponsored foundation programs work to improve the conditions in which their employees live and work. When these organizations discover that their employees are involved in or contribute to a given cause, they may be more inclined to support that cause.

Government grantmaking programs are created through legislation. If you find a program that seems well suited to your organization's work, reviewing the legislation is worth your time. Doing so helps you fully understand the program's context and intentions. You're able to think like a legislator trout!

Build a Donor Pyramid

Earlier in this chapter, we suggest starting by asking people you know. Imagine your fundraising approach as starting with those people at the peak of a pyramid and working your way down to the broader base. After asking people you know, try to enlist those donors in asking their contacts to support your organization as well. Some are likely to respond (in part because people they know also are contributors). Then ask those new donors to ask their friends. If each contributor leads you to two additional contributors, you steadily build your pyramid.

Make It Easy to Respond

You've written a brilliant appeal letter. You've created a compelling Web site. You've delivered a stirring speech to a roomful of prospective donors. You've got them hooked. They want to contribute. But they're glancing around the room with confused looks on their faces. You blew it. You didn't give them an easy way to respond.

Always suggest a specific amount for donors to consider contributing. Connect that amount to what you need and to their potential giving levels (which you can estimate from your research). And always make immediate giving easy for them: Distribute an addressed envelope and reply card with each mailing, allow a reader to click through your e-mail letter to the Donate Now button on your Web site, or set up a labeled box by the exit where they can leave contributions. Give potential donors pens, stamps, e-mail addresses, pledge cards, and any other tools to help them respond when you have their attention.

Keep Good Records

After you begin attracting contributors, your donor records become your most valuable fundraising tools. Individuals who give to your organization once are likely to continue giving for three or more years. If you thank them, address them as if they're part of your organization, and generally treat them well, the size of their gifts is likely to increase over time.

Working with foundations, corporations, and government sources is a different story. In their case, you want to keep clear records of your original project goals and outcomes, project budget, and due dates for any required reports. Although these sources may not be willing or able to support your organization year after year, their future support is more likely if you're a conscientious grantee who submits reports on time and keeps clear records.

You can create a simple database on a set of index cards by recording names, addresses, phone numbers, e-mail addresses, patterns of giving, and personal information (such as whether a donor knows one of your board members or whether he or she is married and has children).

Of course, these days we like to keep databases on computers. You can spend lots of money on commercial database programs known as *fundraising software*. You can find out more about appropriate donor software that's right for your organization's size and systems by following articles in Idealware's electronic newsletter (www.idealware.org) or by searching the information at TechSoup (www.techsoup.org).

However you keep it, guard your donor database carefully and invest the time necessary to keep it up-to-date. It's one of your organization's most valuable resources.

Part V
Appendixes

The 5th Wave   By Rich Tennant

"Business here is good, but the weak dollar is killing my overseas markets!"

In this part . . .

Here we provide some useful tools, including an extensive glossary of nonprofit terms and a selection of print and Web references for further reading. Appendix C is your guide to using the CD that accompanies this book.

Appendix A

Nonprofit Resources

● ●

*H*ere we offer you a cornucopia of reference materials. We don't have room to list every book, magazine, and Web site that may be of interest to nonprofit folks, but these resources will get you heading in the right direction.

Organizations

You'll find the nonprofit organizations (and one government agency) listed here to be helpful for providing guidance and information on everything from the history of nonprofits in America to raising money to support your programs.

Alliance for Nonprofit Management: www.allianceonline.org

American Society of Association Executives: www.asaecenter.org

The Aspen Institute: Program on Philanthropy and Social Innovation: www.aspeninstitute.org/policy-work/nonprofit-philanthropy

Association of Fundraising Professionals: www.afpnet.org

BBB Wise Giving Alliance: www.bbb.org/us/Wise-Giving

BoardSource: www.boardsource.org

Center for Civil Society Studies at the Johns Hopkins Institute for Policy Studies: www.ccss.jhu.edu

The Center on Philanthropy at Indiana University: www.philanthropy.iupui.edu

Community Development Financial Institutions: www.cdfi.org

The Council on Foundations: www.cof.org

The Foundation Center: www.foundationcenter.org

Giving Institute and Giving USA: www.aafrc.org

U.S. Government Printing Office (for regulatory guides): www.gpo.gov

The Grantsmanship Center: www.tgci.com

Independent Sector: www.independentsector.org

Leader to Leader Institute: www.pfdf.org

National Council of Nonprofits: www.councilofnonprofits.org

Nonprofit Finance Fund: www.nonprofitfinancefund.org

State Associations of Nonprofits: www.ncna.org/states

Web Resources

These Web sites have detailed information on a variety of nonprofit topics, including preparing your application for tax exemption for the Internal Revenue Service, finding possible grant sources, and keeping up with the latest news about nonprofits.

Keep in mind that Web site addresses change frequently, so if a page isn't where we say it is, use your favorite search engine to track down the new address.

Affordable or free databases: www.eBase.org; www.salesforce.com; www.eTapestry.com

Blue Avocado (a free electronic newsletter about nonprofits): www.blueavocado.org

The Catalog of Federal Domestic Assistance (a comprehensive directory about federal funding opportunities): www.cfda.gov

Charity Channel (an online network of nonprofit professionals): www.charitychannel.com

CharityVillage (a Canadian center for nonprofits): www.charityvillage.com/cv/main.asp

Chronicle of Philanthropy: philanthropy.com

Congressional Record: www.gpoaccess.gov

Federal government grant applications and information: www.grants.gov

The Foundation Directory Online (available for a monthly fee): www.foundationcenter.org

Foundation News and Commentary (formerly published by the Council on Foundations; past articles are archived): www.foundationnews.org

Free Management Library (for nonprofits and for-profits): `management help.org`

Fundraising Forum Library: `www.raise-funds.com/library.html`

The Giving Institute and Giving USA Foundation: `www.aafrc.org`

The Grant Advisor Plus (subscription required): `www.grantadvisor.com`

Grassroots Fundraising Journal (published by the Grassroots Institute for Fundraising Training): `www.grassrootsfundraising.org`

GreatNonprofits (consumer-generated reviews of nonprofits): `www.great nonprofits.org`

Guerrilla Marketing: `www.gmarketing.com/index.phtml` (Registration is required to access most material on this site.)

GuideStar: `www.guidestar.org`

Idealware (articles about software for nonprofits): `www.idealware.org`

Internal Revenue Service (for information about nonprofits): `www.irs.gov/charities/index.html`

W.K. Kellogg Foundation Evaluation Handbook (downloadable PDF): `www.wkkf.org/Pubs/Tools/Evaluation/Pub770.pdf`

National Technical Information Service: `www.ntis.gov`

Network for Good: `www.networkforgood.org`

Nonprofit Academic Centers Council (academic programs for nonprofit managers): `www.naccouncil.org`

The Nonprofit FAQ (indexed answers to questions about nonprofits): `www.idealist.org/npofaq`

Nonprofit Genie, CompassPoint Nonprofit Services: `www.compasspoint.org/askgenie/index.php`

The Nonprofit Quarterly: `www.nonprofitquarterly.org`

The Nonprofit Times: `www.nptimes.com`

Opportunity Knocks (nonprofit job listings): `www.opportunity knocks.org`

Press Lists (paid subscription): `www.us.cision.com`

Registration forms for soliciting donations: `www.multistate filing.org`

TechSoup (technology information for nonprofits): `www.techsoup.org`

U.S. Census Bureau: `www.census.gov`

United States Department of Labor (for employee benefits information): www.dol.gov

Volunteer Match: www.volunteermatch.org

Web surveying: www.zoomerang.com and www.surveymonkey.com

"What You Should Know About Nonprofits" (booklet): www.independent sector.org/PDFs/WhatUShouldKnow.pdf

Books and Print Materials

Here are some books and other publications that you'll find helpful as you discover the nonprofit sector. You'll also find books to help you through the incorporation process and guides to writing grant proposals.

Accounting For Dummies, 4th Edition, by John A. Tracy, CPA (Wiley)

E-Mail Marketing For Dummies by John Arnold (Wiley)

Facebook For Dummies by Carolyn Abram and Leah Pearlman (Wiley)

Facebook Marketing For Dummies by Paul Dunay and Richard Krueger (Wiley)

FC-Search, CD-ROM (The Foundation Center)

Fiscal Sponsorship: 6 Ways to Do It Right, 2nd Edition, by Gregory L. Colvin (Study Center Press)

The Foundation Center's Guide to Proposal Writing, 5th Edition, by Jane C. Geever (The Foundation Center)

The Grantseekers Guide to Winning Proposals, edited by Judith B. Margolin and Elan K. DiMaio 2008 (The Foundation Center Library) (Third volume of a series of books available in some Foundation Center libraries that provide examples of successful grant proposals.)

The Foundation Directory, Directory Part 2, and *Supplement* (The Foundation Center)

Foundation Yearbook: Facts and Figures on Private and Community Foundations (The Foundation Center)

Fundraising When Money is Tight: A Strategic and Practical Guide to Surviving Tough Times and Thriving in the Future by Mal Warwick (Jossey-Bass)

Getting Funded: The Complete Guide to Writing Grant Proposals, 4th Edition, by Mary S. Hall and Susan Howlett (Continuing Education Press)

Grant Proposal Makeover: Transform Your Request from No to Yes by Cheryl A. Clarke and Susan P. Fox (Jossey-Bass)

The Guide to U.S. Foundations, Their Trustees, Officers, and Donors (The Foundation Center)

How to Form a Nonprofit Corporation, 9th Edition, by Anthony Mancuso (Nolo)

How to Write Successful Fundraising Letters, 2nd Edition, by Mal Warwick (Jossey-Bass)

Human Resources Kit For Dummies, 2nd Edition, by Max Messmer (Wiley)

Managing a Nonprofit Organization in the Twenty-First Century, 3rd Edition, by Thomas Wolf (Free Press)

Marketing For Dummies, 3rd Edition, by Alexander Hiam (Wiley)

Models of Proposal Planning and Writing by Lynn E. Miner and Jeremy T. Miner (Praeger)

National Directory of Corporate Giving (The Foundation Center)

The New Nonprofit Almanac and Desk Reference: The Essential Facts and Figures for Managers, Researchers, and Volunteers by the Independent Sector, Urban Institute (Jossey-Bass)

Nonprofit Almanac 2008 by Kennard T. Wing, et al (Urban Institute Press)

Nonprofit Boards: Roles, Responsibility and Performance by Diane Duca (Wiley)

A Nonprofit Organization Operating Manual: Planning for Survival and Growth by Arnold J. Olenick and Philip R. Olenick (The Foundation Center)

The Nonprofit Sector: A Research Handbook, 2nd Edition, by Walter W. Powell and Richard Steinberg (Yale University Press)

Principles of Professional Fundraising: Useful Foundations for Successful Practice by Joseph R. Mixer (Jossey-Bass)

Public Relations For Dummies, 2nd Edition, by Eric Yaverbaum, Ilise Benun, and Bob Bly (Wiley)

The Public Relations Handbook for Nonprofits: A Comprehensive and Practical Guide by Art Feinglass (Jossey-Bass)

Securing Your Organization's Future: A Complete Guide to Fundraising Strategies, Revised Edition, by Michael Seltzer (The Foundation Center)

Small Business Marketing For Dummies, 2nd Edition, by Barbara Findlay Schenck

Starting and Managing a Nonprofit Organization: A Legal Guide, 5th Edition, by Bruce R. Hopkins (Wiley)

Storytelling for Grantseekers: A Guide to Creative Nonprofit Fundraising, 2nd Edition, by Cheryl A. Clarke (Jossey-Bass)

Twitter For Dummies by Laura Fitton, Michael Gruen, and Leslie Poston (Wiley)

Winning Grants Step by Step, 3rd Edition, by Mim Carlson, Tori O'Neal McElrath, and The Alliance for Nonprofit Management (Jossey-Bass)

Appendix B

Glossary of Nonprofit Terms

annual report: A voluntary report published by a nonprofit organization, foundation, or corporation describing its activities and providing an overview of its finances. A foundation's annual report generally lists the year's grants.

articles of incorporation: A document filed with an appropriate state office by persons establishing a corporation. Generally, this filing is the first legal step in forming a nonprofit corporation.

bylaws: Rules governing a nonprofit organization's operation. Bylaws often outline the methods for selecting directors, forming committees, and conducting meetings.

capacity building: A general term used to describe activities to help a nonprofit organization do its job better. Examples include staff and board training, computer and financial management systems upgrades, and consultant assistance for organizational planning.

capital campaign: An organized drive to raise funds to finance an organization's capital needs — buildings, equipment, renovation projects, land acquisitions, or endowments.

capital support: Funds provided to a capital project.

case statement: A brief, compelling statement about an organization's projects, accomplishments, and vision.

challenge grant: A grant made on the condition that other funds must be secured before it will be paid — usually on a matching basis and within a defined time period.

charitable contribution: A gift of goods, money, property, or services to a nonprofit organization.

charity: The word encompasses religion, education, assistance to the government, promotion of health and the arts, relief from poverty, and other purposes benefiting the community. Nonprofit organizations formed to further one of these purposes generally are recognized as exempt from federal tax under Section 501(c)(3) of the Internal Revenue Code.

community foundation: A grantmaking organization receiving its funds from multiple public sources, focusing its giving on a defined geographic area, and being managed by an appointed, representative board of directors. Technically, it's classified by the Internal Revenue Service as a public charity, not a private foundation.

community fund: An organized community program making annual appeals to the general public for funds that are usually disbursed to charitable organizations rather than retained in an endowment. Also sometimes called a federated giving program.

company-sponsored foundation: A private foundation that derives its grant-making funds primarily from contributions of a profit-making business.

corporate giving program: A grantmaking program established and managed by a profit-making company. Unlike a company-sponsored foundation, gifts of money, goods, and services go directly from the company to grantees.

demonstration grant: A grant made to experiment with an innovative project or program that may serve as a model for others.

distribution committee: A group of individuals responsible for making grant decisions. For community foundations, this committee must be broadly representative of the community to be served by the foundation.

donor advised fund: A fund held by a community foundation or other charitable organization for which the donor, or a committee appointed by the donor, may recommend charitable recipients for grants from the fund.

donor designated funds: Restricted funds in which those contributing the funds specify how the monies will be used.

endowment: Funds intended to be kept permanently and invested to provide income for continued support of an organization.

excise tax: An annual tax of net investment income that private foundations must pay to the Internal Revenue Service.

family foundation: Not a legal term, but commonly used to describe foundations that are managed by family members related to the person or persons from whom the foundation's funds were derived.

federated campaign or federated giving program: Raising funds for an organization that will redistribute them as grants to nonprofit organizations. This fundraising often is led by volunteer groups within clubs and workplaces. United Way and the Combined Federal Campaign are two examples.

fiscal sponsor: A nonprofit 501(c)(3) organization that formally agrees to sponsor a project led by an individual or group from outside the organization that may or may not have nonprofit status. If the outside individual or group receives grants or contributions to conduct an activity, those funds are accepted, approved, and managed on behalf of the project by the fiscal sponsor.

foundation: A nongovernmental, nonprofit organization with funds and a program managed by its own trustees and directors, established to further social, education, religious, or charitable activities by making grants. A private foundation may receive its funds from an individual, family, corporation, or other group consisting of a limited number of members.

gift table: A structured plan for the number and size of contributions needed to meet a fundraising campaign's goals.

grantee: An individual or organization receiving a grant.

grantor: An individual or organization awarding a grant.

independent sector: The portion of the economy that includes all 501(c)(3) and 501(c)(4) tax-exempt organizations as defined by the Internal Revenue Service, all religious institutions, all social responsibility programs of corporations, and all people who give time and money to serve charitable purposes. It's also called the voluntary sector, the charitable sector, the third sector, or the nonprofit sector.

lobbying: Efforts to influence legislation by shaping the opinion of legislators, legislative staff, and government administrators directly involved in drafting legislative policies. The Internal Revenue Code sets limits on lobbying by organizations that are exempt from tax under Section 501(c)(3).

matching gifts program: A grant or contributions program that matches employees' or directors' gifts made to qualifying nonprofit organizations. Each employer or foundation sets specific guidelines.

matching grant: A grant or gift made with the specification that the amount contributed must be matched with revenues from another source on a one-for-one basis or according to another defined formula.

mission statement: A succinct statement of the purpose and key activities of a nonprofit organization.

nonprofit: A term describing the Internal Revenue Service's designation for organizations whose income isn't used for the benefit or private gain of stockholders, directors, or other owners. A nonprofit organization's income is used to support its operations and further its stated mission. It may sometimes be referred to as an NPO, or nonprofit organization.

outcome evaluation: An assessment of whether a project achieved the desired long-term results.

program officer: A staff member of a foundation or corporate giving program who may review grant requests, recommend policy, manage a budget, or process applications for review by a board or committee. Other titles, such as program director or program consultant, also are used.

program related investment: A loan or other investment (not a grant) made by a foundation or corporate giving program to another organization for a project related to the grantmaker's stated charitable interests.

proposal: A written application, often with supporting documents, submitted to a foundation or corporate giving program when requesting a grant.

public charity: A type of organization classified under Section 501(c)(3) of the Internal Revenue Service Code. A public charity normally receives a substantial part of its income from the general public or government. The public support of a public charity must be fairly broad, not limited to a few families or individuals.

restricted funds: Assets or income whose use is restricted by a donor.

tax exempt: A classification granted by the Internal Revenue Service to qualified nonprofit organizations that frees them from the requirement of paying taxes on their income. Private foundations, including endowed company foundations, are tax-exempt; however, they must pay a modest excise tax on net investment income. All 501(c)(3) and 501(c)(4) organizations are tax-exempt, but only contributions to a 501(c)(3) are tax-deductible to the donor.

unrelated business income: Income from an activity that's not within the scope of the organization's mission.

unsolicited proposal: A proposal sent to a foundation without the foundation's invitation or prior knowledge. Some foundations don't accept unsolicited proposals.

venture philanthropy: A style of grantmaking drawing on the business practices of venture capitalists.

Appendix C

About the CD

*U*sing the CD that accompanies this book couldn't be easier. You can pop it into pretty much any Mac or Windows computer made in the last ten years as long as that computer has an optical drive capable of playing good, old-fashioned CDs. If you're the hesitant type, check out the following system requirements.

System Requirements

Make sure that your computer meets the minimum system requirements shown in the following list. If your computer doesn't match up to most of these requirements, you may have problems using the software and files on the CD. You need the following:

- A PC with a Pentium or faster processor; or a Mac OS computer with a 68040 or faster processor

- Microsoft Windows 98 or later; or Mac OS system software 7.6.1 or later

- At least 32MB of total RAM installed on your computer; for best performance, we recommend at least 64MB

- A CD-ROM drive

- A monitor capable of displaying at least 256 colors or grayscale

If you need more information on the basics, check out these books published by Wiley: *PCs For Dummies,* 10th Edition, by Dan Gookin; *Macs For Dummies,* 8th Edition, by David Pogue; *iMac For Dummies,* 4th Edition, by Mark L. Chambers; *Mac OS X Tiger For Dummies,* by Bob LeVitus; *Windows 98 For Dummies,* by Andy Rathbone; *Windows 2000 Professional For Dummies,* by Andy Rathbone and Sharon Crawford; or *Windows XP For Dummies,* 2nd Edition, by Andy Rathbone.

Using the CD

To install the items from the CD to your hard drive, follow these steps.

1. **Insert the CD into your computer's CD-ROM drive.** The license agreement appears.

   Note to Windows users: The interface won't launch if you have autorun disabled. In that case, click Start⇨Run. In the dialog box that appears, type D:\start.exe. (Replace D with the proper letter if your CD-ROM drive uses a different letter. If you don't know the letter, see how your CD-ROM drive is listed under My Computer.) Click OK.

   Note to Mac users: The CD icon will appear on your desktop. Double-click the icon to open the CD and double-click the "Start" icon.

2. **Read through the license agreement, and then click the Accept button if you want to use the CD.** After you click Accept, the license agreement window won't appear again.

   The CD interface appears. The interface allows you to install the programs and run the demos with just a click of a button (or two).

What You'll Find on the CD

The following sections are arranged by category and provide a summary of the software and other goodies you'll find on the CD. If you need help with installing the items provided on the CD, refer to the installation instructions in the preceding section.

✔ *Shareware programs* are fully functional, free, trial versions of copyrighted programs. If you like particular programs, register with their authors for a nominal fee and receive licenses, enhanced versions, and technical support.

✔ *Freeware programs* are free, copyrighted games, applications, and utilities. You can copy them to as many computers as you like — for free — but they offer no technical support.

✔ *GNU software* is governed by its own license, which is included inside the folder of the GNU software. There are no restrictions on distribution of GNU software. See the GNU license at the root of the CD for more details.

✔ *Trial, demo,* or *evaluation* versions of software are usually limited either by time or functionality (such as not letting you save a project after you create it).

Software

You'll find the following software on your CD:

✔ **Adobe Reader:** Adobe Reader is a freeware program that allows you to view, but not edit, Adobe Portable Document Files (PDFs).

✔ **OpenOffice.org:** OpenOffice.org is a free multi-platform office productivity suite. It is similar to Microsoft Office or Lotus SmartSuite, but OpenOffice.org is absolutely free. It includes word processing, spreadsheet, presentation, and drawing applications that enable you to create professional documents, newsletters, reports, and presentations. It supports most file formats of other office software. You should be able to edit and view any files created with other office solutions.

Chapter files

The following list summarizes all the chapter files on the CD:

CD0101   Classification of Nonprofit Activity Types

CD0102   Chapter 1 Web Resources

CD0201   Sample Fiscal Sponsorship Agreement

CD0202   Chapter 2 Web Resources

CD0301   Sample Mission Statement for the Bay Area Discovery Museum, Adopted in 1995, included with permission from Richard Winefield, Executive Director

CD0302   Sample Mission Statement for the Bay Area Discovery Museum, Revised by Its Board in 2002, included with permission from Richard Winefield, Executive Director

CD0303   Chapter 3 Web Resources

CD0401   Checklist for Forming a Nonprofit Organization

CD0402   Directory of State Offices, with Web connections

CD0403   Writing Bylaws

CD0404   Chapter 4 Web Resources

CD0501   Chapter 5 Web Resources

CD0601   Sample Grid for Planning Board Recruitment

CD0602   Board Officer Position Descriptions

CD0603   Sample Board Contract

CD0604   Sample Simple Board Agenda

CD0605   Sample Formal Board Agenda

CD0606   Chapter 6 Web Resources

CD0701   Sample Planning Retreat Agenda

CD0702   Outline of an Organizational Plan

CD0703   Sample Needs Assessment Survey

CD0704   Chapter 7 Web Resources

CD0801   Sample Volunteer Job Description, Food to the Table Delivery Volunteer

CD0802   Sample Volunteer Job Description, Take My Hand Adult Mentor

CD0803   Sample Volunteer Intake Form

CD0804   Sample Volunteer Agreement Form

CD0805   Chapter 8 Web Resources

CD0901   Sample Personnel Policies, used with permission from San Francisco Study Center, Inc.

CD0902   Sample Job Description, Executive Director

CD0903   Sample Job Description, Development Director

CD0904   Sample Job Description, Office Administrator

CD0905   Sample Reference Checking Form

CD0906   Sample Hire Letter

CD0907   Chapter 9 Web Resources

CD1001   Sample Organization Budget, Photography Workshops for Teenagers

CD1002   Sample Organization Budget, Mid-Sized Sheltered Workshop for Persons with Disabilities

CD1003   Sample Organization Budget, Education and Recreation Center for Homeless Children

CD1004   Total Project Costs for Tutoring Center, Including Indirect Costs

CD1005   Tracking Actual Income and Expenses: Sample Organization Simple Budget and Monthly Report of Budget versus Actual Income and Expenses

CD1006   Tracking Actual Income and Expenses: Sample Organization Budget and Monthly Report of Budget versus Actual Income and Expenses with Budget Variance Columns

CD1007   Five Year Trend Line, included with permission from LarsonAllen Nonprofit and Government Group

CD1008   Monthly Information Every Nonprofit Board Needs to Know, included with permission from LarsonAllen Nonprofit and Government Group

CD1009   "A Few Good Accounting Packages," included with permission from TechSoup Global; Copyright @ 2008 CompuMentor. This work is published under a Creative Commons Attribution-NonCommercial-NoDerivs 3.0 License

CD1010   Sample Cash Flow Projection

CD1011   Cash Flow Worksheet Projection

CD1012   Sample Audited Financial Statement

CD1013   Tips for Reading Financial Statements

CD1014   Advice for Reading an Audit

CD1015   Chapter 10 Web Resources

CD1101   Sample Audience Survey, Neighborhood Historical Society

CD1102   Sample Participant/Volunteer Survey

CD1103   Sample Press Release, included with permission from Carla Befera

CD1104   Sample Press Alert

CD1105   Sample Calendar Release

CD1106   Sample Photo Caption

CD1107   Sample Photo Use Permission Form

CD1108   Sample Public Service Announcement

CD1109   Chapter 11 Web Resources

CD1201   List of Required Spaces, included with permission from the Nonprofit Finance Fund, © Nonprofit Finance Fund, `www.nonprofitfinancefund.org`. All rights reserved.

CD1202   Planned Change and Facilities, included with permission from the Nonprofit Finance Fund, © Nonprofit Finance Fund, `www.nonprofitfinancefund.org`. All rights reserved.

CD1203   Organization Capacity Worksheet, included with permission from the Nonprofit Finance Fund, © Nonprofit Finance Fund, `www.nonprofitfinancefund.org`. All rights reserved.

CD1204   Your Project's Relative Size, included with permission from the Nonprofit Finance Fund, © Nonprofit Finance Fund, `www.nonprofitfinancefund.org`. All rights reserved.

CD1205   Chapter 12 Web Resources

CD1301   Acknowledgement letter for contribution over $250, Good or Service Provided

CD1302   Ackowlegement letter for contribution over $250, No Good or Service Provided

CD1303   Sample Fundraising Plan, High School Music Awards Program

CD1304   Sample Fundraising Plan, Neighborhood Park Coalition

CD1305   Sample Fundraising Budget, High School Music Awards Program

CD1306   Sample Fundraising Budget, Neighborhood Park Coalition

CD1307   Chapter 13 Web Resources

CD1401   Sample Donation Letter

CD1402   Sample Donor Information Record

CD1403   Telemarketing "Do's" and "Don'ts" and Two Sample Telemarketing Scripts

CD1404   Tips for Writing an E-mail Fundraising Letter

CD1405   Sample E-Solicitation Letter, included with permission from Jeffrey Lependorf, Executive Director, Small Press Distribution

CD1406   Sample E-Letter for Building a Potential Donor Relationship

CD1407   Ten Tips for Raising Money from Your Web Site

CD1408   Chapter 14 Web Resources

CD1501   Sample Budget for a Tribute Dinner

CD1502   Special Event Budget Form for a Benefit Concert or Performance

CD1503   Sample Benefit Auction Budget

CD1504   Sample Special Event Committee Invitation Letter, Save Our Lakeshore Awards Dinner

CD1505   Sample Special Event Solicitation Letter, Save Our Lakeshore Awards Dinner

CD1506   Sample Special Events Timeline: Tribute Dinner or Luncheon

CD1601   Foundation Research Checklist

CD1602   Federal Government Program Research Checklist

CD1603   Foundation Prospect Evaluation Sheet

CD1604   Chapter 16 Web Resources

CD1701   Sample Letter of Inquiry, Save Mount Artemis

CD1702   Sample Full Proposal, included with permission from Jerome Moskowitz and the Joe Goode Performance Group

CD1703   Sample General Operating Support Grant Proposal, included with permission from UCSF AIDS Health Project

CD1704   Sample Project Grant Proposal Addressed to a City Government Agency, included with permission from Jerome Moskowitz and the San Francisco Mime Troupe

CD1705   Sample Logic Model, included with permission from Harvard Family Resource Center. © 1999 President and Fellows of Harvard College. Published by Harvard Family Research Project, Harvard Graduate School of Education. All rights reserved. No part of this publication may be reproduced without permission of the publisher. Since 1983, HFRP has helped stakeholders develop and evaluate strategies to promote the well being of children, youth, families, and communities. HFRP's work focuses on early childhood education, out-of-school time programming, family and community support in education, complementary learning, and evaluation. Visit www.hfrp.org to access hundreds of resources with practical information for evaluators, practitioners, researchers, and policymakers.

CD1706   Sample Foundation Budget Form

CD1707   Finishing and Submitting Your Proposal

CD1708   Sample Proposal Written in Response to a Foundation's Form and Questions, included with permission from Jerome Moskowitz and the Joe Goode Performance Group

CD1709   Sample Letter Proposal

CD1710   Sample Company Foundation Guidelines

CD1711   Sample Letter Proposal Written to a Corporation, Tech Reuse Center

CD1712   Chapter 17 Web Resources

CD1801   Sample Presentation of Capital Campaign Costs

CD1802   Capital: Hard and Soft Costs, included with permission from the Nonprofit Finance Fund, © Nonprofit Finance Fund, www.nonprofitfinance fund.org. All rights reserved.

CD1803   Sample Capital Campaign Budget, Constructing a Youth Center Within an Existing Building

CD1804   Sample Capital Campaign Budget, Constructing a Small Theater Within an Existing Building

CD1805   Sample Capital Campaign Budget, Constructing a Child Care Center Within an Existing Building

CD1806   Feasibility Study Interview Questionnaire

CD1807   Feasibility Study Overview

CD1808   Capital Campaign Gift Table (Pyramid of Gifts)

CD1809   Chapter 18 Web Resources

Troubleshooting

We tried our best to compile programs that work on most computers with the minimum system requirements. Alas, your computer may differ, and some programs may not work properly for some reason.

The two likeliest problems are that you don't have enough memory (RAM) for the programs you want to use, or you have other programs running that are affecting installation or the running of a program. If you get an error message such as Not enough memory or Setup cannot continue, try one or more of the following suggestions and then try using the software again:

- ✔ **Turn off any antivirus software running on your computer.** Installation programs sometimes mimic virus activity and may make your computer incorrectly believe that it's being infected by a virus.

- ✔ **Close all running programs.** The more programs you have running, the less memory is available to other programs. Installation programs typically update files and programs; so if you keep other programs running, installation may not work properly.

- ✔ **Have your local computer store add more RAM to your computer.** This is, admittedly, a drastic and somewhat expensive step. However, adding more memory can really help the speed of your computer and allow more programs to run at the same time.

If you have trouble with the CD-ROM, please call the Wiley Product Technical Support phone number at 800-762-2974. Outside the United States, call 1-317-572-3994. You can also contact Wiley Product Technical Support at http://support.wiley.com. Wiley Publishing, Inc., will provide technical support only for installation and other general quality control items. For technical support on the applications themselves, consult the program's vendor or author.

To place additional orders or to request information about other Wiley products, please call 877-762-2974.

Index

Wiley Publishing, Inc.
End-User License Agreement

Business/Accounting & Bookkeeping

Bookkeeping For Dummies
978-0-7645-9848-7

eBay Business
All-in-One For Dummies,
2nd Edition
978-0-470-38536-4

Job Interviews
For Dummies,
3rd Edition
978-0-470-17748-8

Resumes For Dummies,
5th Edition
978-0-470-08037-5

Stock Investing
For Dummies,
3rd Edition
978-0-470-40114-9

Successful Time
Management
For Dummies
978-0-470-29034-7

Computer Hardware

BlackBerry For Dummies,
3rd Edition
978-0-470-45762-7

Computers For Seniors
For Dummies
978-0-470-24055-7

iPhone For Dummies,
2nd Edition
978-0-470-42342-4

Laptops For Dummies,
3rd Edition
978-0-470-27759-1

Macs For Dummies,
10th Edition
978-0-470-27817-8

Cooking & Entertaining

Cooking Basics
For Dummies,
3rd Edition
978-0-7645-7206-7

Wine For Dummies,
4th Edition
978-0-470-04579-4

Diet & Nutrition

Dieting For Dummies,
2nd Edition
978-0-7645-4149-0

Nutrition For Dummies,
4th Edition
978-0-471-79868-2

Weight Training
For Dummies,
3rd Edition
978-0-471-76845-6

Digital Photography

Digital Photography
For Dummies,
6th Edition
978-0-470-25074-7

Photoshop Elements 7
For Dummies
978-0-470-39700-8

Gardening

Gardening Basics
For Dummies
978-0-470-03749-2

Organic Gardening
For Dummies,
2nd Edition
978-0-470-43067-5

Green/Sustainable

Green Building
& Remodeling
For Dummies
978-0-470-17559-0

Green Cleaning
For Dummies
978-0-470-39106-8

Green IT For Dummies
978-0-470-38688-0

Health

Diabetes For Dummies,
3rd Edition
978-0-470-27086-8

Food Allergies
For Dummies
978-0-470-09584-3

Living Gluten-Free
For Dummies
978-0-471-77383-2

Hobbies/General

Chess For Dummies,
2nd Edition
978-0-7645-8404-6

Drawing For Dummies
978-0-7645-5476-6

Knitting For Dummies,
2nd Edition
978-0-470-28747-7

Organizing For Dummies
978-0-7645-5300-4

SuDoku For Dummies
978-0-470-01892-7

Home Improvement

Energy Efficient Homes
For Dummies
978-0-470-37602-7

Home Theater
For Dummies,
3rd Edition
978-0-470-41189-6

Living the Country Lifestyle
All-in-One For Dummies
978-0-470-43061-3

Solar Power Your Home
For Dummies
978-0-470-17569-9

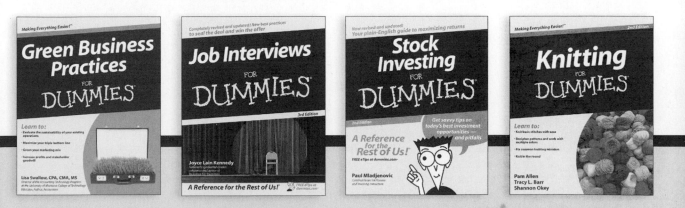

Internet

Blogging For Dummies,
2nd Edition
978-0-470-23017-6

eBay For Dummies,
6th Edition
978-0-470-49741-8

Facebook For Dummies
978-0-470-26273-3

Google Blogger
For Dummies
978-0-470-40742-4

Web Marketing
For Dummies,
2nd Edition
978-0-470-37181-7

WordPress For Dummies,
2nd Edition
978-0-470-40296-2

Language & Foreign Language

French For Dummies
978-0-7645-5193-2

Italian Phrases
For Dummies
978-0-7645-7203-6

Spanish For Dummies
978-0-7645-5194-9

Spanish For Dummies,
Audio Set
978-0-470-09585-0

Macintosh

Mac OS X Snow Leopard
For Dummies
978-0-470-43543-4

Math & Science

Algebra I For Dummies
978-0-7645-5325-7

Biology For Dummies
978-0-7645-5326-4

Calculus For Dummies
978-0-7645-2498-1

Chemistry For Dummies
978-0-7645-5430-8

Microsoft Office

Excel 2007 For Dummies
978-0-470-03737-9

Office 2007 All-in-One
Desk Reference
For Dummies
978-0-471-78279-7

Music

Guitar For Dummies,
2nd Edition
978-0-7645-9904-0

iPod & iTunes
For Dummies,
6th Edition
978-0-470-39062-7

Piano Exercises
For Dummies
978-0-470-38765-8

Parenting & Education

Parenting For Dummies,
2nd Edition
978-0-7645-5418-6

Type 1 Diabetes
For Dummies
978-0-470-17811-9

Pets

Cats For Dummies,
2nd Edition
978-0-7645-5275-5

Dog Training For Dummies,
2nd Edition
978-0-7645-8418-3

Puppies For Dummies,
2nd Edition
978-0-470-03717-1

Religion & Inspiration

The Bible For Dummies
978-0-7645-5296-0

Catholicism For Dummies
978-0-7645-5391-2

Women in the Bible
For Dummies
978-0-7645-8475-6

Self-Help & Relationship

Anger Management
For Dummies
978-0-470-03715-7

Overcoming Anxiety
For Dummies
978-0-7645-5447-6

Sports

Baseball For Dummies,
3rd Edition
978-0-7645-7537-2

Basketball For Dummies,
2nd Edition
978-0-7645-5248-9

Golf For Dummies,
3rd Edition
978-0-471-76871-5

Web Development

Web Design All-in-One
For Dummies
978-0-470-41796-6

Windows Vista

Windows Vista
For Dummies
978-0-471-75421-3

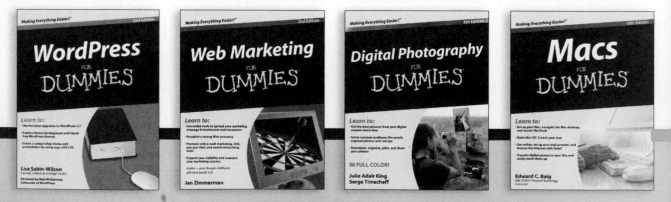